*W*oolf *S*tudies *A*nnual

Volume 11, 2005

PACE UNIVERSITY PRESS • NEW YORK

Copyright © 2005 by
Pace University Press
41 Park Row, Rm. 1510
New York, NY 10038

All rights reserved
Printed in the United States of America

ISSN 1080-9317
ISBN 0-944473-71-7 (pbk: alk.ppr.)

Member

Council of Editors of Learned Journals

∞™ paper used in this publication meets the minimum
requirements of American National Standard for
Information Sciences–Permanence of Paper for Printed Library
Materials,
ANSI Z39.48–1984

Editor

Mark Hussey *Pace University*

Editorial Board

Tuzyline Jita Allan	*Baruch College, CUNY*
Eileen Barrett	*California State University, Hayward*
Kathryn N. Benzel	*University of Nebraska-Kearney*
Pamela L. Caughie	*Loyola University Chicago*
Wayne K. Chapman	*Clemson University*
Patricia Cramer	*University of Connecticut, Stamford*
Beth Rigel Daugherty	*Otterbein College*
Anne Fernald *(Book Review Editor)*	*Fordham University*
Sally Greene	*Independent Scholar*
Leslie Kathleen Hankins	*Cornell College*
Karen Kaivola	*Stetson University*
Jane Lilienfeld	*Lincoln University*
Toni A. H. McNaron	*University of Minnesota*
Patricia Moran	*University of California, Davis*
Vara Neverow	*Southern Connecticut State University*
Annette Oxindine	*Wright State University*
Beth Carole Rosenberg	*University of Nevada-Las Vegas*
Bonnie Kime Scott	*San Diego State University*

Consulting Editors

Nancy Topping Bazin	*Old Dominion University*
Morris Beja	*Ohio State University*
Louise DeSalvo	*Hunter College, CUNY*
Jane Marcus	*Distinguished Professor CCNY and CUNY Graduate Center*
Brenda R. Silver	*Dartmouth College*
Susan Squier	*Pennsylvania State University*
Peter Stansky	*Stanford University*
J. J. Wilson	*Sonoma State University*
Alex Zwerdling	*University of California, Berkeley*

Many thanks to readers for volume 11: June Cummins (San Diego SU), Emily Dalgarno (Boston C), Laura Davis (Kent SU), Jeanne Dubino (Southeastern Louisiana U), David Eberly (Ind. Scholar), Jane Goldman (Edinburgh U), Katherine Hill-Miller (Long Island U), Molly Hite (Cornell U), Georgia Johnston (St. Louis U), Eleanor McNees (U of Denver), Jeanette McVicker (SUNY Fredonia), Diana Royer (Miami U Ohio), Cristina Ruotolo (San Francisco SU), Sonita Sarker (Macalester C), Mark Wollaeger (Vanderbilt U), Rishona Zimring (Lewis & Clark C).

Woolf Studies Annual is indexed in the *American Humanities Index*, *ABELL* and the *MLA Bibliography*.

The Society of Authors has been appointed to act for the Virginia Woolf Estate. Inquiries concerning permissions should be addressed to:

Mr. Jeremy Crow
The Society of Authors
84 Drayton Gardens
London SW10 9SB

Phone: 020 7373 6642
Fax: 020 7373 5768

Email:
info@societyofauthors.org

URL: www.societyofauthors.org

Contents

Woolf Studies Annual

Volume 11, 2005

	viii	Abbreviations
Stuart Clarke	1	Letter to the Editor
Melba Cuddy-Keane	3	From Fan-Mail to Readers' Letters: Locating John Farrelly
Ann Martin	33	Modernist Transformations: Virginia Woolf, Cinderella, and the Legacy of Lady Ritchie
Kathryn Simpson	53	The Paradox of the Gift: Gift-Giving as a Disruptive Force in "Mrs. Dalloway in Bond Street"
Ruth Hoberman	77	Aesthetic Taste, Kitsch and *The Years*
Helen Southworth	99	"Mixed Virginia": Reconciling the "Stigma of Nationality" and the Sting of Nostalgia in Virginia Woolf's Later Fiction
Angela Frattarola	133	Listening for "Found Sound" Samples in the Novels of Virginia Woolf

GUIDE

161 Guide to Library Special Collections

REVIEWS

Patricia Moran	179	*The Katherine Mansfield Notebooks: Complete Edition.* Margaret Scott, Ed.
Erica L. Johnson	186	*A Shrinking Island: Modernism and National Culture in England* by Jed Esty; *Sapphic Primitivism: Productions of Race, Class, and Sexuality in Key Works of Modern Fiction* by Robin Hackett; *Colonial Odysseys: Empire and Epic in the Modernist Novel* by David Adams
Rishona Zimring	193	*Psychoanalysis, Psychiatry, and Modernist Literature* by Kylie Valentine; *Cultures of the Death Drive: Melanie Klein and Modernist Melancholia* by Esther Sanchez-Pardo
Tuzyline Jita Allan	201	*Hearts of Darkness: White Women Write Race* by Jane Marcus
Anne E. Fernald	205	*Virginia Woolf, the Intellectual and the Public Sphere* by Melba Cuddy-Keane
Mary Ann Caws	209	*Bloomsbury Rooms: Modernism, Subculture, and Domesticity* by Christopher Reed
Anna Snaith	212	*Virginia Woolf As Feminist* by Naomi Black
Randi Saloman	216	*Lily Briscoe's Chinese Eyes: Bloomsbury, Modernism, and China* by Patricia Laurence
Celia Marshik	220	*Violence and Modernism: Ibsen, Joyce, and Woolf* by William A. Johnsen

Stuart N. Clarke	**224**	*The Library of Leonard and Virginia Woolf: A Short-title Catalog,* Julia King and Laila Miletic-Vejzovic, Compilers and Eds.
Notes on Contributors	**228**	
Policy	**230**	

Abbreviations

AHH	*A Haunted House*
AROO	*A Room of One's Own*
BP	*Books and Portraits*
BTA	*Between the Acts*
CDB	*The Captain's Death Bed and Other Essays*
CE	*Collected Essays (4 vols.)*
CR1	*The Common Reader*
CR2	*The Common Reader, Second Series*
CSF	*The Complete Shorter Fiction*
D	*The Diary of Virginia Woolf (5 vols.)*
DM	*The Death of the Moth and Other Essays*
E	*The Essays of Virginia Woolf (6 Vols.)*
F	*Flush*
FR	*Freshwater*
GR	*Granite & Rainbow: Essays*
JR	*Jacob's Room*
L	*The Letters of Virginia Woolf (6 Vols.)*
M	*The Moment and Other Essays*
MEL	*Melymbrosia*
MOB	*Moments of Being*
MT	*Monday or Tuesday*
MD	*Mrs. Dalloway*
ND	*Night and Day*
O	*Orlando*
PA	*A Passionate Apprentice*
RF	*Roger Fry: A Biography*
TG	*Three Guineas*
TTL	*To the Lighthouse*
TW	*The Waves*
TY	*The Years*
VO	*The Voyage Out*

To the Editor

I have read with interest Jeanette McVicker's two-part theoretical analysis of Virginia Woolf's six *Good Housekeeping* articles, published in *Woolf Studies Annual*, Vols. 9 and 10 (2003 and 2004). I agree with her that any satisfactory understanding of them must consider the sixth (problematic) essay, "Portrait of a Londoner," as an essential part of the series.

This essay was unfortunately omitted from *The London Scene* collections, first published in a limited edition by Frank Hallman in New York in 1975 and reprinted by both Random House and the Hogarth Press in 1982. There is, however, no evidence to support McVicker's contention that Angelica Garnett and Quentin Bell made a "decision to exclude it" on "editorial (and commercial, one assumes)" grounds (*WSA* 10: 163-4; see also 9: 151).

It is perhaps impossible after so many years to establish exactly how the essays were rediscovered. The sequence is, however, clear from consulting the various editions of B. J. Kirkpatrick's *A Bibliography of Virginia Woolf*. The first five essays appeared for the first time in the second edition of 1967. Although Woolf in a letter of 22 March 1931 referred to six articles, understandably the editors of *The Letters of Virginia Woolf*, Vol. 5 (1978), annotated this as a "series of five essays" (*L5* 301). Independently, I discovered the sixth essay in April 1980, and was relieved to see it listed in the third edition of the *Bibliography* later that year (*pace WSA* 9: 143, n. 1). Anne Olivier Bell used the third edition when preparing Vol. 4 of *The Diary of Virginia Woolf* (1982) and of course confirmed that there were six articles (p. 12).

What is likely is that Frank Hallman was not aware of the sixth essay in 1975 and that Woolf's US and UK publishers, when they reprinted the book in 1982, neither knew nor would have cared had they known of its existence.

Yours faithfully
Stuart N. Clarke

Jeanette McVicker replies:

I am grateful to Stuart Clarke for taking the time to read my two-part essay on Woolf's *Good Housekeeping* articles (*WSA* 9 and 10) and for his usual keen attention to keeping the records straight. I agree completely with his assertion that "It is perhaps impossible after so many years to establish exactly how the essays were rediscovered." My contact with editors at British *Good Housekeeping* several years ago allowed me to obtain a copy of the sixth essay,

"Portrait of a Londoner," as well as the table of contents from each issue in which one of the *London Scene* articles appeared, but they could locate no correspondence or other records that could provide any additional publication history for the series. I thank Clarke for correcting my error about the omission of the sixth essay from the third edition of B.J. Kirkpatrick's bibliography, which I had listed incorrectly in my notes.

While Clarke is right to suggest that there is no direct evidence to support my contention that Angelica Garnett and Quentin Bell made a conscious decision to exclude "Portrait of a Londoner" (I can only presume that they knew of the existence of that sixth essay—another claim for which I have no direct evidence) from the Frank Hallman edition of *The London Scene* in 1975, the language of the dust jacket nevertheless suggests an effort to construct a versioning (Brenda Silver's word) of Woolf's writing in the mid-1970s that would have had difficulty accounting for that strange final essay in the series. I am glad that the essay will finally be republished so that more readers will have the opportunity to see the complete series and draw their own conclusions.

Sincerely,

Jeanette McVicker

A new edition of The London Scene *including all six essays was published by Snowbooks, London, in 2004 (ISBN 0-9545-7592-X)*

From Fan-Mail to Readers' Letters: Locating John Farrelly

Melba Cuddy-Keane

Housed in the Monks House Papers at the University of Sussex, under "Correspondence of Virginia Woolf," are three slight, innocuous, brown folders placed under the intriguing, though possibly surprising, category, "Fan-Mail etc." Inside the folders lie some of the precious few remaining traces of the wide readership that Woolf's writings attracted in their own time.[1] But what does it mean to label these readers "fans"? Is there an implied difference from the letters collected under another category with the heading, "Letters from readers about VW's books"? Do fan letters produce their subject as "celebrity" rather than "author"?[2] And do such fans then use an author's celebrity status to construct narratives of their own lives rather than concentrating on the published narratives they supposedly admire?[3] In truth, the catalogue labels merely distinguish letters of general appreciation from letters about Virginia Woolf's specific works. Yet the labels themselves serve usefully to bring such questions to mind when we ourselves read the letters of one particularly enthusiastic reader: the young American who signs himself "John Farrelly, Jr."

Introducing himself to Virginia Woolf, on the fourth of September 1940, John Farrelly certainly sounds like an adoring fan. He is sending, he writes, "a sort of love letter from a secret young admirer," to tell her that she has "never been out of [his] (literary) mind for the two years since [he] stumbled over The Years on a shelf of second hand books."[4] Love letters and secret admirers emit the warning tones of infatuated response, but the sentence simultaneously rings other notes: the lovely parenthetically inserted "literary" to qualify "mind," and the hints of hours spent hunting for treasure among dusty piles of used books. Then, as the letter proceeds, the literary mind rapidly fleshes out with substance and shape: He states that "whenever the conversation approaches even the neigh-

---

[1] Anna Snaith points to the way the diversity of Woolf's readership is demonstrated in the *Three Guineas* letters ("Wide Circles"). It was also the subject of a special session, organized by Beth Rigel Daugherty, at the Twelfth Annual Virginia Woolf Conference.

[2] For a discussion of constructions of Virginia Woolf as celebrity, see Brenda Silver, *Virginia Woolf Icon* (1999).

[3] For a discussion of the various uses to which celebrity construction is put, see Graeme Turner, *Understanding Celebrity*, (Sage 2004).

[4] This quotation, and other quotations from Farrelly's writings, can be found in his letters and his reviews of Virginia Woolf published in this issue.

borhood of books," he asks, "Have you read Virginia Woolf, Emily Dickinson, and Gerard Hopkins?" He claims he has "bored, even tormented, [his] friends until they have read one or the other of [her] books," and that he persisted with one "singularly stubborn friend" until *Mrs. Dalloway* "broke down his stubbornness last week." He states that Woolf has given him "that all important shove towards Donne and Hazlitt," and contrasts his awkwardness in relation to her as a living author with his uncomplicated admiration for his favorite authors from the past, like Blake or Tolstoi. He may be a fan, but John Farrelly is also clearly a reader.

A similar combination of adoration and perspicuity informs Farrelly's second letter. Farrelly is now writing several months later, on January 18, 1941, and in the intervening time, he has reread *To the Lighthouse* and has read *Roger Fry*. He has come across a reference to Woolf in Yeats's letters to Dorothy Wellesley; he has—and I think I use an appropriate word here—*mooned* over Woolf's photograph in Winifred Holtby's book. But he is also courageous enough to express his initial disappointment with Woolf's biographical method in *Roger Fry*, missing in it the imprint of her characteristic style, and he proceeds to an analysis that perceptively senses the challenge she undertook in writing this work: "Now I see your success lay in your complete absorption in the character to the exclusion of your own personality." Still prone to the lover's excess, he begs for her picture. And he goes into ecstatic raptures over her handwriting, for he is now replying to a letter that Virginia Woolf has written to *him*.

It is hard to imagine anyone reading these letters without being profoundly moved. We might smile at the youthful posturing and naivete, but Farrelly himself seems to grasp the inevitably comic aspect of his role. Noting, in the first letter, the relief that confession will bring, he self-mockingly adds "Consider the Oppressive Burden." And with suitable apologies for himself as "incoherent" and "inexpert," he humbly explains, as if both to excuse and to impress, "I am nineteen." And impress he does, not only with his wide reading but with his bared soul:

> After reading your prose—particularly your novels—I feel dizzy, feverish. Your mind is as sensitive as an open wound, and you so sensitize your readers. Millions of thoughts, impressions, intimations flash through me—I am so completely alive that it is almost painful.

The ground of infatuation is sensitive reading; fan and reader are one.

But what, on reading these letters, passed through Virginia Woolf's mind? Their arrival was uncannily apt, given events in her life at the time. Her diaries record the growing intensification and closeness of the bombing; they also record her terrible sense of separation from her readership. Such isolation was compounded in August of 1940, when Ben Nicolson sent her two fairly strong letters, repeating the hostile accusation that she wrote for a small, elite audience of friends. Ben visited Monks House on September 7; on September 12, Woolf conceived her idea for "a Common History book" of all literature; on September 18, she wrote down a possible title "Reading at Random" (Silver 356). Somewhere around this time, she would have received Farrelly's first letter,[5] conveying, among other things, the inspiration he took from her essays on Hazlitt and Donne. On October 12, she visited the Lewes Library, looked up their copy of *The Common Reader* and recorded her great satisfaction in seeing many signs of its use.[6] While, personally, Woolf may have been grieving for the loss of the reader's "echo" that she feared the war would destroy, she was simultaneously drafting a history of print culture that would testify to the importance of the reader's collaborative role. As for her young admirer's second letter—expressing sympathy for those more immediately experiencing the "mad nightmare" of war—it would likely have arrived approximately two months before Woolf's death.

The part of this story irrevocably lost, it appears, is what Farrelly's letters meant to Virginia Woolf. We know she cared enough to answer his first letter; we don't know what she wrote.[7] From its inclusion in the archives, it appears that the second letter did reach Rodmell but, if Woolf read it, we don't know what she thought. Did she dismiss him for exuberance and brashness? Recoil from his playful allusions to the difficulty of her being alive? Or was she moved by his evident sincerity, and his clear sensitivity to her works? Nothing survives from her writing to let us know. But I take one clue from my own passion that Farrelly stirred. For years, his letters haunted me, and I knew I had to embark on a search. My interest in Woolf's early readers is luckily shared by others, and their work is rapidly making such letters readily available in print: Anna Snaith's wonderful edition of the *Three Guineas* letters in *Woolf Studies Annual* 6 (2000), Sybil Oldfield's collection of the condolence letters written to Leonard Woolf,[8] and the special issue planned next for this journal, in which Beth Rigel Daugherty will edit and introduce numerous other letters written to Woolf on her works. But tracing such readers is a complex and challenging endeavor, as my own story of following such a trail will show.

---

[5] In his second letter, Farrelly explains that there was a delay in posting his first one, so Woolf's receipt of this letter is impossible to date. See the annotation to the letter in this issue for a possible explanation of the circumstances.

[6] For details about this episode and the surrounding events, see my *Virginia Woolf, the Intellectual, and the Private Sphere*, 110-14.

[7] For the possible fate of this letter, see note 15.

[8] *Afterwords: Letters on the Death of Virginia Woolf*, edited by Sybil Oldfield, Rutgers University Press and Edinburgh University Press (2005).

An amateur sleuth, I turned first to the internet to see what I could find. The return address on John Farrelly's first letter is The Hut, Pinook Farm, Fox Creek Road, Allenton, Missouri, but I was unable to find any such address in the present time. Nineteen in 1941, I reasoned, would be seventy-seven in 1999, so I switched to search for a person instead. But a simple name search turned up no likely candidates and, although the Social Security Death Index of the United States, on Ancestry.com, located twenty John Farrellys with birth dates between 1893 and 1940, none was the right fit. But searching the internet white pages identified seven Farrellys in the state of Missouri, so I wrote letters of inquiry to each. This was in March 1999, and in early April I received an envelope containing a four by six card with some jotted notes: the date of his birth (June 3, 1921) and, sadly, the date of his death (January 3, 1972), a few personal details, including the information that he had a son (not named) who was a doctor in England; the information that he had attended both St. Louis University and Cambridge, and that he wrote for "Time Magazine - New Republic"; and a comment that he "struggled with alcohol addiction." And my correspondent added that she had never met Farrelly and that she was writing without her husband's ("Pete" Farrelly's) knowledge.

Excited but perplexed, I decided I could not contact my correspondent without betraying her confidence. The clues, however, gave me two trails. Another internet search identified a George Farrelly living in London, and my cousin in England confirmed that a George Farrelly was indeed listed in the medical registry there. I wrote to him on April 13. My research into publications proved more immediately fruitful. It was the *New York Times*, not *Time Magazine* where Farrelly had published a few reviews, but the *New Republic* evidenced more extensive work. His first review appeared there in 1946; in 1947, he was listed as a Staff Contributor; in 1948, he moved up to the position of a Contributing Editor (along with Malcolm Cowley). In 1949, he published forty-five reviews but, in 1950, his contributions were significantly down, and in 1951, there were none; after March 1952, his name was no longer listed as being on staff. I had found some fascinating confirmation of his literary skills—and more of that to come—but the trail to locate him ran cold.

Through the summer of 1999, I waited for some response from John Farrelly's son. The notes on the 4 by 6 card had given me some indication of a troubled family history, and I feared that my questions might seem an unwelcome intrusion into private life. But in October, needing information for an upcoming talk on historical readers, I decided to risk a call to the woman who stated she was writing without her husband's knowledge, planning to pretend I was conducting a telemarketing survey if her husband answered the phone. To my relief, she answered the phone herself; to my surprise, she did not remember writing to me, and said I really should speak to her husband, John's younger brother. Peter Farrelly then came willingly to the phone—there seemed to be no hidden message in his not knowing about his wife's reply—but, since he would have been only eight years old at the time of his brother John's first letter, he directed me to his older sister, Caroline Gross. A phone call to her, also in St. Louis, Missouri, produced my first specific knowledge of my elusive ghost. And the evening of my conference paper, due to miraculous coincidence—or more likely a long-distance prompting from his aunt—I received an email from George, John Farrelly's son, and we embarked on what has become a long and continuing correspondence. When I finally met George in London, he showed me a bound volume of his father's war-time letters to his family, lovingly typed by his sister Elizabeth (Doodles), despite the growing and debilitating effects of ALS (Lou Gehrig's disease). Sybil Oldfield, who heard about my work, graciously sent me a copy of Farrelly's condolence letter to Leonard Woolf, dated 5 April 1941. John's brother Mark (whose religious name, as a Benedictine Monk, is the Reverend John Farrelly) has also provided valuable help. The ensuing story altered quite a few of my first preconceptions, but the extraordinary passion and sensitivity of those early letters proved to have been the genuine thing.[9]

"The Hut, Pinook Farm," along with the reference, in Farrelly's second letter, to "the school room" had led me to imagine the letter-writer as a young teacher in a small farming community, with few resources other than a shop with used books. The person I discovered was the eldest son in a lively, large, and occasionally impoverished Irish American family, but one who had been well educated in the Jesuit schools (the Joycean parallels are evident elsewhere too).[10] With twelve children, the family had settled on a small farm just outside St. Louis, since—although they did not farm themselves—a large house in the country was easier to afford.[11] Even with an addition, however, the 1840 house was too small, and a separate building was built for the two elder boys, which John romantically named "The Hut." The idea I had constructed of a relatively

---

[9] Since my account of Farrelly's life has been reconstructed from various documents and with the help of numerous exchanges with family members, I have not cited specific sources for the general details of his life.

[10] Just as Stephen Dedalus rhymes off to Cranly the numerous fluctuations and incarnations in Simon Dedalus's career, so John Farrelly senior was first a master printer whose business collapsed during the depression, then a real estate salesman, then the owner of an ice cream parlor producing a superior make of ice cream called "Farrelly's Finest" until that trade collapsed, and finally an oil well broker who underwent radical swings in profits and loss.

[11] Mark Farrelly recalls that they had "cows, chickens, sheep and a man who basically looked after the farm, Herman St. Onge."

unworldly and isolated nineteen-year old also had to be revised. As he indicates in his letter to Leonard Woolf, Farrelly was at the time a freshman at St. Louis University.[12] But he had not revealed that his English professor was none other than Marshall McLuhan, who taught there from 1937 to 1944, before returning to Canada and coming eventually to the University of Toronto, where I heard him lecture many years later, as a student myself. If I had only known that one day I would want to ask him questions about a former protegé! But the family's stories of McLuhan's interest in Farrelly abound—from telling the class that he and John Farrelly should change places in the classroom, to McLuhan's wading through a swollen creek to get to a party at Pinook Farm, to perhaps the most significant detail: McLuhan's offer to help Farrelly continue his studies at Cambridge, where McLuhan himself had obtained a B.A. and M.A., and where—though as a non-resident—he was currently writing his doctoral dissertation.

Farrelly was indeed to proceed to Cambridge, but not easily, and not until 1951. The war intervened, and he bounced from studying with McLuhan to serving in the Merchant Marine. Life became an oscillation between extremes: austere periods of duty at sea alternating with a loose, bohemian life on shore. For Farrelly had reconnected in New York with the brilliant and eccentric Marius Bewley, a close friend from St. Louis whom he had met through Marshall McLuhan when Bewley was back in the United States between taking his undergraduate degree in Cambridge in 1940, and beginning his doctoral work there in 1949. Bewley, who was for a time Peggy Guggenheim's assistant in her New York gallery, was well-connected in literary and artistic circles, and drew Farrelly into his rather exotic life.[13] Thus ship board meant long hours of duty, spaced by reading Henry James, E. M. Forster, T. S. Eliot, and the works of the Early Church Fathers, while shore-leave meant lush, extravagant parties at Peggy Guggenheim's where Farrelly met prominent artists such as Max Ernst, and an equally unconventional life among literary friends, such as the poets "Wystan"

---

[12] The 1950 Directory of St. Louis University High School indicates that John J. Farrelly graduated in 1939. The year 1939-40 saw an interruption in his education due to his father's financial difficulties.

[13] Bewley is misleadingly identified as the "curator of the Guggenheim" in MacKillop (166); he did, however, work at Peggy Guggenheim's gallery, Art of This Century, and he was definitely welcomed into her social circle (Dearborn; Guggenheim). Sexually coded, in his terms, as an "Athenian," he was noted for his flamboyant dress, his curiously formal and theological patterns of speech, his sense of humor, and his brilliance. He went on to become a noted critic of Romantic and American literature and Professor of English at Rutgers University.

Auden and George Barker.[14] Out of this unsettled time, Farrelly's story proceeds to an unfortunate marriage, anxiety over his wife's ability to care for their ailing child (whose birth had occasioned the marriage), the child's death, and that marriage's end. Not surprisingly, his vulnerability to alcohol addiction began to emerge.

There could be no hope of Cambridge studies in such a context. Farrelly put off his dreams, and threw himself instead into writing the *New Republic* reviews. But then he married a second time, to a woman who had inherited substantial wealth, allowing them to buy a home on the newly fashionable Upper East Side of Manhattan—a purchase significant enough to be recorded in the *New York Times*. With these changed circumstances, and the financial advantages from his marriage, Farrelly eventually set off for Cambridge; yet the timing was, from the outset, perhaps already too late. Not that his talent and genius were overlooked. The family recall Leavis's praise of Farrelly as "the best read man of his generation," and Robert Fraser, George Barker's biographer, writes that by 1952, Farrelly was "now firmly ensconced as Leavis's favourite student" (305). In the accounts of Leavis's students at Downing College, Farrelly's name appears as one of the group of Catholics or lapsed Catholics reported to be "the most impressive people around," along with Farrelly's pungent remark, "I sometimes feel as though Downing were becoming an outpost of the Vatican" (Harrison 255). But the war may have taken its toll. Or perhaps there was too much money. And the temptation of alcohol too great. One might draw such conclusions from Ian MacKillop's brief portrait: "Like Bewley, [Farrelly] had been a Catholic, and was from St. Louis, drank (more than Bewley) and wore good suits from Pratt Manning in Trinity Street" (284). And "he rented summer houses, often in France" (but to which, it should be noted, the Leavises invited themselves to stay). In addition, Farrelly's frustrations as a creative writer (he had written a long novel and several short stories, but none had met with any success) produced a sense of failure that ran very deep.[15]

---

[14] My brief summary of this time is based on information in Dearborn, Fraser, and Farrelly's war-time letters.

[15] Mark Farrelly comments, "John wrote a novel in that period [around the time of his letters to Woolf] about a strange friend of his, Paul Gorman, and his mother. I remember Paul—a brooding sort of man who at times visited us. Paul was a man who felt once, probably after that date, that God told him to beat Marius Bewley up, and he did. Paul eventually ended up in an asylum. And that novel, which Cissy read and loved, was with some other possessions of John in a storage compartment in NYC. John was in arrears on payment, so they threw it all out or sold it." It is possible that Woolf's letter was with these papers.

But the failure seems most to have derived from some fatal combination of Farrelly's inner demons and Leavis's recognized repressive effects. In "On a Distant Prospect of English Poetry and Downing College," George Barker uses the phrase "rigor leavis" for the pall cast by Leavis's ruthless and highly critical mode (Fraser 307); Marius Bewley (himself accused by Barker of the rigor-leavis effect) similarly charged Leavis with not taking what was best for his students sufficiently into account (MacKillop 269). And George Farrelly reports, "My mother says she thought he had genius; thinks he would have been another F. Scott Fitzgerald. But his studies under Leavis paralysed his creative side and he felt if he could not produce something on the par with Anna Karenina there was no point even trying." And so Robert Fraser dramatizes Farrelly's inner turmoil with metaphors that could easily come from the third chapter of Joyce's *A Portrait of the Artist as a Young Man*: "To his right loured the puritanical and hortatory features of Leavis; to his left grinned the subversive gargoyle of Barker" (305). But what might be wonderfully effective as schematic metaphors in a literary work are frequently inadequate to the psychological complexities of individual lives. MacKillop, for example, locates a not dissimilar dichotomy *within* Leavis, between a preference for "bohemianism," unorthodoxy, and originality, and an equally strong adherence to respectability, "high thinking," and "plain living" (168-69). Leavis himself is a complex and controversial figure, and his students debate his simultaneously enriching and debilitating effects.

But whether it was the lack of preparation Leavis, in preferring the independent essay, gave his students for the Cambridge exams, or his overly rigid and demanding expectations, or causes emanating from Farrelly's past, the result was that Farrelly took an Upper Second on his exams (Fraser 323), making an academic career like Bewley's unlikely, and further sowing the seeds of insecurity that inhibited his creative work. And so his life proceeds first to a year on the continent that, in Fraser's account, resembles a blend of *The Sun Also Rises* and *Tender is the Night*, followed by numerous short-term jobs that—again, almost like Dick Diver—take him from place to place, until the break-down of his second marriage, jealousy over his wife's subsequent relation with George Barker, the loss of contact with his children, a series of abortive relationships, and increasing problems with alcoholism lead finally, sadly, to his suicide in January of 1972. "Your mind is as sensitive as an open wound, and you so sensitize your readers," he had written to Virginia Woolf. As if in terrible symmetry, his own open wound would lead him, in his death, to follow Virginia Woolf's final path.

The outer signposts of a person's life, however, are but rough markers for the life within. As Woolf shows through the life of Clarissa Dalloway, what people do in their lives is not always equivalent to the effect, the impression, the influence, that makes their mark upon others. The nineteen-year-old writer of "fan-mail" was caught up in an image of himself, transfigured by the glamour of literary life, which failed to come to fruition. But the nineteen-year-old *reader* of Woolf's works was actively inspired by the world of literature and eager to pass on that inspiration to others. When he achieved that, even for a moment, it was a real achievement. And, I would argue, the same inventive quality that allowed him to construct himself as the literary lover of Woolf enabled him to construct, out of her words, a world of literary ideas with meaning and value. On many occasions, fan and reader merged together in fulfilling and productive ways.

The meaning of John Farrelly as a reader of Woolf thus need not be governed by the end of his life; we can seek it instead in his passionate dedication to literature whenever that passion could be expressed. It was expressed in his childhood when, like Woolf, he possessed an easy ability to build up a world around him for others to share. It was expressed, again like Woolf, in an early desire to foster in others an appetite for reading. And it was expressed, in a more disciplined form, in his work as a reviewer, although perhaps nowhere so successfully mingling his critical task with the lover's sensitivity as in his review—the culmination of those early letters—of the essays of Virginia Woolf.

Before turning to these reviews, however, we need to consider not so much the troubles that lay ahead, but the imagination that lay behind them. What we see in this light, is a life rich in its extraordinary impact on other people, characterized by an intensity of interaction that his younger brother Mark put into effective words:

> John certainly had a very perceptive mind and engaged heart, as you can see from his wartime letters. I think he was fascinated by interactions among people, and even much older people shared things about their own lives with him as with an adult. He was articulate about the things that interested him, and expressed himself frequently in a striking way. He had a very creative mind as well, initiating games or conversations that got many of us involved. My mother tried to get us all to read, and John passed this on to some younger siblings. He certainly influenced me.

He adds: "John introduced me to many authors -American (Henry James), Irish (James Joyce) and Russian (Dostoyevsky, Tolstoy and others) primarily. I read these in high school, to the dismay of some of my Jesuit teachers."

John's younger sister Caroline (Cissy) Gross is similarly flooded with memories testifying to his literary influence on their lives. "All during the war," she wrote to me, "well, really all his life, he would give me lists of books to read. . . . He was our mentor and guided us all." But this interest in reading was strongly linked to John's own capacity for invention, when it flowed freely at an early age. When he was six or seven, and in the second grade, he started a cartoon story of the "Bean family" an ongoing saga of an extended family, with all sorts of men and women having the names of different beans: Coffee Bean was the father, while two of the women were Lima and String. "Everyone at the school couldn't wait for the next instalment," Caroline wrote, "and we were the same." And there were numerous times when stories came alive in performative situations. As a great help to his mother, he would crowd about ten children together into a small storage closet, taking them verbally away to "Sugar Plum Town" in a rocket. He could keep them spellbound for two hours before dinner, and not just occasionally. These episodes were almost nightly affairs. He was also not averse to performing as the priest of the imagination. In eighth grade, he would drape himself in his mother's large Spanish Shawl as his vestments, recite homilies to the other children and administer communion, using, for the host, circles cut from fish food wafers.

Farrelly's childhood invention extended as well to the acting out of stories they were reading, one particular favorite being *The Story of the Treasure Seekers* by E. Nesbit—a book that resonates with his own life in innumerable but also uncanny ways. This story of the Bastable children, who inventively formulate plots to find treasure as a way to restore the family's fortunes after their father's business failures, might have appealed subliminally as an imaginative response to family circumstances that the Farrelly children, at this time, could only have glimpsed. But the more extraordinary relevance of this work lies in its narrator's use of his reading as the basis for his inventions. Arguing the ways that children refashion for themselves the constructions imposed by the adult writers of children's books, Marah Gubar shows further how Nesbit herself models such creative appropriation. Treasure hunting can be a plundering of previous texts as material for imaginative recreation, and in Gubar's view, "the fact that Oswald, [the eldest child and imaginative ring-leader of the Bastable children] opens his first three chapters with sharp-eyed critiques of various kinds of literature suggests that reading enables writing; or rather, that *critical* reading releases or empowers one's own creative efforts" (413). As Nesbit herself plunders previous literature for her own creations, so her narrator Oswald plunders his own reading for like effect. And consciously or unconsciously, for Nesbit's reader John Farrelly, his true capabilities seemed to flourish when reader and writer in him were barely distinguishable; and perhaps both became subject to atrophy when the link—for whatever reason—was cut.

What relevance, then, does this childhood facility with narrative have for the young professional's later reviews? Certainly what was requisite for a regular reviewer for the *New Republic* was a broad and catholic interest in books, and the first impressive feature of Farrelly's reviews, as with Virginia Woolf's, is their range. Contemporary fiction—the largest category in the works that

Farrelly covered—brought sufficient diversity on its own, and he also reviewed reprints of canonical works, and translations of foreign novels. At one point, he even interviewed E. M. Forster, who was impishly most willing to talk about his views on American undergraduate life and the problems, in England after the war, of not having enough to eat ("Distinguished Visitor"). In their approach, Farrelly's early reviews evidence a Jamesian interest in *method*, highlighting such aspects as the use of perspective, the problems of either lack of, or exaggerated, detachment, and the importance of conveying lived experience as opposed to writing formulaic or propagandistic prose. And each book is weighed on its own merits, regardless of the writer's reputation; "pretentious" and "unpretentious" are two of his guides, and while he can be devastating about meaningless stories that read like "a text of carefully arranged punctuation marks" or war writers who have swarmed over Europe "picking up themes as souvenirs," he can entrance by describing "not a story that has ended but a spell that is broken" or chillingly warn, "the plot is only the hors-d'oeuvres to this supper of horrors."[16]

Literary criticism then develops as one of his specialties, and he ranges widely through L. C. Knights, V. S. Pritchett, Sir Arthur Quiller-Couch, Stanley Hyman, Philip Rahv, Edmund Wilson, and critics on Samuel Butler, Henry Fielding, the Brontës, Robert Louis Stevenson, as well as Keats, Poe, Yeats, Joyce, Proust, and Eliot. Not unexpectedly, Farrelly is most adulatory when he comes to F. R. Leavis's *Revaluation: Tradition and Development in English Poetry* (1947) and *The Great Tradition* (1948), and Eric Bentley's selection from *Scrutiny* (1948). Although Farrelly had yet to go to Cambridge himself, we can safely assume some influence here of Marius Bewley, who was included in Bentley's selection and had indeed been publishing in *Scrutiny* since 1939. But Farrelly is also clear on his reasons for elevating Leavis: a rejection of loose emotionalism in favor of a focus on language and close attention to the text, a defense of serious writing against a general deprecation of the intellectual in the culture at large, discriminating judgements of different works according to their human awareness and their moral intensity, and a pedagogic approach aimed at teaching students to make judgments for themselves. Against a system too frequently dependent on the memorization of facts and the acceptance of established opinion, Leavis brought a new emphasis to the critical intelligence, and it was one that Farrelly readily embraced.

---

[16] These remarks apply respectively to *Three* by William Sampson (9 June 1947); a selection of war novels (Apr 28, 1947); *Titus Groan* by Mervyn Peake (2 Dec. 1946); and *The End is Not Yet* by Fritz von Unruh (2 June 1947). For reasons of space, I have not listed these relatively minor reviews in my Works Cited.

But there were other, more ominous elements in Leavis's writing, making it difficult to read these reviews now without hindsight: Farrelly quotes, for example, Leavis's disparaging judgement that Shelley's "surrendering to inspiration" was scarcely "distinguishable from surrendering to temptation" (Leavis 216) and one is left contemplating, in some horror, the full impact of Leavis's withering corrective of readers who have been falsely "intoxicated by Shelley's poetry at the age of fifteen" (203). Despite Leavis's theory of enabling the readers' thinking, his propensity toward categorical judgement and his distaste for "lyrical" emotion may have had, for Farrelly, precisely the opposite effect.[17] The emphasis Leavis gave to the primary text may have led Farrelly into a practice of giving too much lengthy quotation, while Leavis's strictures against imaginative identification may have repressed Farrelly's special ability sympathetically to convey the essence of a literary work. Whatever the reason, there seem to be more reviews in the later period that are perfunctory or purely negative—with the striking exception, however, of one particular genre. Farrelly's extraordinary sensitivity, his astonishing perceptiveness, his evocative ability to translate experience into words emerge with the same moving quality of his early letters in a series of reviews, largely in the spring of 1948, on life-writing and personal essays: Rainer Maria Rilke's letters, Franz Kafka's diaries, André Gide's journals, and Paul Valéry's later-life reflections. In these remarkable reviews, Farrelly illuminates these writers' own *self*-perceptions, in words inspired by both emotional identification and thoughtful analysis—the fan and the reader working together to create a luminous world. Again, speculation is hard to resist: was Farrelly's true métier biography, where he might have allowed both creative imagination and critical intelligence free play?

In this fertile period of early 1948, I finally found the review that I sought. It was a featured article, as the first review in a special expanded literary section; and it further stood out from Farrelly's usual reviews in being printed as a center-fold, on facing rather than successive pages, and with his name as a by-line

---

[17] A change in Farrelly's approach is certainly evident if we compare a review that predates his work for the *New Republic* and what was possibly the last piece of literary criticism that he wrote. In a 1946 *New York Times* review of stories by Elizabeth Bowen, Farrelly argues that American readers must draw on the creative imagination to understand the British experience of "war as a territory rather than as a page of history." But in his 1968 introduction to *Moby Dick*, his one publication as a "critic," he argues that the reader must abandon the "irresistible temptation to the creative urge" (12). Yet Farrelly brings back the creative imagination by positing first that Melville makes a link of imaginative identification with his narrator Ishmael, and then that the whole work is "contained in Ishmael's 'meditating mind'" (26)—the mind of "the schoolmaster-seaman-writer of imaginative genius" (25). What Farrelly displaces in himself he relocates in the text.

rather than a signature at the end. But what struck me most was the evolution of fan into fully-fledged reader—or, rather, the fine integration of the sensitive and intelligent reader with the commitment and enthusiasm of the fan. The promise of those early letters here blossoms into maturity, as each side tempers the threatened extremes of the other: the result is a penetrating critical analysis animated with the glow of literary love.

"The Pursuit of Reading" (26 April 1948) concerns two recently published volumes of Woolf's essays: the American edition of *The Moment and Other Essays* and the combined edition of *The Common Reader: First and Second Series* (both issued by Harcourt Brace on 22 March 1948). Farrelly would thus have had to move quickly to write this review, but he was also returning, in part, to works that had inspired his freshman year, when Woolf's essays impelled him toward Hazlitt and Donne. As if perhaps even remembering that youthful enthusiasm, he begins with the reflection that Woolf's reputation has suffered from "a kind of hypnotized adulation"; yet he writes not to disclaim the fan's admiration, but to counter the inevitable "backlash" against such excess. No longer relying on her picture or her handwriting, he now renders his mature critical judgement: "her best work is unexcelled by anything of its kind in English letters."

For a short review (well under 1500 words), "The Pursuit of Reading" astounds with the number of crucial and significant features it identifies in Woolf's work. Farrelly grasps Woolf's contextual approach to literary criticism through her exploration of the relation between writing and its environment, and the significance of this approach for her feminism as she connects women's writing and the conditions of their lives. He highlights her sympathy for outsiders and eccentrics and grasps her dream of a classless society, understanding that she means not the loss of individual differences or the sacrifice of leisure and privacy, but rather the extension of these "privileges" to all. And Farrelly is extraordinarily perceptive about her aims, reading through her "mock-veneration" to perceive her incisive critique of the "vested interest" of male professionalism, and her "insistent amateur's" devotion to the activity of reading for the broad pleasures it gives. Above all, Farrelly understands what we might call the "phatic" dimension of Woolf's essays: the way they provide "an incentive to reading" and stimulate her readers' abilities to read. The urgency underlying Woolf's words, "We have got to teach ourselves to understand literature,"[18] is for him all the more meaningful, stemming as it does from "a lifetime devoted to books."

---

[18] Quoted from "The Leaning Tower," *The Moment and Other Essays* (153).

Surely Farrelly's description of Woolf as one "passionately addicted to the reading of books" captures as well the ghostly figure of that dreaming and hopeful nineteen-year-old lurking still within the battle- and life-scarred writer of twenty-six. But when I first read Farrelly's words, I had the oddest sensation that he was articulating my own thoughts. "But the minor or obscure figures most engage her talents," he wrote, "some half-forgotten diarist, some stillborn monster of literature, some odd member of a vanished *beau monde*." And then he quoted, "For one likes romantically to feel oneself a deliverer advancing with lights across the waste of years to the rescue of some stranded ghost.... Possibly they hear one coming. They shuffle, they preen, they bridle. Old secrets well to their lips. The divine gift of communication will soon again be theirs."[19] Farrelly's words—describing Woolf's obscure and stranded ghosts—became, for me, words about himself. And, in a further shift, the objective researcher calmly turning the pages of the *New Republic* in the University of Toronto Library, suddenly recognized herself as a figure in the narrative—ironically amused by the self-reflection in liking "romantically to feel oneself a deliverer" and at the same time now irrevocably under the spell that binds the listener to ghostly speech.

That spell kept me faithful, through the years, to my search. Some time ago, when I included this project as part of a grant application, I received, from one reviewer, some discouraging words: "What makes these readers, whoever they were, representative of Woolf's audience? How can their responses fifty or more years ago be accurately recreated at this time?" and "It seems to me very unlikely that such a limited research base can tell us anything reliable about 'modernism's historical audience'." Certainly much of our history has been lost, and retrieving it is a hazardous matter of chance—as indeed my ability to tell even part of this story has depended on the chance finding of Farrelly's first letter to Woolf, after he discarded it, by some kind person who dropped it in the post. Certainly no one reader is representative, but my discovering just how extraordinary John Farrelly was led me also to realize this: common readers are often, maybe always, extraordinary people, and their individuality is what makes the pool of common readers such a fascinating, complex reflection of a book's multiple and plural life. And the more we discover such readers, the more we dispel the narrow views of Woolf's limited appeal that once held such sway. Finally, both Farrelly's story *and* the story of discovering it will, I hope, testify to Woolf's own example, showing that the border between common and professional reading is not fixed; we may fall at various times to one side or the other,

---

[19] Quoted from "The Lives of the Obscure" (*CR1*: 106-07).

but the porousness of that border will help us to keep the cool light on the object while fanning the flame that makes it an object of pursuit.

The mixed nature of our resulting knowledge—an ambiguity that indeed belongs to life itself—is encapsulated in one final review of Farrelly's that must be mentioned here. It usefully prevents us from making a simplistic, heroic narrative out of Woolf and her readers; at the same time, it traces the ghostly outline of Woolf's continuing legacy to us. Again it is a lead article with his name as a by-line; again it is a review of Woolf's work. It is, moreover, a review in which Farrelly explicitly revisits his earlier enthusiasm and, sadly, finds it has—at least partially—dimmed. Yet the diminishment, he considers, is an effect in himself rather than in her works: the distance from his youthful reading is too great to revive the earlier passion yet, for a truly fresh reading, the distance is not far enough. And so, while admitting his critical reactions may be temporary, he advances certain negative views: *Orlando* is a fine joke that, in its extension, becomes too frivolous; *The Waves* is a sensitive experiment that similarly extends for too long. Rereading *Mrs. Dalloway*, however, his enthusiasm begins to revive and he perceptively analyses both Clarissa's vibrancy and her class limitations, and the way, through Peter, the novel *itself* is "ruthlessly honest" in revealing this double view. But diminishing Clarissa for weakness, he fruitlessly seeks the explicit "values" he expects the novel to insert in her place. There is an evident presence of Leavis and *Scrutiny*, but the review at least raises interesting, controversial points.

Then, moving from *Mrs. Dalloway* to *To the Lighthouse*, Farrelly's early rapture returns. This is a book about love, he ventures, and he traces the theme in its myriad forms. And then his prose becomes a celebration, in keeping with his title, "The Landscape of the Heart." And I can think of no more fitting place to end this essay than by quoting his final lines, where he in turn quotes Virginia Woolf: "Love had a thousand shapes. There might be lovers whose gift it was to choose out the elements of things and place them together and so, giving them a wholeness not theirs in life, make of some scene, or meeting of people (all now gone and separate), one of those globed compacted things over which thought lingers, and love plays."[20]

---

[20] Quoted from *To the Lighthouse* (192). I have slightly revised Farrelly's quotation to present it as it is in Woolf's text.

I am deeply indebted to Dr. George Farrelly for permission to publish his father's letters and reviews, to Jeanne Farrelly for responding to my initial query, and to John Farrelly, Jr.'s family—especially his brother Mark (the Reverend John Farrelly), his sister Caroline, and his son George—for their generosity in providing further information and their patience with my many questions and requests. I would also like to thank Elizabeth Inglis and Dorothy Sheridan of the University of Sussex Library for their assistance, and the Social Sciences and Humanities Research Council of Canada for a grant for a larger project on Woolf and reading that helped to support this research. Finally, I would like to express my profound gratitude to the editor of this journal, Mark Hussey, for his help with the preparation of these materials, and his belief in the value of publishing them.

Works Cited

Cuddy-Keane, Melba. *Virginia Woolf, the Intellectual, and the Public Sphere.* Cambridge: Cambridge UP, 2003.
Dearborn, Mary V. *The Life of Peggy Guggenheim.* Boston, New York: Houghton Mifflin, 2004.
Farrelly, George. Emails to the author. 8 Oct. 1999-30 Nov. 2004.
Farrelly, Jeanne. Correspondence to the author. Postmarked 29 Mar. 1999.
Farrelly, John. "The Art of Elizabeth Bowen: Her Short Stories of War and its Repercussions in the Life of England." Rev. of Elizabeth Bowen, *Ivy Gripped the Steps and Other Stories. New York Times* 7 Apr. 1946, sec. 7: 1, 37.
———. "Distinguished Visitor." Interview with E. M. Forster. *New Republic* 28 July 1947: 28-29.
———. "The Landscape of the Heart." Rev. of Virginia Woolf, *Mrs. Dalloway, Orlando, To the Lighthouse, The Waves. New Republic* 6 Sept. 1948: 21-22.
———. Introduction. *Moby Dick or the White Whale.* By Herman Melville. London: Panther 1968. 11-27.
———. Letter to Leonard Woolf. 5 April 1941. Leonard Woolf Papers, Part II: D13 Virginia, ms. Letters of condolence received by LW on VW's death. U of Sussex Library.
———. Letter to Virginia Woolf. 18 January 1941. Correspondence of Virginia Woolf. Letters: III. Fan mail folder 2, ms. Monks House Papers. U of Sussex Library.

———. Letter to Virginia Woolf. 4 September 1940. Correspondence of Virginia Woolf. Letters: III. Fan mail folder 2, ts. (signed). Monks House Papers. U of Sussex Library.

———. *Letters of J. Farrelly Jr. (1942-5)*. Ed. Elizabeth Farrelly Kavanagh. St Louis: Genealogical R & P, 1986.

———. "Practical Criticism." Rev. of F. R. Leavis, *Revaluation: Tradition and Development in English Poetry*. *New Republic* 16 Feb. 1948: 36-37.

———. "The Pursuit of Reading." Rev. of Virginia Woolf, *The Moment and Other Essays* and *The Common Reader: First and Second Series*. *New Republic* 26 April 1948: 20-21.

Farrelly, Mark (Rev. John Farrelly). Emails to the author. 19 Sept.-30 Nov., 2004.

Fraser, Robert. *The Chameleon Poet: A Life of George Barker*. London: Jonathan Cape, 2001.

Gross, Caroline Farrelly. Letter to the author. 3 July 2002.

Gubar, Marah. "Partners in Crime: E. Nesbit and the Art of Thieving." *Style* 35 (2001): 410-29.

Guggenheim, Peggy. *Confessions of an Art Addict*. New York: Macmillan, 1960.

Harrison, Patrick. "Downing After the War." *F. R. Leavis: Essays and Documents*. Ed. Ian MacKillop and Richard Storer. Sheffield: Sheffield Academic Press, 1995.

Leavis, F. R. *Revaluation: Tradition and Development in English Poetry*. 1936. New York, G. W. Stewart, 1947.

MacKillop, Ian. *F. R. Leavis: A Life in Criticism*. London: Allen Lane, 1995.

Silver, Brenda. Introduction. "'Anon' and 'The Reader': Virginia Woolf's Last Essays." *Twentieth Century Literature* 25 (1979): 356-68.

———. *Virginia Woolf Icon*. Chicago: U of Chicago P., 1999.

Snaith, Anna. "Wide Circles: The *Three Guineas* Letters." *Woolf Studies Annual* 6 (2000): 1-12.

Snaith, Anna, ed. "*Three Guineas* Letters." Woolf Studies Annual 6 (2000): 13-168.

Turner, Graeme. *Understanding Celebrity*. London: Sage, 2004.

Woolf, Virginia. *The Common Reader: First Series*. 1925. Ed. Andrew McNeillie. New York: Harcourt, 1984.

———. *The Moment and Other Essays*. 1947. San Diego: Harcourt Brace, 1975.

———. *To the Lighthouse*. 1927. San Diego: Harcourt Brace Jovanovich, 1981.

Typed
September 4, 1940

The Hut, Pinook Farm; Fox Creek Road, Allenton, Missouri

Dear Mrs. Woolf,

This is a sort of love letter from a secret young admirer to tell you that you have never been out of my (literary) mind for the two years since I stumbled over The Years on a shelf of second hand books.

That the first thing I say whenever the conversation approaches even the neighborhood of books is: Have you read Virginia Woolf, Emily Dickinson, and Gerard Hopkins?

That I have bored, even tormented, my friends until they have read one or the other of your books.

That I have spent more than one night discussing you (and related subjects) with a singularly stubborn friend-who refused to read you simply because I suggested you. However, Mrs. Dalloway broke down his stubborness [sic] last week.

That "my heart leaps up" whenever I read or hear your name, and that I have searched for those ~~sea~~ thirteen letters through innumerable indexes.

Moreover, you have done me the invaluable favor of giving me that all important shove towards Donne and Hazlitt in the Common Reader. Those two have a favored place in my estimation and on my shelf. Thank you.

This sort of letter may appear ridiculous to the receiver; I have always thought it so in the writer. But now I understand what compels the fools. You see, I can never forget that there you are-- alive (unlike my other favorites, except Shaw and T.S. Eliot) in England. And here am I-- admiring you so much. Why shouldn't I take advantage of your accessibility to tell you so?

At any rate, after this is sent away in the morning I will be relieved of an oppressive burden of-- is it gratitude?-- that I feel I owe you. And I shall feel that my relationship with you (How you complicate matters by being alive! I read Blake or Tolstoi, admire them, and peacefully accept them.) shall be clearer, much easier.

FROM FAN-MAIL

If I am incoherent, consider that I am inexpert, never having written this sort of letter before- in my life. (I am nineteen.) And it shall not matter greatly, for it means more to me to write it (Consider the Oppressive Burden) than it could mean to you to receive it.

> Your admirer and champion,
> [signed] John Farrelly, Jr.

4 September, 1940

---

[1] Farrelly presumably refers to *The Hogarth Letters* (twelve letters by various writers), published by the Hogarth Press in 1933.

Typed
January 18, 1941

> Pinook Farm
> Allenton Missouri
> U.S.A
> 18 January, 1941

Dear Mrs Woolf,

My brother brought your letter in to school for me.[1] When he said "You have a letter from Virginia Woolf" I only stared at him. I turned the envelope round and round in my hand, noting the return adress [sic], the post-mark, the time the letter was mailed-and studied your handwriting.[2]

Can you believe that anyone could be so excited -so unreasonably elated about a letter? My delight is composed of so many things - simply holding the paper, trying to build up around the few details a whole background; your house, your routine. I imagined all sorts of silly things - how the same hand that guided the pen in forming these letters, wrote "To The Lighthouse-" (How crushing if you typewrite your manuscripts!)[3]

I examined each word as carefully as if the letter had been a love letter. Of course I had become very fond of the person I had constructed from your writing - and it wasn't hard. There's such a definite imprint of a personality on your every page. Nevertheless, you would probably be amazed at yourself as you exist in my mind.

You see, I was so knocked off balance because you caught me by surprize [sic]. I wrote but never mailed the letter you answered. After carrying it about with me for several days, I decided against sending it - (such self consciousness at nineteen!) and threw the letter away. Someone evidently found and stamped it![4]

Of course I wrote another letter immediately. But I put it aside until I had read "Roger Fry" - I'm glad now that I did. You've never seen such rot as I wrote-and at what length!

I enjoyed "Roger Fry" so much. ~~Of co~~ At first I was disappointed because I had read it for <u>you</u> not for <u>Fry.</u> But as I became engrossed in the man, I forgot my disappointment. Now I see that your success lay in your complete absorption in the character to the exclusion of your own personality.

How I love that man from your book! He was so <u>good,</u> so <u>wise.</u> So beautifully and completely developed, realizing to a great extent man's possibilities as they are so seldom realized. He was a man as ~~mean~~ men were meant to be. It is a compliment to your skill that you portrayed him so clearly. His whole personality has been transported into my mind. I feel him; not just identify the thought of him with a few facts and dates.

Since I received your letter I have re-read "To the Lighthouse." After reading your prose-particularly your novels, I feel dizzy - feverish. Your mind is as sensitive as an open wound and you so sensitize your readers. Millions of thoughts, impressions, intimations flash through me - I am so completely alive that it is almost painful. How can one live all the time that way? I am almost thankful for the protective coating of sluggishness which ~~yo~~ usually coats my nerves.

Can you identify for me these lines from "To the Lighthouse?" I have tried, but I can't find them. Nobody recognizes them.

> "All the lives we ever lived
> And all the lives to be
> Are full of trees and changing leaves" etc.[5]

I want to ask if you one more thing. Is there any place where I can buy a picture of you? Is there anybody who deals in such goods? Could you give me the adress [sic]? Or if not-is this really too insolent? -could you send me one? Anything - perhaps a clipping from a magazine or paper. I found a lovely one in Winifred Holtby's study of your work - But the book does not belong to me and I hesitate at vandalism.

I have just read Yeats' letters to Dorothy Wellesl[e]y. In one letter she says that you believe poetry is the only thing worth writing.[6] Now that isn't strictly so, is it? Surely prose has advantages which poetry does not have, and much of your prose holds what effects poetry does have.

Well, this letter is very long after all. And not quite sane. However, I will mail it.

I hope for the complete success of "Roger Fry" - every sort of success, and for health and happiness (or at least pleasure) for you. These days must be dreadful for all of you. Its [sic] like a mad nightmare even from this viewpoint. How everyone here sympathizes!

Yours very sincerely,
John Farrelly, Jr

---

[1] Farrelly was at the time a freshman at St. Louis University, and would stay in St. Louis with relatives or friends. According to Mark Farrelly, it was his brother William, who was a year younger than John but also at the university in 1940-1941, who brought in the letter from Pinook Farm. (John had taken a year out from schooling for financial reasons). For the possible fate of Woolf's letter, see "From Fan-Mail to Readers' Letters," note 15.

[2] Pierre-Eric Villeneuve drew my attention to the striking resemblance between Farrelly's handwriting in this letter (indeed, his signature suggests a change from the first) and Virginia Woolf's own.

[3] The first version of *To the Lighthouse* is indeed in Woolf's handwriting.

[4] John's brother Mark comments: "A story I recall from the time you are mentioning (1940-1941) is that after John wrote a letter to Woolf—either to Virginia Woolf or her husband, though I presume it was the first of his letters—he thought who am I to write this letter. And he threw it out of the car window as my father was driving them back to Pinook one day. He was so surprised when he got a response; someone had picked up the letter and put stamps on it and sent it on. If this happened, and I do not know why I would recall such a story if it had not, it is characteristic of John."

[5] The lines come from "Luriana, Lurilee" by Charles Elton, a poem that Virginia Woolf discovered through Lytton Strachey and that was still unpublished at the time Farrelly wrote. For details of its later publication see the Shakespeare Head edition of *To the Lighthouse* (Oxford: Blackwell, 1992), edited by Susan Dick.

[6] In a letter dated 6 July 1936, Dorothy Wellesley wrote, "I had a charming letter from Virginia Woolf, saying that 'praise from Yeats is the only solid thing of its kind now existing' . . . .Of course when all is said and done poetry is the only stuff [except very little prose] worth writing, most especially now, and I think she, Virginia, knows it." See W.B. Yeats, *Letters on Poetry from W. B. Yeats to Dorothy Wellesley* (London: Oxford UP, 1940): 78-79. But Wellesley also advised Yeats to study "all" of Woolf's works, noting that Woolf possessed both "rhythm" and "genius" (62-63).

Handwritten
April 5, 1941

Virginia Woolf drowned herself in the river Ouse on March 28, 1941. On April 3, the St. Louis Post-Dispatch *carried a news item from the Associated Press, announcing that she was missing and presumed dead. On April 4, the* Post-Dispatch *published an editorial, as Farrelly mentions below, linking her suicide with that of Count Paul Teleki, the Hungarian prime minister, on the same day. Rather than pathologizing Woolf as a special case, the editorial argued that the common fate of "one of the most sensitive, most delicate contemporary practitioners of the art of English prose writing" and "a seasoned statesman" who was "an old hand at Europe's international poker game," in addition to "the thousands and thousands of unrecorded suicides," testified to the toll being exacted by the tragedy and madness of war.[1] One can only guess the impact of this editorial on Farrelly, who had written to Woolf not only about their shared sensitivities, but also about his sympathy for what she must be enduring at the time.*

Pinook Farm
Allenton Missouri
5[2] April, 1941

My Dear Mr. Woolf,
 I was shocked and saddened by the news of your wife's death. For two days I have been stunned and sick at the thought. You may question this from a person who knew absolutely [nothing] of Mrs. Woolf's private life, who had never even met her. But I think that anyone who has known her books feels the same. Through all her writing runs the thread of a lovely and loveable person, so that one naturally felt a personal affection for Mrs. Woolf herself. And we knew her at her very best.
 I know that so many felt this from the way many of my friends speak. Her's [sic] is not just the death of a public figure for them. The Post Dispatch (our main newspaper - and a hard-boiled political sheet, at that) ran a sympathetic and admiring editorial about her last night. My English professor (I am a freshman at college) devoted yesterday's class to an enthusiastic lecture on her.[3] They all felt a deep personal loss.
 So if it is any consolation to you to know that so many everywhere share your sorrow, draw upon that consolation.

I wrote a letter to Mrs. Woolf last Fall which she answered. I mailed another from St. Louis about January 15. I wonder if she ever received it.[4]

Sympathy is a weak and inadequate thing - particularly from a stranger, but one needs to do or say something - yet is left gaping. I know that I feel much that words would only falsify and make clumsy and ridiculous. In a sense, I write this for myself - Not only for you am I grieved, but with you.

Sincerely yours,
John Farrelly Jr.

[1] "A Measure of Today's Tragedy," *Post-Dispatch* [St. Louis] 4 April 1941: E3. I would like to express my sincere thanks to Mike Meiners, Director of News Research at the *Post-Dispatch*, for providing me with this information and with a copy of the editorial.

[2] The 5 appears to have been written over a 1, most likely the beginning of "1941."

[3] Presumably, this professor was Herbert Marshall McLuhan.

[4] While it might seem that Farrelly wrote somewhat precipitously on the news of Virginia's presumed death (her body was not recovered until April 18), the *Post-Dispatch* editorial had written of her suicide. Furthermore, Farrelly's quick response seems motivated by a deep anxiety to know whether his second letter to her had arrived—whether, with its words of sympathy about the war, it had reached its *reader*.

New Republic, 26 April 1948: 20-21

THE PURSUIT OF READING
By John Farrelly

THE MOMENT AND OTHER ESSAYS, by Virginia Woolf (Harcourt, Brace and Company; $3).
THE COMMON READER: FIRST AND SECOND SERIES, by Virginia Woolf (Harcourt, Brace and Company; $4).

THE SECOND posthumous volume of Virginia Woolf's essays has been published, and her husband, Leonard Woolf, says that a sufficient number remain to make another book. If *The Moment and Other Essays* does not, as a whole, come up to the First and Second Series of *The Common Reader* (now published for the first time in one volume), it is perhaps because they have not been chosen "according to some scale of merit," but as representative of the variety of her subject matter. And it must be admitted that there is variety enough in such topics as D. H. Lawrence, Ellen Terry, Ring Lardner and Queen Marie. However, this reservation scarcely needs to be qualified by saying that when Virginia Woolf suffers it is only by comparison with herself; that her best work is unexcelled by anything of its kind in English letters.

Her writing is supremely personal, but the triumph of the personal is charm, that quality so unsettling to critical evaluation. Virginia Woolf has suffered from a kind of hypnotized adulation; on the other hand, she has suffered (and will continue to suffer) from the inevitable reversal when the critical intelligence does penance for its excesses. The usual accusation is that she lacks seriousness, and this is frequently untrue. She has the kind of civilized mind that maintains its subtle balance between a witty manner and a serious purpose. And when she does err it is by a kind of excess of virtue: her manner dazzles her subject out of countenance so that it seems to diminish by comparison with her celebration of it.

The essays in *The Moment*, as in *The Common Reader*, are for the most part on literary subjects, and, taken together, these volumes form a high tribute to the "pursuit of reading." "Of all men," wrote Mrs. Woolf, "great scholars are the most mysterious, the most august." This is mock-serious veneration from a lady of wit and fine intelligence, blessed with leisure and passionately addicted to the reading of books. It is the tribute of the insistent amateur, implying an aristocratic disdain of professional inclusiveness or finality. Her position is neither academic nor editorial, but that of the modest common reader who " reads for his own pleasure." With an exquisite courtesy, she assumes a like industry "in all those rooms, too humble to be called libraries, yet full of books, where the pursuit of reading is carried on by private people." But when she describes the common reader she does him too great justice, and the description fits herself more exactly than any reader likely to be common today.

"Above all," she says, "he is guided by an instinct to create for himself . . . a portrait of a man, a sketch of an age, a theory of the art of writing. He never ceases, as he reads, to run up some rickety and ramshackle fabric which shall give him the temporary satisfaction of looking sufficiently like the real object to allow of affection, laughter and argument." That is her method-to recreate the subject of her reading through her own keen perceptions and appreciation, and by communicating her enthusiasm "to allow of affection."

To create "a portrait of a man"—thus she often penetrates through writing to the writer himself, and by solidly establishing the figure of the artist, illumines his work. This is her treatment of Montaigne, Donne, Thomas Browne and George Eliot, for example. But the minor or obscure figures most engage her talents— some half-forgotten diarist, some stillborn monster of literature, some odd member of a vanished *beau monde*. "For one likes romantically to feel oneself a deliverer advancing with lights across the waste of years to the rescue of some stranded ghost. . . . Possibly they hear one coming. They shuffle, they preen, they bridle. Old secrets well to their lips. The divine gift of communication will soon again be theirs." The wit of such a passage lies in its perfect description of her intention, her attitude and her achievement.

And what an animated lot they are, especially her women: the Duchess of Newcastle, Laetitia Pilkington, Miss Mitford, Geraldine Jewsbury. She particularly favors the eccentrics, those capricious, erratic and extravagant personalities so fitted to her own prose. In her hands they loom as significant figures. Reading these essays consecutively, one is surprised by the extent to which they accumulate as a history of manners, particularly of the eighteenth and early nineteenth centuries. And as the same figures appear and reappear, like characters in a novel, the whole forms a social comedy in exquisite miniature.

Any "theory of the art of writing" is advanced tentatively by Virginia Woolf. When such inquiries occur they are usually on the connection between writing and the environment in which it is produced. What is, for example, the connection between women's writing and "their condition itself . . . the privacy they lacked, the incomes they had not, the conventions which stifled them and the education they never received"? In her last essays the war has forced comparison between its writers and the traditional novelists; Jane Austen and Scott, for example, who never "heard Napoleon's voice as we hear Hitler's voice as we sit at home of an evening."

Finally there are class distinctions: "The Elizabethan age was far more elastic in this respect than our own," but as everyone knows, almost all writers from Chaucer's time to the present have "been raised above the mass of people upon a tower of stucco—that is their middle-class birth; and of gold—that is their expensive education." But for the writers between the two wars the tower began to lean, and "directly we feel that a tower leans, we become acutely conscious that we are on a tower." Socially conscious, in short, with the ironic result that the leaning-tower writers "do not look any class straight in the face," and their tendencies she sums up as "discomfort; pity for themselves; anger against society."

The woman, she would seem to imply, is classless. If excluded from the professions open to men, she is (or can be) by the same token independent of the class interests, that is, the vested interests, of the men of the family. Again the amateur, but again free of the pretensions of male professionalism, a freer citizen of the "republic of letters." Of course, she speaks here for her own generation, now passing, and it is for some such broad republic that she hopes when she speaks (in 1940) of a classless, but scarcely uniform society in which "only natural differences such as those of brain and character will serve to distinguish us."

But no hope that Virginia Woolf ever entertained could relinquish those precious privileges: leisure and privacy—for reading. In a society of equal opportunity for literacy, the price, indeed the purpose, is a general lucidity and discernment. And the great ordinary means is to hand: "We have got to teach ourselves to understand literature." The advice that follows is inevitable; it is the only one which fits the case, yet it is all the more urgent and touching for its reiteration during a lifetime devoted to books: "We can begin . . . by reading omnivorously, simultaneously, poems, plays, novels, histories, biographies, the old and the new. We must sample before we can select. It never does to be a nice feeder."

If the purpose of criticism is an appropriate appreciation of the subject, the common reader will find in few critics the instruction, the delight and the incentive to reading present in almost every page of Virginia Woolf.

Books in Review, *New Republic*, 6 September 1948: 21-22

THE LANDSCAPE OF THE HEART
by John Farrelly

TO THE LIGHTHOUSE; MRS. DALLOWAY; THE WAVES; ORLANDO, by Virginia Woolf (Harcourt, Brace and Company; $3 each).

THE RE-ISSUE of these four books in handsome bindings answers no urgent need: three of them are already available in less expensive editions. Nevertheless, it is an occasion to reread several of Mrs. Woolf's books at the same time. Inevitably, I found the spell of the old enchantment considerably diminished. Inevitable, in part, because we are at that awkward distance which prevents either a fresh reading of her work or an impersonal detachment. In so far as our disaffection is caused by a temporary impatience with the elaborate, the playful, the idiosyncratic, we are the losers.

Orlando has always seemed to me embarrassingly frivolous. Of course, it is a very ingenious joke, very "literary" and scholarly, and the frivolity mocks itself, as when, after exercising a few lines in an archaic manner, the author breaks off: "(and so on for six pages if you will, but the style is tedious and may well be dropped)." It would have been delightful as one of her shorter, light pieces, but in this form the joke is stretched beyond the fun in it, and the fun was always more for the writer than the reader.

The Waves is a serious novel, of course, about six children who are brought up together and whose lives are interwoven until the book leaves them in middle age. They reveal themselves (and one another) in alternating interior monologues. Never has Mrs. Woolf (or any other writer, for that matter, in quite this way) employed this technique so exclusively. It is not an attempt to imitate the processes of the unconscious or of involuntary association, but a determined concentration on the self, expressed in a formal poetic style: "'Now let me try,' said Louis, 'before we rise, before we go to tea, to fix the moment in one supreme endeavor. This will endure'."

In this sort of fixity, consciousness is a continual surrender to a stream of sense-impressions and related memories. It is an end in itself; sensitivity is the supreme value. The result is often very lovely; nevertheless, the rhythm of monologue is finally monotonous and the characters of the novel are apt to fade into the anonymity of mere sensitized plates. Any continuity or interrelation of their reveries is too frequently only a trick of composition. *The Waves* (like most of its author's work) has been compared to music—a useful simile, as it suggests a thematic structure unusual in English fiction. But literature is no more music than music is literature, and the obtrusion of a formal scheme risks the chilling or even paralysis of a novel.

Mrs. Dalloway and *To the Lighthouse* are Virginia Woolf's most successful novels. The former is brilliant; it originates on the surface of things—"the silver, the chairs"; "there was a beating, a stirring of galloping ponies, tapping of cricket bats"—and the impulse of these impressions to the reflective mind constructs the sense of "life; London; this moment in June." Appropriately in this world of surfaces, "the supreme mystery . . . was simply this: here was one room, there another." It is a rare creative stroke that recognizes the mood, despite the flash and gayety, as one of ineffable sadness and futility: "This late age of the world's experience had bred in them all, all men and women, a well of tears." The most Clarissa Dalloway can do is give a party.

So far, the work is a triumph of the visual imagination; the following reference to Clarissa's courageous and inane high-mindedness is another matter: "Not for a moment did she believe in God; but all the more, she thought, . . . must one repay in daily life to servants, yes, to dogs and canaries, above all to Richard her husband, who was the foundation of it." And again: "Thank you, thank you, she went on saying in gratitude to her servants generally for helping her to be like this, to be what she wanted, gentle, generous-hearted."

There is here, at the very least, an ambiguity; at most, a failure of the ironic intelligence. How can one judge the passages quoted above? There are too few clues. This failure, if it is failure, is all the more baffling because it is intermittent; Sir William Bradshaw and Hugh Whitbread are disposed of swiftly and keenly.

That is not to say that Clarissa goes scot-free. Peter Walsh, her old love, recognizes in her something "timid; hard; something arrogant; unimaginative; prudish." And "Clarissa had grown . . . a trifle sentimental into the bargain, he suspected." She herself "could see what she lacked. . . . It was something central which permeated; something warm. . . ."

Thus, she is *diminished* as thoroughly as ruthless honesty could demand; in fact, she is diminished until she scarcely fills her place in the center of the book. But what we miss are values other than Clarissa's own by which she can be *placed*. In their absence, and with Clarissa reduced, contracted, the book tends to lapse in places, then to race a bit, and here and there to gush slightly: words like "delicious," "enchanting," "extraordinary" are not infrequent.

At this point, all previous reservations must be suspended: *To the Lighthouse* seems to me among the few near perfect novels in the language. If *Mrs. Dalloway* is dazzling, this book is luminous. It is unique among Virginia

Woolf's writing for its warmth and sympathy. It contains her two most substantial characters: Mr. and Mrs. Ramsay. Its theme, which fills every page with vitality, is expressed by Lily Briscoe at their summer house in the Hebrides, "staying with the Ramsays. Directly she looked up and saw them, what she called 'being in love' flooded them. They became a part of that unreal but penetrating and exciting universe which is the world seen through the eyes of love . . . life, from being made up of little separate incidents which one lived one by one, became curled and whole like a wave which bore one up with it and threw one down with it, there, with a dash, on the beach."

The theme of the book is "love"; the word itself recurs persistently, but with such subtle variations in meaning that one might not recognize its presence. Mrs. Ramsay herself, the central character, personifies the numerous aspects of love. In more general, suggestive terms, there is "the astonishing power that Mrs. Ramsay had over one." Again: "Knowledge and wisdom were stored up in [her] heart." In another place, she is beautifully compared to a bee-hive: "Like a bee, drawn by some sweetness or sharpness in the air intangible to touch or taste, one haunted the dome-shaped hive." "Her capacity to surround and protect" her eight children extends in a wider maternalism: "She had the whole of the other sex under her protection." And like some humble, domestic goddess of love, she is forever match-making: "She was driven on, too quickly she knew, almost as if it were an escape for her too, to say that people must marry; people must have children." She and Mr. Ramsay are themselves "the symbols of marriage, husband and wife." Finally, she is identified, after her death, with "the fertility, the insensibility of nature."

What aerates and lightens this pervasive theme, this almost oppressive love, is the stirring life of the book: the natural summer life of the garden, the dunes, the bay; the quick, sly humor; the gigantic figure of Mr. Ramsay; the gayety of the holiday; the odd assortment of visitors; the many children. Nothing suggests the domestic scene better than the following: "The great clangor of the gong announced solemnly, authoritatively, that all those scattered about, in attics, in bedrooms, on little perches of their own, reading, writing, putting the last smooth to their hair, or fastening dresses, must leave all that, and the little odds and ends on their washing-tables and dressing-tables, and the diaries which were so private, and assemble in the dining-room for dinner"—the wonderful dinner, most festive of the many parties in Virginia Woolf's books, the dinner of the *Boeuf en Daube*.

But if Mrs. Ramsay is the source and repository of love, she is complemented by Lily Briscoe, the artist, whose homage and devotion reflect that life and so create the book: "Love had a thousand shapes. There might be loves whose gift it was to choose out the elements of things and place them together and so, giving them a wholeness not theirs in life, make of some scene, or meeting of people (all now gone and separate) one of those globed compacted things over which thought lingers, and love plays."

Modernist Transformations: Virginia Woolf, Cinderella, and the Legacy of Lady Ritchie

Ann Martin

> At twelve my horses turn into rats and off I go. The illusion fades. But I accept my fate. I make hay while the sun shines.
> —Virginia Woolf, *Night and Day*

> And the twelfth stroke of midnight sounded; the twelfth stroke of midnight, Thursday, the eleventh of October, Nineteen hundred and Twenty-eight.
> —Virginia Woolf, *Orlando*

Virginia Woolf's allusions to Continental fairy tales such as "Cinderella" are informed by personal and cultural associations that complicate our interpretations of both the tales and their significance in her works. Mrs. Ramsay's reading of the Grimms' "The Fisherman and His Wife" in *To the Lighthouse*, for instance, is a realistic detail, echoing the storytellings that took place at 22 Hyde Park Gate (see Annan 109). It is also a thematic detail, presenting a vision of Victorian marriage that "hints" at some of the tensions in the Ramsays' union (Kaehele and German 194). As importantly, it gestures towards the interactive nature of the transmission and reception of inherited texts, where James's and Cam's different responses to the story mirror Woolf's own multifaceted engagements with and uses of literary tradition.[1] In her versions and subversions of fairy tales, Woolf participates in a mode of citation that involves complicity and resistance, as she negotiates the implications of narratives that speak to other times and ideologies as well as to her own.

While a layered response to texts and traditions is typical of any form of intertextuality, Woolf's references to fairy tales become particularly significant in relation to the literary legacy of her aunt, Lady Anne Thackeray Ritchie. Though Ritchie's influence on Woolf has been explored by a number of critics, her adaptations of fairy tales have not been afforded as much attention, nor have they been connected to Woolf's own uses of works by Charles Perrault or the Brothers Grimm. As points of entry for exploring Woolf's "literary transformations" of her Victorian heritage (Paul 6), Ritchie's short stories exemplify perspectives on writing, class, and gender that Woolf's prose would seem to chal-

---

[1] Cam's random movements are, for example, contrasted throughout the reading scene to James's apparent quiescence (see *TTL* 49).

lenge. At the same time, the relationship that emerges from Woolf's often conflicted portrayals of her aunt's life and work testifies to more than a generational divide. Her responses to Ritchie demonstrate what Janis Paul has called "the dynamic of rebellion and return," which characterizes Woolf's attitudes towards the artistic conventions of the previous era (5). In this sense, Woolf's allusions to fairy tales, a genre that she knew her aunt had written in and about,[2] allow her to acknowledge and to alter the legacy of her precursor.

But fairy tales are also texts through which Woolf plays with multiple strands of Victorian and Modern culture. The forms in which Woolf herself encountered fairy tales—as oral stories, commercial children's literature, ballets, operas, and especially pantomimes—indicate the variety of conventions and ideologies, both contemporary and inherited, that influenced her writing, and testify to the cultural diversity that exists within as well as between generations of writers. The sense of plurality associated with fairy tales has particular resonance in a novel such as *Orlando*, with its multiple references to "Cinderella" and to the social normatives with which that story becomes associated. Where Lady Ritchie updates Perrault's seminal version of the fairy tale, reinforcing the stability of the social order that is signified by the heroine's marriage to the Prince, Woolf combines this literary legacy with references to other conventions, most notably those from the British pantomime. Her repeated allusions to the carnivalesque aspects of "Cinderella" are derived, then, not just from the dominant written variants of the tale, but also from the traditions of the *commedia dell'arte*, as the trickster figure of the Harlequin informs Orlando's own performance of identity. The closure implied by the structure of the novel, with its ties to "the Bildungsroman and the biography" (Paul 187), is thus complicated by the gender confusion of both Cinderella and the Principal Boy, as Woolf simultaneously cites and subverts the artistic and social status quo. Like Harlequin's motley, *Orlando*'s patchwork of legitimate and illegitimate art forms both signals and troubles cultural patrimony, as Woolf's allusions to fairy tales challenge the primacy of a single line of literary inheritance.

Woolf had been immersed in the language and culture of Victorian children's literature and fairy tales from an early age.[3] As she states in a 1925 letter to the *Nation* regarding the influence of Charles Dickens,

---

[2] As well as adapting Continental fairy tales, Ritchie wrote an introduction, for example, to *The Fairy Tales of Madame d'Aulnoy* in 1892.

[3] Julia Duckworth Stephen wrote children's stories, which Leslie Stephen illustrated (King 36). Through her mother, Maria Jackson, and her aunt, Sara Prinsep, she knew William Makepeace Thackeray, whose *The Rose and the Ring* Leslie Stephen read to their children (Spalding 7), and John Ruskin, author of *The King of the Golden River*. Woolf herself wrote tales that circulated in the nursery (see V. Bell), as well as in the *Hyde Park Gate News* (Lee 108-109), and among friends like Violet Dickinson (169). Later in life

> [*David Copperfield*] is a book of such astonishing vividness that parents will read it aloud to their children before they can quite distinguish fact from fiction, and they will never in later life be able to recall the first time they read it. *Grimm's Fairy Tales* and *Robinson Crusoe* are for many people in the same case. ("*David Copperfield*" 69)

Woolf's use of fairy tales in her writing is thus a resurfacing of culturally latent imagery and diction, including but not restricted to works of literature. Invoking a figure from Perrault's collection of fairy tales, for instance, she refers to Lady Cunard as a "stringy old hop o' my thumb" (*D3* 202). She draws upon a more general knowledge of the stories when she describes Phil Burne Jones as being a "fairy God father to [...] fashionable young ladies" (*D3* 248). Her familiarity with fairy tales stems also from her enjoyment of the British pantomime, a Christmas theatrical tradition that, by the turn of the century, was an amalgamation of conventions from the *commedia dell'arte*, the music-hall, the fairy tale extravaganzas of J. R. Planché, the commodity culture of the modern city, and of course, the stories popularized by Perrault and the Grimms.[4] Her experiences with the pantomime are echoed in her diary. For example, she compares *The Voyage Out* to "a harlequinade" (*D2*17) and decides that her next novel will "be very Arabian nights" (*D3* 236).[5] In her essays too, fairy tales, be they written or staged, are used as metaphors. Woolf compares John Ruskin to a Sleeping Beauty who has been given "gifts" by fairies but still succumbs to his position as an "outsider" to literature ("Ruskin" 50). In a piece on Jane Austen, she suggests that "One of those fairies who perch upon cradles must have taken her on a flight through the world directly she was born" ("Jane Austen" 136). The sto-

---

she wrote *Nurse Lugton's Curtain* for her niece, Ann Stephen, and *The Widow and the Parrot: A True Story* for Julian and Quentin Bell's *Charleston Bulletin*. According to Quentin Bell, his Aunt's story was "a tease. We had hoped vaguely for something as funny, as subversive, and as frivolous as Virginia's conversation. Knowing this, she sent us an 'improving story' with a moral, based on the very worst Victorian examples" (Afterword).

[4] The popularity of the British pantomime cannot be understated. In December of 1897, for instance, at least 25 pantomimes, including "Cinderella," "Beauty and the Beast," and "Red Riding Hood," were staged in London and its suburbs (Archer 424-425). Woolf notes in her diaries that she attended a performance of *Aladdin* in January of 1897 and went to the first run of *Peter Pan* in January of 1905 (*PA* 6, 228). George Duckworth, it seems, "took children to the pantomime" regularly (*MOB* 144-45). In 1918 she seems to have done the same for Julian and Quentin Bell when they visited her in London (381), and in 1930 she went with Angelica to the Lyceum for the pantomime *Puss in Boots* (*D3* 284-285).

[5] Indeed, in Chapter IX of *The Voyage Out*, Ridley actually mentions "sitting on a rock thinking of nothing at all when Elliot started up like a fairy in a pantomime" (111).

ries are part of Woolf's working vocabulary, be it as unconscious points of reference or as deliberately chosen intertexts. As cultural common ground, they enable her to bridge the gap between author and reader, as well as between "high art" and popular culture.

Whether in the form of published stories or pantomimes, films or advertisements, fairy tales pervade almost every area of British cultural production in the twentieth century, representing tradition and continuity as much as their own adaptability and ideological malleability. While the most familiar fairy tales arrived in England through translations of Charles Perrault's *Histoires, ou contes du temps passé, avec des Moralitez* in the eighteenth century, and of *Kinder- und Hausmärchen* by the Brothers Grimm in the early nineteenth century, they reached an unprecedented popularity in the Victorian period. By the end of the nineteenth century, writers such as Ruskin, Lewis Carroll, George MacDonald, Jean Ingelow, and Oscar Wilde had written new fairy stories for children that presented lessons in socialism, feminism, and environmentalism, as well as more conservative political perspectives. Using traditional fairy tales to achieve similar pedagogical goals also had Victorian antecedents. While Planché's fairy tale extravaganzas were oriented primarily towards satiric entertainment, literary adaptations of the same stories were published by Woolf's aunt, Anne Thackeray Ritchie, and had rather different aims. Diane Gillespie notes that Woolf owned "the volume of *Five Old Friends and a Young Prince* (1876) that Anny inscribed and gave to Julia [Stephen]" (7). This text was originally published in 1868, and features a number of Ritchie's reworkings of Perrault's tales, including "The Sleeping Beauty in the Wood," "Cinderella," and "Little Red Riding Hood," as well as "Jack the Giant-Killer," probably inspired by a Grimms' story, and Madame de Beaumont's "Beauty and the Beast." It was followed by another volume, *Bluebeard's Keys and Other Stories*, published in 1874, which contains versions of "Bluebeard," "Riquet à la Houppe," "Jack and the Bean-Stalk," and "The White Cat" ("Thackeray" 182).

The sister of Leslie Stephen's first wife, Minny, and the eldest child of William Makepeace Thackeray, Anne Isabella Thackeray Ritchie established a lasting connection with the Stephens. During her marriage to Richmond Ritchie, later Lord Ritchie, Anny stayed in touch with her brother-in-law (Fuller 156), and after Minny's death, introduced to him his future second wife, Julia Duckworth. After Julia's death in 1895, Ritchie became a frequent visitor to the Stephen household and an important support system for Leslie Stephen and his children (Gérin 241). Stephen's feelings for her were somewhat conflicted. Though his irritation with Anny's "absurd or contradictory" behavior was often accompanied by genuine affection (Stephen 14), Hermione Lee suggests that

Ritchie was "treated by the Stephen children (under parental guidance) as a figure of fun" (76). The Anny Thackeray Ritchie that Quentin Bell presents, for instance, is associated with an "extraordinary youthful, vigorous and resilient optimism," but also with an "ebullience [that] must have been overwhelming" and "exasperating" (*Woolf* I 11).

Virginia Woolf's portraits of Ritchie as an author participate in this Stephenish ambivalence. Her appreciation of Ritchie's energetic style is layered, for instance, with her doubts regarding Ritchie's approach to writing itself. On one hand, Ritchie is "a writer of genius" and "a true artist" ("Lady Ritchie" 13, 14); on the other, she is a charming woman who seems more often than not to be "scribbling brilliant nonsense" ("Enchanted" 399). The figure of Mrs. Hilbery encapsulates this doubled vision, particularly in light of her non-academic approach to the genre of biography in *Night and Day*. Like Ritchie, who represents for Woolf a "female tradition," Mrs. Hilbery is an alternative to the patriarchal and homosocial Oxbridge system of Richard Alardyce (Marcus, "Enchanted" 104). Their shared emphasis on personal and ephemeral details challenges the official public version of the father in question, and is echoed in Woolf's own rather irreverent works of biography: *Flush*, *Freshwater*, and of course, *Orlando*. However, this resistance is limited by the very legacy that the fictional woman and her model inherit. Mrs. Hilbery is described as "a child who is surrounding itself with a building of bricks" (88), as the Father continues to exert his authority in *Night and Day*: "All the books and pictures, even the chairs and tables, had belonged to him, or had reference to him" (89). She remains officially the daughter of an educated man, supporting and constrained by his powerful reputation.

Woolf herself is faced with a similar situation, though she must negotiate not just the immediate influence of her Aunt Anny, but also the somewhat dubious legacy of the Victorian woman writer, whom Woolf associates with Ritchie through the recurring image of the thrush. In 1919's "Lady Ritchie," the bird is associated with the light and natural tone of Ritchie's sketches of the past:

> Again and again it has happened to us to trace down our conception of one of the great figures of the past not to the stout official biography consecrated to him, but to some little hint or fact or fancy dropped lightly by Lady Ritchie in passing, as a bird alights on a branch, picks off the fruit and leaves the husk for another. (18)

In *Night and Day*, the same image is associated with Mrs. Hilbery's almost capricious approach to writing, where she fills "a page every morning as instinctively as a thrush sings" (27).[6] In *Orlando*, such music is connected with female emotion rather than with intellectual rigor: "At one moment we deplore our birth and state and aspire to an ascetic exaltation; the next we are overcome by the smell of some old garden path and weep to hear the thrushes sing" (102). In "Women and Fiction," the image of the bird is tied directly to the liabilities of feminine writing:

> In the past, the virtue of women's writing often lay in its divine spontaneity, like that of the blackbird's song or the thrush's. It was untaught; it was from the heart. But it was also, and much more often, chattering and garrulous—mere talk spilt over paper and left to dry in pools and blots. (51)

As Ellen Rosenman suggests in her reading of *A Room of One's Own*, "The female 'temperament' expressed in Mrs. Hilbery's giddiness and lack of discipline either disfigures art with personal grievance or prevents it from taking shape altogether" (64).[7] By the late twenties, the cluster of images that connect Ritchie, women's writing, and birds has come to signify the limitations of the Victorian precursor.

The ambivalence surrounding the inspired but flighty song of the thrush provides an interesting backdrop to Woolf's statement that "we think back through our mothers if we are women" (*AROO* 69). Because the woman writer fears that there is no strong female tradition to engage with, she faces an "'anxiety of authorship'—a radical fear that she cannot create, that because she can never become a 'precursor' the act of writing will isolate or destroy her" (Gilbert and Gubar, *Madwoman* 49). The solution is to find female role models who will "legitimize her own rebellious endeavors" (50), since the precursor, by "acting as mother and mirror, affirms the daughter's identity as an artist" (Rosenman 139). This female literary tradition involves not only a recognition that "each generation of women writers influences each other," but also an acknowledgement that "style evolves historically and is determined by class and sex" (Marcus, *Art* 80). Evolution is a process predicated upon natural, or in this case, literary selection; that is, it involves a rejection of some women writers and a dependence upon others. In this sense, it becomes necessary for the Modernist

---

[6] The image is applied directly to Ritchie by Carol Hanberry MacKay (75) and by Winifred Gérin (241).

[7] Similarly, Elizabeth Boyd suggests that, for Woolf, Ritchie writes "as naturally as the bird sings," but does not "rewrite, select, and perfect," a distinction that represents the crucial difference between the two artists (89).

to determine which woman is an "empowering ancestress" and which is only a "trivial" or "silly lady writer" (Gilbert and Gubar, *No Man's Land* 203).[8]

In Woolf's portraits of Ritchie, however, Aunt Anny occupies both of these roles: she is an important female influence, but also a feminine writer of limited abilities. Instead of choosing between a powerful precursor and a "weaker talent," then, it would seem that Woolf chooses both in a layered presentation of the same writer (Bloom 5). This "double positionality," to use Melba Cuddy-Keane's terminology, speaks not just to a sense of ambivalence towards Ritchie and her writing, but to a deliberate rhetorical strategy in which Woolf herself occupies two positions (148). The "multilevel discourse," through which Woolf self-reflexively disrupts the transparency and stability of her own voice, has obvious significance in relation to *Orlando*, in which the layering of authorial presence is echoed by the layering of literary styles and genres, as well as by the layering of motifs from "Cinderella." By combining different responses to Ritchie in her biographical sketches, and by combining in *Orlando* Ritchie's interpretations of fairy tales with other versions of "Cinderella," Woolf troubles a model of artistic production that is based upon a single, evolving line of inheritance. Instead of consolidating the legitimacy of the father or mother figure, and thus of the heir, Woolf patches together a different vision of legacy, where the multiple cultural influences that are connected through fairy tales provide an alternative to a naturalized patrilineal tradition.

As I will suggest in my reading of *Orlando*, Woolf puts into play the more disruptive aspects and forms of "Cinderella" to undercut inherited cultural assumptions regarding the performance and policing of gender roles, and thus the stability and the hegemony of heteronormative legacies. In contrast, Ritchie's aim in her stories is to reform and improve society through established Victorian narratives and strictures. Fairy tales are connected in Ritchie's work to the family unit, wherein women navigate the possibilities and pitfalls of courtship, marriage, and childrearing. Not surprisingly, Ritchie was exposed to fairy tales in part through her father, William Makepeace Thackeray, whose Christmas book of 1855, *The Rose and the Ring,* is one of a series of stories he wrote for children.[9] Where her father's absurdly playful fairy story is clearly intended to entertain, Ritchie's tales are intended not just to delight but to

---

[8] Ritchie's works certainly echo the plots of the "*mind-and-millinery* species" of novel that George Eliot critiques (301), just as Ritchie's lack of "patient diligence" places her in proximity to the lady novelists from whom Woolf would seem to distance herself (323).

[9] Though the delightfully silly adventures of Prince Giglio of Paflagonia are subtitled a "Fire-side Pantomime for Great and Small Children" (Thackeray 197), Thackeray emphasizes less the theatrical conventions of the pantomime form, and more its fairy-tale plot, which ends through magical interventions in marriage.

instruct. Her adaptations of Perrault are directed not necessarily towards children but more towards women, and are inspired, perhaps, by her journalism for the *Cornhill Magazine*, which "encouraged" the women who wrote for it "to identify with key social issues of their own times" (Harris 389). Her essays are also social commentaries through which she addresses topics such as marriage, and women's careers and educational opportunities. "Toilers and Spinsters" (1874), for instance, explores the issue of women's employment, which Woolf later addresses in *A Room of One's Own* and "Professions for Women." Unlike Woolf, however, Ritchie does not encourage resistance to a patriarchal order that forces women to rely financially and emotionally upon often unreliable men, but rather offers ways in which women can work within the system. It is a pragmatic approach, but one that accepts the status quo despite a recognition of its inherent or systemic flaws.

Another influence on Ritchie's adaptations of the stories is the literary tradition of "'domestic fiction'" (Boyd 77), which is echoed in her depiction of the growth and often the love-life of the heroine. Though she presents insightful commentaries on economics and gender within this form, Ritchie's emphasis on the marriage plot tends to overshadow the more overtly political aspects of her texts. In "Jack and the Bean-Stalk" from *Bluebeard's Keys and Other Stories*, for instance, the updated title character leads a labor revolt against the local squire. The portrayal of social reform is, however, gradually supplanted by Ritchie's focus on a romance that remains grounded in patriarchal norms. Her version of "Sleeping Beauty in the Wood" involves a similarly conservative vision of gender relations. The heroine is Cecilia Lulworth, who has been lulled into an intellectual and emotional slumber by her overprotective and ignorant mother:

> though Mrs. Lulworth had grown up stupid, suspicious, narrow-minded, soured, and overbearing, and had married for an establishment, and Miss Bowley, her governess's daughter, had turned out nervous, undecided, melancholy, and anxious, and had never married at all, yet they determined to bring up Cecilia as they themselves had been brought up, and sincerely thought they could not do better. (*Five* 8-9)

The issue is education, but the focus of the critique is the individual, rather than the larger social factors that contribute to these flawed versions of femininity. Indeed, the spell is broken not by a direct challenge to a system in which poorly educated women are expected to turn children into productive citizens, but by Cecilia's cousin, who visits, falls in love with, and eventually marries the heroine. Cecilia becomes a symbol of the proper bourgeois wife and mother, whose rewards are "her children and her husband" (28).

Ritchie's version of Perrault's "Cinderella" in *Five Old Friends and a Young Prince* also features the happy marriage of a rescuing hero and a rescued heroine. At twelve years of age, Ella Ashford is a budding Angel in the House: "She was a cheery, happy little creature, looking at everything from the sunny side, adoring her father, running wild out of doors, but with an odd turn for housekeeping, and order and method at home" (42). The Evil Stepmother, however, turns her into a servant. It is only when Ella is fostered by Lady Jane Peppercorne, who outfits the "hesitating, flushing, blushing" girl in appropriate clothing (56) and takes her out to make her debut in society, that the situation changes. In a powerful echo of the second moral to Perrault's version of the story, the wealth and social connections of Ella's Fairy Godmother make the girl's beauty meaningful.[10] Similarly, although Ella's Prince Charming is "a short ugly man," he is desirable in large part because he is "the next heir to a baronetcy" (61). Ritchie makes a point, of course, of informing her readers that the girl falls in love with the man rather than with his money, and that the would-be baronet falls in love with Ella's fairy-like perfection. Even so, the hero's desire is most obvious when Ella wears a "beautiful white net dress" and her "pearl necklace with the diamond clasp" (70). In ending the tale with a benediction encouraging "happiness, content and plenty," the narrator proposes a vision of marital bliss that is very much linked to the financial issues that have informed the story throughout (78).

As in most variants of "Cinderella," Ella's upward social shift depends upon the Prince's gaze and his recognition not just of her beauty, but of the class position that her beautiful dress signifies. In Perrault's tale, for example, Cinderella's performance of a sexually appealing identity arises from her gown, according to which she is identified as a "beautiful princess" (72). Similarly, Ella Ashford's beauty seems incongruous to the Prince of Ritchie's tale when she is wearing dusty working clothes, but appropriate when she dons her white dress and diamonds. In other words, Cinderella's heterosexual appeal can be acknowledged only when she is properly—that is, wealthily—clothed, whether by the ball

---

[10] Godmothers are useful things
Even when without the wings.
Wisdom may be yours and wit,
Courage, industry, and grit—
What's the use of these at all,
If you lack at friend at call? (78)

gown or the glass slipper.[11] As Arthur Rackham and Edmund Gosse's adaptation of Perrault's "Cinderella" suggests, the Prince cannot recognize the appeal of the heroine if she is not in costume:

> Amazed, the prince followed, but could not catch her. Indeed, he missed his lovely princess altogether, and only saw running out of the palace doors a little dirty lass whom he had never beheld before, and of whom he certainly would never have taken the least notice. (230)

The ending of the Grimms' version makes the same point, as it is the slipper that prompts the Prince's recognition of desirable femininity (127). Clothes make the woman or man, and money makes the clothes; thus money makes gender material, or makes it matter in a society where the body is almost secondary to its social markings.

The connection between fashion and social identity, and the performative nature of gender are at the heart of *Orlando* and Woolf's multifaceted use of "Cinderella." But where Cinderella's transformation and social ascension consolidate an aristocratic, heterosexual, and patriarchal order in Perrault's story, or a bourgeois version of the same in Ritchie's domestic romance, Orlando's transformations subvert the naturalized status of the system and parody its assumptions of control and consistency. Such instability is suggested in Woolf's opening description of the title character:

> When he put his hand on the window-sill to push the window open, it was instantly coloured red, blue, and yellow like a butterfly's wings. Thus, those who like symbols, and have a turn for the deciphering of them, might observe that though the shapely legs, the handsome body, and the well-set shoulders were all of them decorated with various tints of heraldic light, Orlando's face, as he threw the window open, was lit solely by the sun itself. (12)

Orlando's body mocks the solidity of patriarchy, as the father's coat of arms is reduced here to "various tints of heraldic light": identity becomes a temporary projection rather than an embodiment of inherited, propertied, gendered position. Like Cinderella, whose status depends upon her clothing, Orlando's social role seems about as stable as the shifting colors on his body. In this image, the family line, and the heterosexual gender roles upon which it rests, become a patchwork of conflicting subject positions and cultural impulses that, like the colors of the stained glass windows, shift according to time and context.

---

[11] In contemporary films predicated upon the basic plot of "Cinderella," we see the same movement. In *Maid in Manhattan*, for example, the Jennifer Lopez character is acknowledged by the wealthy politician "when he catches her trying on a Dolce & Gabbana suit worth several thousand dollars" (Gordon J3).

The motley array of tints and hues also marks Orlando as Harlequin, a figure that symbolizes a "temporary liberation from the prevailing truth and from the established order" (Bakhtin 10).[12] Woolf's allusion to Harlequin arises, I would suggest, in large part from her experiences of the British pantomime, a bastard form of theatre that was heavily influenced not just by fairy tales, but by the *commedia dell'arte*. Indeed, the Harlequin was a prominent image in turn-of-the-century British society. As Martin Green and John Swan note, Pierrot and Harlequin appear in a wide range of Modernist art. In texts as diverse as Picasso's *The Two Saltimbanques*, Diaghilev's ballet *Le Carnaval*, and Wyndham Lewis's *The Wild Body*, the commedia, with its roots in street theatre, comes to represent an alternative to "society's dominant respectable values" (xiii). Edith Sitwell's *Façade*, which Woolf reviewed in the 1920s (Lee 470), contains a number of commedic references (Hunter 15). Indeed, Sacheverell Sitwell would issue *The Hundred and One Harlequins* in 1922, and Edith and Osbert Sitwell would publish a collection of poetry entitled *Twentieth Century Harlequinade* (Green and Swan 43). One of the most striking Harlequins in Modernist literature, though, appears in Joseph Conrad's *Heart of Darkness* from 1902. The "motley appearance, clownish mannerisms, and conspicuous gullibility" of the Russian sailor that Marlow encounters in the Congo mark him as a "harlequinesque character" (Canario 225), and the costume becomes emblematic of the "confused lack of order" at the heart of the novel (Helder 364). Conrad's use of the figure is informed also by the traditional associations of Harlequin with "death and the underworld" (Yoder 90), a connection that resonates in Dorothy L. Sayers's *Murder Must Advertise* from 1933. In the novel, Lord Peter Wimsey masquerades as Death Bredon by day and as Harlequin by night, linking a murder that has taken place at an advertising agency to the local drug trade. Wimsey's masquerades recall Orlando's shifts in identity, as Sayers presents the instability of modern subjectivity, for which the opiates of capitalism and cocaine would seem to compensate. A trickster figure, with one foot in the subversive space of the carnival and the other in the realm of death, the Modernist Harlequin signifies the shifting border territories of human experience.[13]

---

[12] Martin Green and John Swan suggest, in fact, that *Orlando* is a "commedic novel" in which Woolf adapts "the archetypal figures to the subject matter of literature and history" in the text (9).

[13] We can think here particularly of Pablo Picasso's use of Harlequin: not just the playful designs he produced for *Parade* in 1917, the commedic performance piece on which he collaborated with Eric Satie and Jean Cocteau (Nichols 38), but also two specific Harlequin paintings he produced in 1901 and 1915 that are connected with the deaths of Casagemas and Eva Gouel (Green and Swan 164, 179).

The role of Harlequin in the British pantomime speaks to the same sense of liminality, inversion, and potential social critique, but in an overtly comic way. Harlequin is traditionally a servant, "loyal, credulous, greedy, always amorous, always getting his master or himself into a scrape" (Nicoll 73-74). Remaining within the traditions of the *commedia dell'arte*, the Harlequin of nineteenth-century pantomime is "always in love, always in trouble, easily despairing, easily consoled" ("Harlequin"). He is at the center of the harlequinade, or transformation scene of the panto, in which the lovers from the main narrative line, usually based upon a fairy tale, are transformed into Harlequin and Columbine. In this topsy-turvy world, where Harlequin's magical bat or "slapstick" gives him control, the love that is otherwise prohibited by the elder blocking characters from the main plot can be expressed. The bat becomes a carnivalesque phallus that enables play and parody, where the servant becomes the master and overturns the existing social order (Holland 198).[14] But the harlequinade marks only a temporary shift in position. The pantomime ends in a reassertion of order, as both Harlequin and Columbine reenter the existing social structure in their proper guises when the Good Fairy reestablishes the status quo.

Less easily contained by the ending of the pantomime, however, is the gender trouble posed by the figure of the Principal Boy. Orlando's "shapely legs," which Woolf notes in her opening description of his body, suggest this cross-dressed figure of the actress who would play the role of the hero of the fairy tale and the harlequinade. While later influenced by male impersonators from the music hall, such as Vesta Tilley, the Principal Boy was traditionally played by women who "were ample of figure" and whose "considerable embonpoint" contrasted with the gender of the character's costume (Garber 176, 177).[15] The incongruous combination of female-gendered body and male-gendered clothing represents another form of transformation and staged cultural confusion, suggesting the instability of social status and gender, however much this play with sexed roles was disavowed or limited to the space of the theatre.

---

[14] As Cheryl Herr points out, this is the impulse and the cultural discourse that James Joyce plays with at the end of the "Circe" section of *Ulysses*. The spectre of Rudy Bloom "is both silent harlequin and the hero of a twentieth-century panto": a dream figure who straddles life and death, having been transformed by his father's imagination into an idealized figure of innocence and redemption (176).

[15] The Dame role, such as the Wicked Stepmother or Ugly Stepsister, was played by men (see Booth 59; Garber 176). Interestingly, though the Dame remains the same in contemporary pantomime, "Principal Boys became slimmer, more 'boyish'" (Garber 176), and the male lead is now usually played by a man, with the exception of some performances of *Peter Pan*.

The British pantomime's repressed challenge to social normatives is extended in *Orlando* through Woolf's multiple allusions to "Cinderella." Indeed, like the harlequinade—a tradition that "satirically and crazily reflected [the] real world and simultaneously laughed at it" (Booth 6)—the appeal of "Cinderella" lies in its representation of social inversion. The servant becomes the mistress in this fairy tale, though paradoxically, the power of the role reversal is not undercut by the reader's knowledge of Cinderella's original privileged class position. The ball that Cinderella attends is like a carnival, which enables disguise and transformation, a plot point that is echoed in the celebration that takes place in *Orlando* during the extraordinary weather of the Great Frost. The challenge to the normal order is symbolized in Woolf's text by the setting of the sun:

> Various churches and noblemen's palaces, whose fronts were of white stone showed in streaks and patches as if floating on the air. Of St Paul's, in particular, nothing was left but a gilt cross. The Abbey appeared like the grey skeleton of a leaf. Everything suffered emaciation and transformation. (34)

The church and its laws become "nothing" in this scene, subject to the same kind of arbitrary power that the cold exerts on the countryside and the city, or that Harlequin's bat exerts in the harlequinade. This temporary overthrow allows for the disruption of other social normatives on the frozen Thames, echoing the Prince's ball in which he can make his choice of bride.

The Elizabethan carnival setting that enables Orlando to fall in love with the Russian Princess also allows for the logic of the fairy tale itself to be overturned. According to Ritchie's version of the story, for example, the Prince recognizes his Cinderella and establishes her in a stable and privileged social position according to the authority of the marriage ceremony. In *Orlando*, however, Sasha's identity remains as unstable as the carnival and its setting. Indeed, she is associated most powerfully with the actors who present *Othello* at the fair, a theatrical performance that spills commedically onto the street.[16] Though the intertext suggests a gender correspondence, where Orlando identifies with the title character of Shakespeare's tragedy and Sasha becomes his female victim, the parallels only emphasize the performative nature of gendered identity (35).[17] The Desdemona with which Sasha is associated is a fictional part. As impor-

---

[16] Significantly, the staging of the play is compared to a Punch and Judy show, another connection to the *commedia dell'arte*, Punch being derived from the character Pulcinella (Nicoll 84).

[17] See Jane de Gay's work on theatrical allusions in *Orlando*, and their connection to moments at which "conventions of gender" are disrupted (31).

tantly, in echoing the role of the wife who Othello believes has played him for a cuckold, Sasha is associated with infidelity. Moreover, in occupying the place of the boy-actor who would have played the wife in the theatre of the day, Sasha's position is triply false. Like the Principal Boy, Sasha's social, sexual, and gender roles are in flux, lying somewhere between, rather than firmly within, heteronormative binaries. Though Orlando names her (28), she shifts beyond his reach, embodying the carnival nature of this topsy-turvy world. Her final evasion of the power of the male gaze comes when she flees the ball and the Prince, or rather, the city and Orlando. Though this Cinderella does not leave behind a shoe, she does leave on the heels of another transformation, and the ice that breaks up on the Thames seems to represent a shattering of the glass slipper that might secure Sasha's identity and Orlando's own place in the fairy tale. As the clock strikes midnight and the party ends, she continues to slip away, and Orlando sees her ship "standing out to sea" (62).

The carnivalesque aspects of "Cinderella" with which Woolf plays here, particularly in terms of the characters' performances of gendered identities, complicate the tale's own textual role as an interpretative anchor or reliable point of reference. The next stage of the novel continues this complication of readerly expectations, as Woolf depicts a second and rather different use of "Cinderella," with a second and rather different leading lady. In another midnight transformation, Orlando descends from his privileged, masculine ambassadorial role: "He stood upright in complete nakedness before us, and while the trumpets pealed Truth! Truth! Truth! we have no choice left but confess—he was a woman" (81). Here, the Prince becomes the servant girl, echoing the alteration of Cinderella's own classed and sexed position after the ball. The shifting uses of the fairy tale, applied to different characters within the novel, thus parallel the shifting relationships between cultural markings and bodies. In other words, just as *Orlando*'s layered references to the fairy tale disrupt the concept of a stable intertext, so Orlando's layered identities disrupt "all concepts of a stable 'self'" (Lee 523). It is the "slippage" of these binaries that undermines the power of the social structures which command their correspondence and underwrite their significance (Butler 122).

Such multiplicity and flexibility is expressed in *Orlando*, as it is in "Cinderella," in the various uses of fashion on the part of various figures. As Orlando suggests, clothes "change our view of the world and the world's view of us" (108). Orlando's freedom from inherited British class and gender roles in the gypsy community, for example, is enabled and symbolized by the Russian and Turkish trousers that are "worn indifferently by either sex" (82). In contrast, her/his reentry into the inherited social order is enabled and symbolized by the dress s/he wears upon returning to England and to Knole. In Orlando's Britain, clothes signal gender, and gender stands for sex, and, as Rachel Bowlby points out, "the assignment of a sex is a prerequisite for any socially recognizable identity" (Introduction, xxxix). This poses a significant problem, of course, as Orlando's multiply classed and sexed body comes into conflict with the system of patrimony that demands singularity and stability. Because Orlando cannot be recognized as the male heir, s/he must "reside in a state of incognito or incognita, as the case might turn out to be" (98), and remains in a state of limbo, unable to claim the property that grounds her social place, if not her gender. Even so, in this "ambiguous" role, Orlando occupies not a marginalized but a doubled position that is less a punishment and more a reprieve. By virtue of Orlando's harlequinesque confusion of the legal system, where her/his motley identity combines the oppositional binaries that would define him/her as "alive or dead, man or woman, Duke or nonentity," s/he defers the final decision of the law, or the final wand-waving of the Good Fairy. Unable to be finally classified, but able to draw upon her financial, familial legacy, Orlando continues his/her topsy-turvy performance of identity in Britain. Money and the privacy of his/her own room enables Orlando in one scene to change out of "a morning gown of sprigged cotton" and into a "dove grey taffeta," then into "one of peach bloom; thence to a wine-coloured brocade" before changing into "the neat black silk knickerbockers of an ordinary nobleman" (107-108). Echoing Cinderella's tactical uses of fashion, as well as the conflicting social markings of Principal Boy's body and clothes, Orlando resists the singularity of identity that this society's gendered language and laws demand.

What results is a challenge to the logic of patrimony in both its literary and lineal senses. Just as Woolf's use of "Cinderella" is not restricted to Ritchie's version of the inherited story, so Orlando is not constrained to the monogamous heterosexuality upon which a line of inheritance is based. Orlando's autoerotic fantasy upon viewing him/herself in a mirror offers an onanistic figuration of sexuality: "the glass was green water, and she a mermaid, slung with pearls, a siren in a cave [...]; so dark, so bright, so hard, so soft, was she, so astonishingly seductive" (107). Orlando's fascination with the prostitute whom s/he desires when, as a woman, s/he is dressed as a man adds another dimension to her/his sexual identity. The prostitute's appearance—the "exquisite shapeliness" of her head and the "lustre" of her eyes—"rouse[s]" Orlando, and evokes Orlando's previous sexual encounters in male form (124). Even the Victorian Prince Charming, who rescues Orlando from a broken ankle rather than a lost slipper, does not so much stabilize Orlando's sexuality as enable its continuing slide: "'You're a woman, Shel!' she cried. / 'You're a man, Orlando!' he cried" (143).

Instead of the stability of the marriage plot of "Cinderella," Woolf presents the inconsistency of the harlequinade, which spills into the main fairy tale narrative. The combination of artistic conventions and sexual desires that inform the story's possible endings suggests also the provisionality of the social institutions that (cannot fully) regulate them.

The Victorian-encoded version of Orlando's story that ends in marriage is further layered at the end of *Orlando* with a modern-day variant of "Cinderella." In its twentieth-century incarnation, the pumpkin-coach becomes a car, "an absurd truncated carriage without any horses" (168), and the search for the glass slipper becomes Orlando's search for "boy's boots" (170) at Marshall & Snelgrove's. Woolf layerings of fairy-tale intertexts, like her layerings of time and genre, extend the possibilities of the source of reference, and complicate a sense of cultural inheritance as a singular line of literary influence, just as the different applications of "Cinderella" in *Orlando* disrupt the ostensible stability and singularity of gendered identity. The novel ends on this note of simultaneous difference, when Big Ben, the clock that signals to Clarissa Dalloway the organization of time and the control of the hours by a patriarchal system, also marks the countdown to Orlando's next metamorphosis and disruption of the status quo. At "the twelfth stroke of midnight, Thursday, the eleventh of October, Nineteen hundred and Twenty-eight," Woolf presents her own turn with tradition, participating in a Modernist transformation of the multiple legacies implicit in Lady Ritchie's fairy tales (187).

Many thanks to Mark Hussey, to Melba Cuddy-Keane, to Heather Murray, and to the anonymous reviewers who have provided me with invaluable feedback on this article.

Works Cited

Annan, Noel. *Leslie Stephen: The Godless Victorian*. New York: Random House, 1984.
Archer, William. *The Theatrical 'World' of 1897*. London: Walter Scott, 1898.
Bakhtin, Mikhail. *Rabelais and His World*. 1965. Trans. Hélène Iswolsky. Bloomington: Indiana UP, 1984.
Bell, Quentin. Afterword. *The Widow and the Parrot*. By Virginia Woolf. Illus. Julian Bell. New York: Harcourt, 1988.
———. *Virginia Woolf: A Biography*. 2 vols. 1972. London: Pimlico, 1996.
Bell, Vanessa. *Notes on Virginia's Childhood*. Ed. Richard J. Schaubeck, Jr. New York: Hallman, 1974.
Bloom, Harold. *The Anxiety of Influence: A Theory of Poetry*. 2nd ed. New York: Oxford UP, 1997.
Booth, Michael. Introduction. *Pantomimes, Extravaganzas and Burlesques*. Ed. Michael Booth. Oxford: Clarendon, 1976. 1-63.
Bowlby, Rachel. Introduction. *Orlando: A Biography*. 1928. Ed. Rachel Bowlby. Oxford: Oxford UP, 1992. xii-xlvii.
Boyd, Elizabeth French. *Bloomsbury Heritage: Their Mothers and Their Aunts*. London: Hamilton, 1976.
Butler, Judith. *Bodies That Matter: On the Discursive Limits of "Sex."* New York: Routledge, 1993.
Canario, John W. "The Harlequin in *Heart of Darkness*." *Studies in Short Fiction* 4 (1967): 225-33.
Cuddy-Keane, Melba. "The Rhetoric of Feminist Conversation: Virginia Woolf and the Trope of the Twist." *Ambiguous Discourse: Feminist Narratology and British Women Writers*. Ed. Kathy Mezei. Chapel Hill: U of North Carolina P, 1996. 137-61.
de Gay, Jane. "'though the fashion of the time did something to disguise it': Staging Gender in Woolf's *Orlando*." *Virginia Woolf Out of Bounds: Selected Papers from the Tenth Annual Conference on Virginia Woolf*. New York: Pace UP, 2001. 31-39.
Eliot, George. "Silly Novels by Lady Novelists." 1856. *Essays of George Eliot*. Ed. Thomas Pinney. London: Routledge, 1968. 300-24.
Fuller, Hester Thackeray and Violet Hammersley, eds. *Thackeray's Daughter*. 2nd ed. Dublin: Euphorian, 1952.
Garber, Marjorie. *Vested Interests: Cross-dressing and Cultural Anxiety*. 1992. New York: Routledge, 1997.
Guérin, Winifred. *Anne Thackeray Ritchie: A Biography*. Oxford: Oxford UP, 1981.

Gilbert, Sandra M. and Susan Gubar. *The Madwoman in the Attic: The Woman Writer and the Nineteenth-Century Literary Imagination.* New Haven: Yale UP, 1979.

——. *No Man's Land: The Place of the Woman Writer in the Twentieth Century.* Volume 1: The *War of the Words.* New Haven: Yale UP, 1988.

Gillespie, Diane F. "The Elusive Julia Stephen." *Stories for Children, Essays for Adults.* By Julia Duckworth Stephen. Ed. Diane F. Gillespie and Elizabeth Steele. Syracuse: Syracuse UP, 1987. 1-27.

Gordon, Daphne. "Makeovers: Why Women Bite." *Toronto Star* 28 Dec. 2002: J3.

Green, Martin and Josh Swan. *The Triumph of Pierrot: The Commedia dell'Arte and the Modern Imagination.* Rev. ed. University Park, Pennsylvania: Pennsylvania State UP, 1993.

Grimm, Jakob and Wilhelm Grimm. "Cinderella." *The Complete Grimm's Fairy Tales.* Trans. Margaret Hunt and James Stern. New York: Random, 1972. 121-128.

"Harlequin." *Oxford Reference Dictionary.* Ed. Joyce M. Hawkins. Oxford: Clarendon, 1989. 372.

Harris, Janice H. "Not Suffering and Not Still: Women Writers at the *Cornhill Magazine*, 1860-1900." *Modern Language Quarterly* 47.4 (1986): 382-92.

Helder, Jack. "Fool Convention and Conrad's Hollow Harlequin." *Studies in Short Fiction* 12 (1975): 361-68.

Herr, Cheryl. *Joyce's Anatomy of Culture.* Urbana: U of Illinois P, 1986.

Holland, Peter. "The Play of Eros: Paradoxes of Gender in English Pantomime." *New Theatre Quarterly* 13.51 (1997): 195-204.

Hunter, Pamela. Introduction. *Façade, with an interpretation by Pamela Hunter.* By Edith Sitwell. London: Duckworth, 1987. 9-18.

Kaehele, Sharon and Howard German. "'To the Lighthouse': Symbol and Vision." 1962. *Virginia Woolf To the Lighthouse: A Casebook.* Ed. Morris Beja. London: Macmillan, 1970. 189-209.

King, James. *Virginia Woolf.* 1994. London: Penguin, 1995.

Lee, Hermione. *Virginia Woolf.* 1996. London: Vintage, 1997.

MacKay, Carol Hanbery. "The Thackeray Connection: Virginia Woolf's Aunt Anny." *Virginia Woolf and Bloomsbury: A Centenary Celebration.* Ed. Jane Marcus. London: Macmillan, 1987. 68-95.

Marcus, Jane. *Art and Anger: Reading Like a Woman.* Columbus: Ohio State UP, 1988.

———. "Enchanted Organs, Magic Bells: *Night and Day* as Comic Opera." *Virginia Woolf: Revaluation and Continuity*. Ed. Ralph Freedman. Berkeley: U of California P, 1980. 97-122.

Nicoll, Allardyce. *The World of Harlequin: A Critical Study of the Commedia dell'Arte*. Cambridge: Cambridge UP, 1963.

Nichols, Roger. *The Harlequin Years: Music in Paris 1917-1929*. Berkeley: U of California P, 2002.

Paul, Janis M. *The Victorian Heritage of Virginia Woolf: The External World in her Novels*. Norman, Oklahoma: Pilgrim, 1987.

Perrault, Charles. "Cinderella." *Perrault's Fairy Tales*. Trans. A. E. Johnson. New York: Dover, 1969. 65-78.

Rackham, Arthur and Edmund Gosse. *The Allies' Fairy Book / Fairy Tales from Many Lands*. 1916. London: Heineman, 1974.

Ritchie, Anne Thackeray. *Bluebeard's Keys and Other Stories*. London: Smith, 1902.

———. *Five Old Friends and a Young Prince*. London: Smith, 1905.

———. "Toilers and Spinsters." 1874. *Toilers and Spinsters and Other Essays*. London: Smith, 1890. 1-35.

Rosenman, Ellen Bayuk. *The Invisible Presence: Virginia Woolf and the Mother-Daughter Relationship*. Baton Rouge: Louisiana State UP, 1986.

Sayers, Dorothy L. *Murder Must Advertise*. 1933. London: New English, 1978.

Spalding, Frances. *Vanessa Bell*. London: Weidenfeld, 1983.

Stephen, Leslie. *Mausoleum Book*. Oxford: Clarendon, 1977.

"Thackeray (Anne Isabella)." *British Library General Catalogue of Printed Books to 1975*. Vol. 323: *Terju-Theve*. London: Saur, 1986. 181-82.

Thackeray, William Makepeace. *The Rose and the Ring; or, the History of Prince Giglio and Prince Bulbo. Miscellanies*. Vol. 8. London: Smith, Elder, 1877. 197-328.

Woolf, Virginia. "*David Copperfield*." *The Moment and Other Essays*. 1947. London: Hogarth, 1952. 65-69.

———. *The Diary of Virginia Woolf*. Ed. Anne Olivier Bell and Andrew McNeillie. 5 vols. New York: Harcourt, 1977-84.

———. "The Enchanted Organ." *The Essays of Virginia Woolf*. Ed. Andrew McNeillie. Vol. 3. London: Hogarth, 1991. 399-403.

———. "Jane Austen." *The Common Reader, First Series*. 1925. Ed. Andrew McNeillie. San Diego: Harcourt, 1984. 134-45.

———. "Lady Ritchie." *The Essays of Virginia Woolf*. Ed. Andrew McNeillie. Vol. 3. London: Hogarth, 1991. 13-20.

———. *Moments of Being: Unpublished Autobiographical Writings*. Ed. Jeanne Schulkind. Sussex: Sussex UP, 1976.
———. *Night and Day*. 1919. Ed. J. H. Stape. London: Blackwell, 1994.
———. *Orlando: A Biography*. 1928. Ed. J. H. Stape. London: Blackwell, 1998.
———. *A Passionate Apprentice: The Early Journals, 1897-1909*. Ed. Mitchell A. Leaska. San Diego: Harcourt, 1990.
———. *A Room of One's Own*. 1929. A Room of One's Own *and* Three Guineas. Ed. Michèle Barrett. London: Penguin, 1993. 1-114.
———. "Ruskin." *The Captain's Death Bed and Other Essays*. London: Hogarth, 1950. 49-52.
———. *To the Lighthouse*. Ed. Susan Dick. London: Blackwell, 1992.
———. *The Voyage Out*. Ed. C. Ruth Miller and Lawrence Miller. Oxford: Blackwell, 1995.
———. "Women and Fiction." *Women and Writing*. Ed. Michèle Barrett. London: Women's P, 1979. 43-52.
Yoder, Emily K. "The Demon Harlequin in Conrad's Hell." *Conradiana* 12 (1980): 88-92.

The Paradox of the Gift: Gift-Giving as a Disruptive Force in "Mrs. Dalloway in Bond Street"

Kathryn Simpson

"[O]ne bright new sixpence": Woolf and the Market Economy

From the mid-1980s onwards there has been a sustained critical focus on modernism's relation to the market, encompassing the "great divide" between modernist art and mass production, and the quintessential modernity of commodity culture. As Reginald Abbott notes, work which, for example, examines James Joyce's engagement with advertising has "irrevocably opened the modernist canon to consumer theory" (194).[1] Such critical examinations have begun to explode the myth, mapped out in earlier influential studies such as Andreas Huyssen's *After the Great Divide*, of modernist writers' and artists' absolute disinterest in, detachment from and contempt for popular and consumer culture. The easy and gendered distinction this myth assumes between "high" (masculine) and "low" (feminine) art and the polarization of art in this way is undermined by more recent studies which have begun to uncover, in Lawrence Rainey's words, "the growing complexity of cultural exchange and circulation in modern society" (2).[2] Rainey's study, along with others, significantly explores the contradictory and ambiguous interrelationships between modernist artists, the cultural institutions which produce art, the market, readers, and modernist art as a "commodity of a special sort" (3). He argues that "[m]odernism marks neither a straightforward resistance nor an outright capitulation to commodification but a momentary equivocation that incorporates elements of both in a brief, necessarily unstable synthesis" (3).

---

[1] Abbott cites Jennifer Wicke's *Advertising Fictions: Literature, Advertisement, and Social Reading* and Jonathan Freedman's *Professions of Taste: Henry James, British Aestheticism, and Commodity Culture* in this respect. Michael Tratner suggests that Cheryl Herr's *Joyce's Anatomy of Culture*, R.B. Kershner's *Joyce, Bakhtin and Popular Literature* and Franco Moretti's *Signs Taken for Wonders* continue this focus on Joyce and the market.

[2] Other studies include Jennifer Wicke's "Mrs. Dalloway Goes to Market: Woolf, Keynes, and Modern Markets," in which she argues that "modernism contributed profoundly to a sea-change in market consciousness" (5); Paul Delany's *Literature, Money and the Market*; Ian Willison, et al's *Modernist Writers and the Marketplace*; Jane Garrity's "Selling Culture to the 'Civilized': Bloomsbury, British *Vogue*, and the Marketing of National Identity" and "Virginia Woolf, Intellectual Harlotry, and 1920s British *Vogue*"; and Leslie Hankins' "Virginia Woolf and Walter Benjamin Selling Out(siders)."

This position of equivocation is a useful one from which to consider Woolf's relationship to commodity culture. Whereas for Abbott in 1992 "Woolf could only be an ambivalent witness to commodity culture,"[3] more recent studies explore Woolf's place *in* the commercial world. Studies continue to focus on some of the same issues, but in ways which problematize earlier assumptions about Woolf's position so as to more fully engage with the deeply rooted sense of contradiction about market economies found in her writing.[4] As co-owner of the Hogarth Press and as a woman writer intent on making money from her pen, Woolf was interested in markets and profit margins.[5] Sales figures feature significantly in her diaries, as both a marker of her artistic achievement and an indication of her financial success. Clearly, profits from her work enabled her to

---

[3] Because of her "upper-middle class background, her cultural heritage as part of Britain's intellectual elite, her peculiar socialism/pacificism, her personal temperament, and . . . her gender" (Abbott 194).

[4] Leslie Hankins has argued that the contradictions are such that Woolf is located on an "ideological fault line" (18). This location on an ideological fault line can be detected, for instance, in Woolf's need to draw a distinction between making money in the marketplace and her own profits. In one example, profits from sales of *To the Lighthouse* are put at a remove from the market economy by their literal and symbolic transformation into a gift: "We have a nice little shut up car.... The world gave me this for writing The Lighthouse, I reflect, a book which has now sold 3,160 (perhaps) copies" (*D*3 147).

[5] Several critics have considered the various ways in which the Woolfs' ownership of the press influenced Woolf's career. It is often seen as being an escape from the taint of the market place and from some of the pressures of publication. Laura Marcus, for instance, suggests that it provides a buffer between Woolf and the market, and as such formed a liminal space in which Woolf could feel more at ease to work: "The Hogarth Press represented work, but work that cut out the middleman and escaped literary commodification. It gave Woolf a way of negotiating the terms of literary publicity, and a space somewhere between the private, the coteries, and the public sphere" (144). Similarly, it seemed to provide an alternative to capitalist enterprise; as Michael Tratner argues, "Woolf...sees the demise of capitalism not in the elimination of private experience, but in the elimination of property, of the ownership of private space by a single dominant individual. Joint ownership and multiply generated private experience mark the step beyond capitalism" ("Why" 132). Jane Garrity also argues that co-ownership of the Hogarth Press allowed Woolf "to perceive herself as separate from the market place," yet Woolf was "deeply immersed in issues of literary circulation and capital" ("Virginia Woolf"197). She goes on to argue that "[f]or Woolf, making money is both an act of subversion—precisely because she's a woman—and a form of contamination, because it exposes the economic basis of her literary production" (197). Woolf herself discusses the Press in terms of enabling her to be herself, to write what she wants: "[a]s I write, there rises somewhere in my head that queer, & very pleasant sense, of something which I want to write; my own point of view" (*D*2 107). By the mid-1920s the Press is more than simply this, however—it "becomes a serious business," as Woolf records in her *Diary* (*D*2 307).

gain greater financial independence, to have purchasing power and to experience the pleasure of commodity culture. However, she also felt considerably uncomfortable about her own place in the commercial world (her writing for *Vogue*, for instance, brought anxiety and concern about the debasement that mass production and commercialism can imply).[6]

For Woolf, participation in the market and being active in the public domain are also clearly bound up with her feminist politics, but in a problematic way. Such participation in the public realm is seen as part of the experience of modernity from which women should not be excluded. Her texts capture the impact of these aspects of modernity on perception and experience, and participation in the market as shopper/ consumer figures significantly (if sometimes ambivalently) in several of Woolf's texts (*Mrs. Dalloway*, "Mrs. Dalloway in Bond Street," "Street Haunting," "Oxford Street Tide" and others).[7] In *Three Guineas*, Woolf describes middle-class women's engagement with capitalist economies as being caught "between the devil and the deep blue sea" (*TG* 86). Women's right to earn money and to have a profession is liberating and brings a changed perception of the world, a freedom to express opinions and, importantly, a freedom from the need to charm and allure men. With increased earning power and career opportunities women have a different sphere of action and vision: "[i]n every purse there was, or might be, one bright new sixpence in whose light every thought, every sight, every action looked different" (*TG* 19). However, participation in capitalist market economies also signals a complicity in a patriarchal system, a system that Woolf sees as tyrannous and as operating in a way similar to a European Fascist state.[8] Woolf is clearly resistant to the politics and sexual politics of the market place and, as critics Bridget Elliot and Jo-Ann Wallace argue, for Woolf the exchange of commodities in a capitalist economy and the exchange of women in a patriarchal sexual economy are interrelated (73).

Participation in market economies, then, seems to be in tension in Woolf's work with a resistance to the male-dominated capitalist system, based as it is on possession of things, money and people. It is a rational system focused on calculation and fixing of value, intent on maintaining clear boundaries and distinctions (between buyer and seller), and rigorously organized by the laws of

---

[6] See Jane Garrity, above. Indeed, Woolf refers to commercial writing in *Three Guineas* as "brain prostitution" (*TG* 108).

[7] These works have been discussed in terms of Woolf's relation to commodity culture by a number of critics including Rachel Bowlby, Leslie Hankins, Ruth Hoberman and Jeanette McVicker, and in terms of the interaction of the aesthetic and the socio-economic system by Caughie (*Postmodernism*).

[8] For Woolf, notably in *Three Guineas*, patriarchal capitalism is bound up in a dangerous nexus of patriotism, fascism and war.

profit and loss. As Tratner argues, Woolf (along with Joyce, Eliot and Yeats) is critical of hegemonic capitalism and the limitations it imposes. He argues that capitalism hides and represses certain aspects of the social order, silences and denies certain groups of people, and represses elements of the psyche which Woolf (and other modernists) sought to release (*Modernism* 11).[9] However, the operation of commodity culture also stimulates and mobilizes a profusion of desires in the consumer, as it fuels fantasy and excites imagination. Participation in mass, consumer culture—characterized as feminized, fluid, shifting, in which flows of desires are equated with commodity flows—can be experienced as positive and pleasurable. The exhilarating proliferation of commodities in such an economy not only engenders new desires for objects and experiences, but simultaneously creates spaces and opportunities for potentially subversive sexual desires to surface. In this way, capitalist commodity culture can be seen to elicit desires which it cannot contain or control, desires which can endanger the hierarchies and heteropatriarchal social order capitalism seems to keep in place.

In her discussion of consumer culture in the late nineteenth century, Rita Felski discusses the cultural anxieties provoked by the awakened appetites and desires of consumers, characterized as "insatiable female shopper[s]," and the fear that such appetites "would have disturbing and unforeseeable effects, reaching out to subvert the social fabric and to undermine patriarchal authority within the family" (62, 65). She sees these desires as being ultimately managed and "manipulated by a logic of calculation and rationalization in the interests of the profit motive" (62). However, Woolf's writing seems to challenge and revise this power dynamic; her shoppers are far from passive and commodities are not their only source of satisfaction. As Jennifer Wicke argues, Woolf's sense of the market economy, which her modernist work helped to revise (like that of Woolf's friend the economist John Maynard Keynes), was of a more fluid and chaotic entity, one which is interconnected to "a strong rewriting of gender" and to "Bloomsbury's comfortable response to homosexuality" ("Mrs. Dalloway Goes to Market" 14).

---

[9] Tratner argues that Woolf's response to hegemonic capitalism, and to the right wing attempts to reduce the power of capitalism via political investment in monarchy and nationalism, was to embrace "alternative traditions of oppressed groups: Jews, women, homosexuals, the working class, all the members of Woolf's 'outsiders' society'" (*Modernism* 14). Although Woolf's representation of all of these 'outsiders' remains ambivalent at times, their involvement with commodity culture and market exchange opens up a space in which dominant cultural values and the social order are significantly undermined and brought into question (in "Street Haunting" and "The Duchess and the Jeweller," for instance).

"And she felt that she had been given a present": Woolf and the Gift Economy

Existing critiques, then, elucidate Woolf's complex and contradictory engagement with the marketplace and relate this to the sexual and class politics of her writing, to her own practice of publication, to her personal attitude to the commercial world, and to her sense of herself as a modernist writer. However, what I want to explore here is another economy at play in Woolf's work—the gift economy. The gift economy can be read as running counter to, but also contiguous with, capitalist systems, and brings another dimension to the equivocal relationship to the marketplace others have detected in Woolf's writing. My focus on the gift economy aims, in part, to offer another angle from which to consider Woolf's ambivalent relationship to and representation of market economies and consumer culture. However, this focus on the gift also opens up a new avenue for exploring the sexual politics and homoeroticism of Woolf's work and suggests that far from simply opposing heteropatriarchal and capitalist systems, Woolf's writing works to question and subvert them from within. As I will argue, the operation of a gift economy acts as a disruptive force—not only upsetting heteropatriarchal social structures and potentially subverting the operation of dominant capitalist economies, but, crucially, articulating an alternative feminine libidinal economy. Feminist critic Hélène Cixous characterizes the gift economy as feminine, and as one which offers a resistance to the commodifying impulse of capitalism.[10] It emphasizes fluidity, indeterminacy, a destabilization of hierarchies and rational systems, and a disturbance of property rights. It doesn't try to recover its expenses or to recuperate its losses—in fact giving, excess and overflow are recognized as sources of pleasure and *jouissance*. I want to suggest that a focus on the gifts exchanged in Woolf's texts, and consideration of the symbolic operation of the two economies in conjunction, can realize a different economy of desire. This economy of desire is fundamentally at odds with and subversive of a heteropatriarchal social order and the repressive institutions of capitalism. The rigid structures of capitalist exchange can, paradoxically, be significantly compromised or undermined by the (over)flows of desires and libidinal longings commodity culture can engender and release. However, the gift economy at work in Woolf's texts signals another dimension to the wants, needs and appetites that commodity culture provokes. Displacing the emphasis from the possession of commodities to the giving and dispersal of the pleasures commodities signify and embody, the gift economy works to facilitate the realization and satisfaction of women's more subversive libidinal desires.

---

[10] See "Castration or Decapitation?" and "The Laugh of the Medusa," for example.

Gifts and gift-giving figure quite significantly in Woolf's writing and in her experience of coming to writing. Gifts from female relatives and friends literally and symbolically facilitated Woolf's entry into the public domain, providing her with the degree of independence and confidence she needed to write.[11] Her fiction has many instances of gifts exchanged between her female characters. These gifts are sometimes literary texts—*Persuasion* (*The Voyage Out*) and *Cranford* ("Mrs. Dalloway in Bond Street")—but other, often erotically charged, gifts are also made which mark the bond between women, notably Sally's kiss in *Mrs. Dalloway* and the ambiguously coded bottle of crème de menthe (whose seal is not broken, its intoxicating pleasures never tasted) in *The Voyage Out*. Woolf also, famously, made a gift of her own writing in giving the original manuscript of *Orlando* to Vita Sackville-West. However, what is in Nigel Nicolson's estimation the "longest and most charming love-letter in literature" may possibly be Woolf's most ambiguous gift (186).[12] It has been seen simultaneously as a sign of Woolf's love and desire for Sackville-West and as a punishment for her infidelity (as Suzanne Raitt and Anna Snaith have argued). Sackville-West's "thank you" letter suggests both her gratitude and a sense of entrapment. She tells Woolf that she feels like "one of the those wax figures in a shop window, on which you have hung a robe stitched with jewels" (cited in DeSalvo and Leaska, 305; also in Raitt 40).

Gift-giving, then, can be ambivalent and problematic. The issues of motivation, the imperative to respond with reciprocal gift or gratitude, or the sense of obligation generated by a gift are also issues that trouble Cixous's thinking about the gift. For Cixous this is "the paradox of the gift that takes," a gift given with the hope of return, or a gift whose value is "annulled" by a "countergift" ("Laugh" 263; Conley 158, cited in Still 167). There is also the danger of colluding with heteropatriarchal power structures which identify woman *as* a gift to

---

[11] Importantly, these include her legacy from her aunt Caroline Emelia and the inkpot from Violet Dickinson, her first present to Woolf in her new independent life at Gordon Square. These gifts are mentioned by Snaith in relation to Woolf's negotiation of the public/private boundary (25).

[12] Not least because it also became Woolf's most lucrative novel and ensured her commercial success. As Robin Majumdar and Allen McLaurin remark, with the increase in sales after *Orlando* the Woolfs were "always well off" (6). Woolf enjoyed the financial freedoms this "gift" brought, as she notes in her *Diary*, "[f]or the first time since I married 1912 – 1928 – 16 years – I have been spending money" (*D3* 212). Although her "spending muscle does not work naturally yet," spending money freely "lubricates" her soul and stimulates her creativity (*D3* 212). Ironically, then, her gift to her Sapphic lover generates more profit than any of her other texts, bringing her more consumer pleasure than she has experienced throughout her marriage. Crucially, though, the profits from this lesbian gift also enable her to "keep [her] brain on the boil" – "to spend freely, & then write" (*D3* 212).

be exchanged between men.[13] However, gift-giving also creates a utopian and liminal space; it has a disruptive effect in suggestively and ambiguously side stepping the calculation of market exchange and eluding the fixity of heteropatriarchal economies. The gift, to retain its identity and integrity as a gift, must remain in circulation. Drawing on a number of anthropological studies Lewis Hyde remarks, "[t]he only essential is this: *the gift must always move*. There are other forms of property that stand still, that mark a boundary or resist momentum, but the gift keeps going" (4, Hyde's emphasis). In Woolf's writing gifts, and the intention to give gifts, facilitate fluidity and the transgression of boundaries, opening up subversive possibilities. The operation of the gift economy in Woolf's texts, I will argue, encodes lesbian libidinal currents.

"Mrs. Dalloway in Bond Street"

A close reading of Woolf's short story "Mrs. Dalloway in Bond Street" enables the disruptive potential of the intersection of gift and market economies in Woolf's work to be explored. Located in commercial London, this story in many ways encapsulates Woolf's ambivalence about consumerism, capitalism and commodity culture, but also seems to explore the subversive potential of women entering the market place with money to buy and give gifts, and to satisfy their own consumer and libidinal desires. Initially intended to be the first chapter of *Mrs. Dalloway*, the story is premised on Clarissa's shopping trip to buy a pair of gloves. It would seem that the cultural anxiety generated by the increased visibility of women in the public realm, "invading" male spaces and participating in male activities, is ameliorated here by Clarissa's apparent class and gender conformity, summed up in the object she intends to purchase. However, a central issue in Woolf's story is a significantly revised connection between libidinal and monetary economies, and the street itself, with its history-

---

[13] In her influential essay, "The Traffic in Women: Notes on the 'Political Economy' of Sex," Gayle Rubin takes issue with the work of structural anthropologist Claude Lévi-Strauss on the importance of gift exchange in primitive societies, notably the exchange of women as gifts to consolidate bonds of kinship, in his study *The Elementary Structures of Kinship*. Writing from a feminist perspective, Rubin argues that because women are "sexual semi-objects—gifts," rather than "exchange partners" or "sexual subjects," they cannot "realize the [social] benefits of their own circulation" (542-3). She suggests that the practice of the "'exchange of women'" is "more pronounced and commercialized in more 'civilized' societies" and goes on to discuss such practice as fundamental to the constitution of dualistic gender identities, socio-economic relations and "obligatory heterosexuality" in a range of male-dominated societies (543, 545, 548). Significantly, she argues that "[t]he asymmetry of gender—the difference between exchanger and exchanged—entails the constraint of female sexuality" (548).

of being "regarded as a man's street" and "on the prostitute beat" seems to be a significant location for this story of subversive female desire (Adburgham 254).[14] The libidinal economy at play in this story is exclusive of men and resistant to the commodification of female bodies for the sole gratification of male heterosexual desires.

In a forthcoming essay, Ruth Hoberman identifies shopping in this story as good but problematic (91). Significantly, she argues, shopping promotes relationships and social exchanges, "human contact is the story's subject" (92). She suggests that window shopping is especially positive because it gives free rein to the imagination, facilitating fantasies of the transformation of identities that commodities can bring (84). Window shopping is also in some ways a "free gift" as Clarissa indulges in the pleasure of the spectacle without purchase (indeed, Clarissa's "shopping trip" as a whole revolves around the pleasure of looking). In particular, though, the subject of this story is *female* contact, of bonds between women which differ from the bonds implied in the street's name. What seems significant in Woolf's story is Clarissa's ability to empathize with other women, to feel admiration for women and possibly attraction to them. What we see in this story is the ways the usual bonds (of exchange, business and personal relationship) can, in Cixous's words, "function otherwise" so as to destabilize market and heterosexual economies ("Castration" 50). Shopping in Bond Street provides opportunities for Clarissa's bonds with other women to surface in an ambiguous way through what she *almost* purchases, and, importantly, through the gifts she considers giving. At odds with capitalist consumerism and the flow of cash and commodities, Clarissa's actual concerns for most of the story focus on "flows" of other kinds as she expresses her wishes to give gifts to women.

---

[14] Alison Adburgham discusses the transformation of Bond Street from being "for most of the nineteenth century ... a man's street," with expensive shops catering exclusively to men, to one selling expensive, bespoke commodities and services for women (*Shops* 254-5). Abbott cites this and another work by Adburgham (*Shopping in Style: London from the Restoration to Edwardian Elegance*, London: Thames, 1979) and argues that by the time Woolf was writing *Mrs. Dalloway* and "Mrs. Dalloway in Bond Street," Bond Street "had succumbed ... to the democratising rules of the new marketplace" (fn 8, 199). However, Clarissa's occupation of a space recognized as a "man's street" because previously it was part of the prostitute beat (Adburgham, *Shops* 254, cited also in Abbott, 198) also signals a potentially threatening "trespass" into male territory—a possible transgression of a site where both male-dominated market and libidinal economies powerfully intersect. As Judith R. Walkowitz argues, "By venturing into the city centre, women entered a place traditionally imagined as the site of exchange and erotic activity, a place symbolically opposed to orderly domestic life" ("The Making of an Outcast Group" in Vicinus, ed. *A Widening Sphere*, 1977, cited in Snaith 23).

In her essay "Castration or Decapitation?" Cixous outlines the ways in which a masculine social, psychic and libidinal economy "decapitates" women, silences the feminine and the female body. But she also considers how this system could be disrupted through, in her words, "resistance to a masculine desire conducted by woman as hysteric, as distracted" ("Castration" 50). In "Mrs. Dalloway in Bond Street," Clarissa isn't exactly a "hysteric" but she is "distracted" from her participation in the masculine market economy by a preoccupation with the womb and menstrual flows. Significantly, this preoccupation is what seems to motivate her desire to give gifts to women. She seems to want to compensate Milly Whitbread for the difficulties with her menopause (implied by Hugh's explanation of their visit to the city) and to compensate the shop assistant in the glove shop for the pains and discomfort of her monthly losses. The roots of Clarissa's generosity and sympathy, then, are bodily as well as emotional, and they are exclusive to women. However, like the Clarissa Dalloways of Woolf's other texts (*The Voyage Out*, *Mrs. Dalloway*, and other short fictions), Clarissa here remains an ambiguous character. She isn't located in one or other economy but moves between gift and market economies, between homoerotic possibility and heterosexual conformity.

The gifts Clarissa considers giving to Milly and the shop assistant offer an escape from daily life, and involve Clarissa in recollections of her past.[15] Standing outside Hatchard's bookshop Clarissa contemplates buying a copy of Elizabeth Gaskell's *Cranford* for Milly. For Clarissa this novel conjures up a simpler, idyllic world and she becomes lost in a nostalgic reverie about her youth—a time of transition, a liminal state in which her desires and mature emotional bonds were emerging and in a state of possibility. Although Clarissa's choice of novel here signals her conventionality and lack of modern sensibility (as we also see in her attitudes to visual art and fashion),[16] this text, centered firmly on a community of women from which men are largely excluded, helps to emphasize the female specific space of Woolf's story. Although Woolf is scathing about

---

[15] Abbott similarly suggests that commodities signify more than their materiality for Clarissa in *Mrs. Dalloway*: "Clarissa transforms the commodity before her into part of her past, her own identity, rather than relying on the commodity as a signifier of her lifestyle or as something to transform her lifestyle" (200).

[16] Woolf seems to be self-consciously ironic concerning what Clarissa admires about this realist novel: "the sentences ending; the characters—how one talked about them as if they were real," and about Clarissa's assessment of the mid-Victorian novel as far surpassing anything produced by "the moderns," especially anything modern written "about death," given that Woolf's story itself is also profoundly concerned with death and loss ("Mrs. Dalloway" 155).

Gaskell at times,[17] this gift for Milly may be significant in terms of *Cranford*'s focus on women and the "economy" which maintains their bonds.

At the beginning of the novel we are told that Cranford is "in the possession of amazons" and that the relationships between the women of this community are sustained by the practising of "elegant economy" so that even those of "moderate means" can participate in entertaining their neighbors (*Cranford* 39, 42). This "economy" acts to bolster the immense class snobbery, antagonism and pretension (represented as absurd by the ironic narrator, Mary Smith), but also perpetuates a near exclusively female community. Later in the novel, having lost her investments, one of the characters, Matilda Jenkyns, sets up a shop. This is far from being a capitalist enterprise, however, and only makes a "profit" because of the generosity of her community. In his analysis of *Cranford*, John Kucich considers this novel's transgressive potential in a way which seems significant here. Having considered both Gaskell's conformity to and divergence from gender norms he argues that

> [f]ar from being a nostalgic glance at a provincial backwater, *Cranford* reaffirms a purely female, contemporary cultural authority, based on feminine affiliations with genteel pretension. It is largely about the feminized power of nineteenth-century culture (or 'pretence' or 'refinement') to ascend the social scale, with or without the assistance of male economic power (207)

He argues that "solidarity is accomplished through one of Gaskell's basic signs of social disorder—the lie" (207) and earlier in his essay claims "lying is defined as a characteristically female transgression" (190). So just as in Cranford we have a community of women based on transgression, in "Mrs. Dalloway in Bond Street" the same case can be made—the women shoppers form a community exclusive of men, practise an "elegant economy" of glances and gestures, and their bonds may well be transgressive in a sexual way. Another possible significance that Cranford may have for Woolf's story is the narrative strand which conveys the meeting of old lovers (Matilda Jenkyns and Thomas Holbrook) who were separated by family snobbery years previously. They meet when Thomas comes to town to buy gloves (gloves which are not purchased). Bringing to the surface desires not fulfilled, possibilities unexplored and, for a short time, the possibility of love being renewed, this may in itself be a deeply encoded reminder for Milly of "A Love Affair of Long Ago" (the title of the chapter in which Thomas and Matilda meet again).

---

[17] For instance, in a review of *Mam Linda* by Will N. Harden, *TLS* 3rd October 1907, cited in Kirkpatrick, 292.

Once Clarissa is inside the glove shop, the flow of empathy and generosity extends to the shop assistant, for whom menstrual flows seem to be causing discomfort. Clarissa considers giving a gift of a holiday to this woman, a holiday better than any the shop assistant would be able to afford, giving her experiences and pleasures beyond the scope of her class bound situation. Her gift of a holiday Clarissa feels would save the shop woman from the loneliness and discomfort of the kind of holiday Clarissa imagines her taking "[i]n some stuffy lodging. [where] [t]he landlady takes the sugar" ("Mrs. Dalloway" 157). Like the gift for Milly, this imagined gift for the shop woman is also prompted by a sense of connection to the past. Clarissa remembers the woman but is surprised at how much older she looks. Clarissa thinks, "if it's the girl I remember, she's twenty years older . . . .," again recalling an earlier period of Clarissa's life, possibly a pre-marital state ("Mrs. Dalloway" 156).

There is a parallel scene in *Mrs. Dalloway* which takes place in a florists shop. It is, on the whole, more explicitly erotically charged (the shop is full of flowers which are more evidently sensual and sexual) and there is a more obvious sense of prior connection between Clarissa and the shop assistant, and possibly an earlier exchange for which the shop assistant, Miss Pym, expresses gratitude.[18] However, there is eroticism implicit in the glove shop too, and this context adds greater significance to the idea of gift-giving, further suggesting the way gifts can function as markers of lesbian desire. Like the florists of *Mrs. Dalloway*, the glove shop is a feminine space. The masculine economy, signalled by Bond Street, is marginalized, and is merely a distant hum, a sound which can only intrude in a dulled way, apparently stifled by the atmosphere of expectation and the female-specific commodities (gloves and silk stockings) for sale: "[t]hey [Clarissa and the other shoppers] waited; a clock ticked; Bond Street hummed, dulled, distant" ("Mrs. Dalloway" 156). It is a space of female intimacy and has a potentially erotic atmosphere as gloves are fitted and removed by the female

---

[18] Critics have read this moment in the novel in a variety of ways. Abbott sees "something more meaningful to both [Clarissa and Miss Pym] and quite different from the professional façade of shop women" but doesn't speculate about *how* this could be more meaningful, except to liken it to the more personalized commercial exchanges of the Victorian period (201). Others have commented more explicitly on the lesbian eroticism of this scene; see Eileen Barrett for instance. Patricia Juliana Smith comments that Miss Pym, "presumably independent ... in her florists shop, connected with the 'lesbian' image of flowers," is one of "the minor 'queer' characters in the novel, whose own romantic or sexual histories go unrevealed and unremarked" (fn 30, 194.) She reads the significance of "this brief idyll" of "female homosocial/homoerotic pleasure" as a key moment in Clarissa's experience of lesbian bliss which acts as a parallel scene to that experienced earlier by the urn with Sally (43).

shop assistants, and as the women shoppers look at each other, exchanging glances. It is a space in which Clarissa expresses her admiration and implicitly her desire for women as she gazes at them "through the hanging silk stockings quivering silver," an image vibrating with sexual suggestion ("Mrs. Dalloway" 157).

Clarissa's entry to the shop is also suggestive as she makes an instant, possibly flirtatious, connection with the shop woman:

> 'Good morning,' said Clarissa in her charming voice. 'Gloves,' she said with her exquisite friendliness and putting her bag on the counter began, very slowly, to undo the buttons. 'White gloves,' she said. 'Above the elbow,' and she looked straight into the shop woman's face... ("Mrs. Dalloway" 156).

The unnecessary lingering over removing her gloves, her bag on the counter and her direct gaze add a sense of suggestiveness to this exchange.[19] Gift exchange continues to operate suggestively as a code for articulating lesbian desires as the shop assistant remarks admiringly on the slenderness of Clarissa's hands, a compliment given whilst "drawing the glove firmly, smoothly, down over her rings," and as Clarissa considers offering the gift of a holiday ("Mrs. Dalloway" 157). It seems significant that the *specific* context in which Clarissa imagines and rules out her gift is the physically intimate one of having a glove fitted and drawn off. This context is only implicit in the story—this particular fitting isn't "present" at the textual surface—but in this feminine space, in which eroticism is already evoked, this detail makes Clarissa's fantasy of a gift even more subversive.

That Clarissa doesn't buy *Cranford* and doesn't pay for a holiday for the shop assistant might suggest her lack of commitment to the feminine gift economy—her lack of investment in such bonds. However, this could also indicate a refusal to participate in a system of property and possessions.[20] The fact that she only considers buying Milly a "little *cheap* book" could indicate that the gift and the bond it represents is trivial ("Mrs. Dalloway" 155, my emphasis). However, it is also significant in representing only a minimal investment in a masculine capitalist economy. The paradox of the gift here is not that it is given with the expectation of a return, but that the gift *isn't* given.

---

[19] Clarissa's actions here can also be read as a self-conscious mockery of the usual process of capitalist exchange. Her actions seem deliberate and exaggerated, so as to signal a mocking imitation of the procedure of transaction, just as she seems to subvert the whole purpose of going shopping—not to purchase but to participate in erotic exchanges with other women.

[20] Abbott attributes the lack of purchasing in Woolf's texts to what he calls an "'acommodity aesthetic,'" defined as "balanced patterns of shopping without spending and consumption without commodities" (209).

Yet, Clarissa's *imagined* gift-giving still retains a disruptive potential. On their honeymoon, Clarissa's husband, Dick, dismisses her desire to give impulsively as "folly" and asserts that trade with China is "much more important" ("Mrs. Dalloway" 157). Dick's economic lesson, presumably forcefully delivered given the long-term impact on Clarissa, hints at a sense of threat and draws attention to the idea that gift giving does have the potential to scupper the economy and trade. It threatens the economic system by undermining the notion of a fixed hierarchy and certain measurement of value, and by disrupting the controlled flows of profit and loss. In a sense, the exchange of gifts between women also scuppers the heterosexual economy in which women are the gifts exchanged between men, not the givers or the receivers. In gift exchange between women, then, women are agents ("exchange partners" and "sexual subjects"[21]) with the power to negotiate their own pleasures, and to give pleasures to other women. Although Clarissa's gifts also have a market value, what they really promise is not readily calculable but is dangerously subversive. In this story gift exchanges have the potential to satisfy women's unspoken desires and to facilitate escape from prevalent heteropatriarchal structures.

Dick's choice of the word "folly" is quite apt when we consider its meaning in the architectural sense—that is of a mock building constructed to satisfy someone's fancy or conceit—or, here, to satisfy other kinds of longing. In this sense, a folly can function as a mocking imitation (and subversion of) the "architecture" of the capitalist economy; the "folly" of giving impulsively, then, can mockingly undermine the foundations of capitalist and heterosexual economies. That Dick tries to prohibit Clarissa's impulsive behavior on their honeymoon seems to be a recognition that such "impulses" have the potential to bring the disorder of flux and fluidity to market and sexual paradigms. In this story the flow of people and commodities, the bodily flows of women (menstrual blood and also tears), and the more fluid economy of the gift have the potential to blur and to even dissolve capitalist and heteropatriarchal structures.[22]

---

[21] See Rubin, above footnote 13.

[22] Jennifer Wicke, arguing that there is a more fluid sense of the market economy in *Mrs. Dalloway*, discusses the overlapping of gift and market economies in a way which also addresses the blurring of distinctions and the collapsing of hierarchies. She argues that "the generosity of her [Clarissa's] gendered acts of consumption" means that "consumption is reformulated as the nature of the gift" ("Mrs. Dalloway Goes to Market" 18). As such, Clarissa's consumption has the potential to liquefy distinctions and hierarchies: "[t]he city of women—Clarissa's London, for instance—is the site not only of all the hierarchies and divisions of the gendered social world, but also their liquefaction in gifts of consumption" ("Mrs. Dalloway Goes to Market" 19).

"Mrs. Dalloway in Bond Street" explicitly puts the market and gift economies into opposition, but Clarissa's negotiation of and participation in the two economies remains ambiguous. Dick's system keeps everyone in their place—in terms of class, gender and role in the process of capitalist exchange—and Clarissa seems to agree: "Of course he was right. And she could feel the girl wouldn't want to be given things. There she was in her place. So was Dick. Selling gloves was her job" ("Mrs. Dalloway" 157). In many ways, Clarissa's gift is problematic anyway—it is patronizing and motivated by class prejudice, and it is also a possible slight on the shop woman's hard-earned independence. It too could be considered as a means of maintaining social hierarchies and keeping hierarchies of value in place. Her obvious placing of her bag on the shop counter, far from being a facet of her flirtation, could also function as a sign of her superior status and authority, immediately making blatant the power dynamic between these two women and emphasizing the shop woman's obligation to satisfy this customer's desires.[23]

In reneging on her gift, Clarissa seems to comply with a masculine economy which silences the feminine and, in Cixous's theory, denies women's erotic and emotional needs and desires. Clarissa stifles her impulse to give a gift to the shop assistant (and presumably to Milly), and, seeming to favor Dick's economic sense, also becomes more "business-like" in her attitude to the shop assistant, more "thrifty" with her time and attentions, more focused on bringing the transaction to a close:

> At last! Half an inch above the elbow; pearl buttons; five and a quarter. My dear slow coach, thought Clarissa, do you think I can sit here the whole morning? Now you'll take twenty-five minutes to bring me my change! ("Mrs. Dalloway" 159).

However, the ambiguity and potential for destabilization of heteropatriarchal systems continues *as part of* the capitalist transaction, as part of the process of purchasing of the gloves. Clarissa's impulses toward the shop assistant dissipate, but her serial desires for women continue and her attention is diverted by the entrance of a woman she recognizes. This woman's entrance is announced by the roar of traffic as the door opens (a reminder of the busy city and the operation of the masculine economy), but also by the brightening of the silk stockings in the shop. The two economies are neatly balanced in a sentence structured around a caesura: "[t]he traffic suddenly roared; the silk stockings brightened" ("Mrs. Dalloway" 158). However, the balance tips in favor of the feminine and "[a] cus-

---

[23] I'd like to thank those participating in discussion of an earlier version of this essay, given as a paper at the 13th Annual Woolf Conference in June 2003, for this suggestion.

tomer came in" ("Mrs. Dalloway" 158). Immediately this woman "distracts" Clarissa, a certain "ring in her voice" triggers emotive memories for Clarissa; again she recalls a pre-marital state, a youthful pastoral idyll indicated here by the reference to Sylvia. This could be referring either to Sylvia Hunt, mocked earlier in this story for her dowdiness by a now deceased friend of Clarissa's youth (154), or to Clarissa's sister, Sylvia Parry, a connection more evocative of a sense of female intimacy.[24] This memory immediately leads Clarissa to thoughts of an imagined future, after the death of her husband. Although apparently this is Clarissa's fantasy about her own stoicism, both remembered and imagined times are significantly times when Clarissa is at a remove from heterosexual structures. Following this stream of thought, and still immersed in the fantasy of a future free from her marital bonds, the other customer's exclamation as she splits a glove draws Clarissa's attention. Clarissa's lesbian gaze lingers admiringly on this "sensual, clever" woman, objectifying her as a "Sargent drawing," and trying to find the point of connection in order to capitalize on this momentary meeting. The end of the story is Clarissa's recollection of the woman's name, Miss Anstruther, but this is clearly only the beginning of further exchanges between them.[25] The final words of the story affirm her connection with this unmarried woman, and the pleasure this affords Clarissa, as she smilingly speaks this woman's name.

---

[24] The early and tragic death of Sylvia is sketchily revealed in *Mrs. Dalloway*. Peter Walsh reflects on Clarissa's loss of her sister due to her father's negligence and notes Clarissa's appraisal of Sylvia as "the most gifted of them" (*MD* 87). If we read this reference to Sylvia in "Mrs. Dalloway in Bond Street" as referring to Clarissa's sister, the brevity of this reference to the female intimacy of Clarissa's past represents, as in *Mrs. Dalloway*, the marginalization and dismissal of exclusive female intimacy, other libidinal possibilities, and the "gifts" of the feminine in Clarissa's society. See Elizabeth Abel for a more detailed discussion. See also Joseph Allen Boone, who discusses this aspect of the novel in his persuasive exploration of the interrelations of Woolf's narrative techniques and form and the libidinal currents at play in *Mrs. Dalloway*.

[25] In contrast to the similar scene of feminine consumption in *Mrs. Dalloway*, where the spell of eroticized female intimacy is interrupted by the intrusion of the dominant social order in the form of a noise from a car outside, even the "violent explosion in the street outside" at the end of "Mrs. Dalloway in Bond Street" does not distract Clarissa from her flirtation with Miss Anstruther ("Mrs. Dalloway" 159). Indeed, the noise—possibly a "Bond Street" protest against such female intimacy—seems only to compound Clarissa's transgressive behavior in triggering her memory of Miss Anstruther's name. Corinne E. Blackmer uncovers a further lesbian encoding in this story when she suggests that the character of Miss Anstruther is a reference to Vernon Lee's longtime companion, C. Anstruther-Thomas. Blackmer comments that "[w]hile Lee was reluctant to acknowledge her lesbianism even to her close friends, her writings on aesthetics, which influenced Woolf, were replete with encoded homosexual references" (86).

However, the story's attention to the object of Clarissa's venture into the marketplace—the gloves—also maintains our sense of Clarissa as a highly ambiguous figure. On the one hand, gloves represent propriety and are firmly coded in the story as a signifier of a specific class, gender and attitude, and signify social barriers and differences. They endorse Clarissa's role as Mrs. Richard Dalloway, and signal her complicity in the dominant social order. What becomes clear, though, is that this isn't their only function in this story. They too "function otherwise" (Cixous, "Castration" 50).

The gloves Clarissa purchases are French with a pearl button (explicitly feminine), and the purchase is overlaid with her recollection of her uncle's Victorian measure of femininity, as Clarissa recalls, "[a] lady is known by her gloves and shoes, old uncle William used to say" ("Mrs. Dalloway" 157). They are what Abbott refers to in his discussion of the flowers in *Mrs. Dalloway* as "aristocratic commodities" and a "fixed symbol" of Clarissa's upper class status, and Clarissa apparently readily colludes in traditional attitudes and systems of value (201). Indeed, much of the story is preoccupied with the fitting of gloves, and getting gloves that fit properly seems to suggest a sense of "fitting in" socially, of being seen to be "proper(ty)" in the heterosocial order. [26] For Cixous "[t]he realm of the proper" is both heterosocial and phallocentric, with "proper" etymologically bound to the concept of "property" ("Castration" 50). Significantly for Woolf's story, Cixous goes on to say that the "proper may be the opposite of improper, and also of unfitting" (ibid). That the customer who can't get gloves to fit is very sad and mournful seems to signify more than the frustration of not being able to find a pair of gloves in the right size. Indeed this response seems to be more a concern with not fitting into, being appropriate in, or complying with heterosocial and heterosexual norms—as both of Clarissa's responses to her suggest. At first Clarissa's gaze lingers on this "improper," "unfitting" woman, whose sideways pose seems to invite the objectifying gaze. She acknowledges this woman's beauty and attraction, likening her to "a figure on a Japanese fan," an object of the heterosexual male gaze "some men would adore," but equally here an object of Clarissa's eroticizing gaze ("Mrs. Dalloway" 156). In her role as upper-class hostess, however, Clarissa conforms to dominant social norms and values and we see the way that this woman prompts Clarissa to think about the

---

[26] We see Clarissa's willingness to collude in this system and to accept her identity as property exchanged between the men of two families in her brief recollection of her family history: "Down Bond Street the Parrys had walked for a hundred years, and might have met the Dalloways (Leighs on the mother's side) going up" ("Mrs. Dalloway" 155). As she herself walks down "the narrow crooked street" she seems happy to locate her identity between these patriarchal family lines.

"dowdy women" whom it would be "intolerable" to have at her party ("Mrs. Dalloway" 156-7).

Clarissa's rapid retreat from her erotic gaze on this woman to the safe haven of what is proper and conventional (her party guests and her Uncle William's measurement of ladylike femininity) could also mark a moment of what Patricia Juliana Smith calls "lesbian panic" (2). Smith argues that lesbian panic is "the uncertainty of the female protagonist (or antagonist) about *her* own sexual identity" and "occurs when a character—or, conceivably, an author—is either unable or unwilling to confront or reveal her own lesbianism or lesbian desire" (3-4, 2, Smith's emphasis). Significantly for my essay, Smith argues that lesbian panic stems from a fear of loss of value and identity in a heterocentric social order:

> what is at stake for a woman under such conditions is nothing less than economic survival, as the object of exchange is inevitably dependent on the exchanger for her continued perceived worth. ... the fear of the loss of identity and value as an object of exchange, often combined with the fear of responsibility for one's own sexuality, is a characteristic response (6).

Clarissa's retreat from her fantasy of giving gifts to Milly and the shop assistant, of being an active sexual subject rather than an object of exchange, could equally be read in this light.

In many ways, Clarissa's attitude and scopophilia seem to concur with Felski's assessment of the effect of consumer culture which "made it possible for women to articulate needs and wants in defiance of traditional patriarchal prohibitions," but which simultaneously "subject[ed] women to norms of eroticized femininity that encouraged constant practices of self-surveillance" and "provided a conduit through which heterogeneous forms of desire could often be deflected and channeled into the imperative to buy ever more commodities" (90). However, Clarissa is clearly not compelled to purchase and discourse about gloves continues to articulate Clarissa's erotic longings for women, even as it operates as a screen for these desires. Far from being simply a "fixed symbol" of Clarissa's class and gender, or as a commodity via which potentially transgressive desires are safely channelled, we can read gloves in this story as having subversive potential.[27] Indeed, the style of glove Clarissa desires may also be a highly encoded reference to her more subversive sexual desires. That the gloves are

---

[27] Discussing the increasing public awareness and visibility of lesbian sexuality in the post-World War 1 period, Laura Doan focuses on fashion: "[t]he meaning of clothing in the decade after the First World War, a time of unprecedented cultural confusion over constructions of gender and sexual identities, was a good deal more fluid than fixed" (96). Clarissa's gloves, then, do not necessarily construct her gender and sexuality in a fixed and unproblematic way, but can signal other possibilities. As Woolf herself suggests in

French suggests romance, even a sense of the risqué (possibly evoking the lesbian chic of Paris in the 1920s), and pearls and buttons can be read as an erotic lesbian code in some of Woolf's texts.[28]

As we have seen, having gloves fitted can be a sensuous, seductive experience, but Clarissa's desires for women, unconventionally masculine women, are also associated with the fit of gloves. Clarissa's admiration for Lady Bexborough, for her superior, aloof status, her "regal" demeanor, and her masculine authority ("talking politics like a man") is summed up in the improper fit of her gloves ("Mrs. Dalloway" 156). Lady Bexborough's gloves are "loose at the wrist" (and her dress is "quite shabby," "Mrs. Dalloway" 156). Yet, far from considering her "dowdy," Clarissa seems to want to imitate her stoicism and as she considers her determination to "go on" should Dick die, she significantly "tak[es] the glove in her hand" ("Mrs. Dalloway" 158). Similarly, Clarissa's attraction to Miss Anstruther becomes focused on her authoritative tone as she tries on different pairs of gloves.

Although a symbolic (class) barrier and an actual barrier to physical contact— a commodity designed to reduce the tactile sensation of even the most restrained and polite touch—in Miss Anstruther's hands gloves actually split, bursting literal and symbolic barriers.[29] The image of the skin splitting recalls the orgasmic moment in *Mrs. Dalloway*, encoded as a thin skin splitting, an overflow of desire, passion and *jouissance*.[30] Although in "Mrs. Dalloway in Bond Street" this potentially erotic moment of splitting is immediately recuperated into the market economy, "'But it's an awful swindle to ask two pound ten!'" ("Mrs. Dalloway" 158), it does occasion a significant exchange of glances between Clarissa and the object of her attention at that point in the story, Miss Anstruther. The seductive impact of this moment is signalled by the symmetrical structure of

---

Orlando, "[c]lothes are but a symbol of something hid deep beneath," which may or may not reveal a consistent gender identity or sexuality (*O* 117).

[28] See my forthcoming essay, "Pearl-Diving: Inscriptions of Desire and Creativity in H.D. and Woolf" for further discussion of this idea.

[29] The shop assistant apologetically explains that "'[g]loves have never been quite so reliable since the war'" ("Mrs. Dalloway" 158). During the war women occupied traditional male roles, gaining a sense of independence and sexual autonomy, and so in this post-war period the unreliablity and inconsistency of gloves is possibly not the only thing being referred to here.

[30] "It was a sudden revelation, a tinge like a blush which one tried to check and then, as it spread, one yielded to its expansion, and rushed to the farthest verge and there quivered and felt the world come closer, swollen with some astonishing significance, some pressure of rapture, which split its thin skin and gushed and poured with an extraordinary alleviation over the cracks and sores" (*MD* 36).

the sentence which describes and exaggerates the mirroring behavior of the two women, intensifying the effect of this glance: "Clarissa looked at the lady; the lady looked at Clarissa" ("Mrs. Dalloway" 158).

Clarissa's attraction to a range of different women in this story repeatedly distracts her from her ostensible mission to make a purchase of gloves—to accept a distinct role, participate in a controlled and rational exchange of objects, and to fulfil her "proper" role as an upper-middle class heterosexual woman. In many ways, Clarissa's role as a female shopper seems merely a masquerade of heterosexual femininity, however, to allay cultural anxieties and to screen Clarissa's more disruptive desires. Far from being a passive female consumer "seduced by the glittering phantasmagoria of an emerging consumer culture," Clarissa's participation in the masculine monetary economy continues to facilitate her activities in a feminine libidinal economy, beyond the ending of this narrative (Felski 62). Earlier in the story we're told that Clarissa takes great pleasure in the "endless—endless—endless" stream of people and sights in the city; equally what we see in this story is the endless flow of Clarissa's desires ("Mrs. Dalloway" 154). The story ultimately resists closure: the capitalist transaction is incomplete (the gloves are not yet purchased) and a bond with another woman just renewed.

Clarissa's participation in gift and market economies is not fixed and specific; she isn't constrained by either a masculine (capitalist and heterosexual) economy, nor limited to a feminine, potentially lesbian, gift economy, but she shifts between the two. Indeed, her "proper" participation in the market economy provides a space for other "improper" economies to function. She takes erotic pleasure from shopping and window shopping, gazing at women, exchanging glances, "bonding" with them, and contemplating giving gifts to enhance the pleasure of women, but ultimately she stakes no claim. She neither gives gifts nor makes a purchase, but takes pleasure in the possibility and processes of both. Certainly the story provides plenty of scope for "speculation" and Clarissa's activities in the marketplace give rise to a good deal of "interest." What seems to be the case is that whether participating in market or gift economies, Clarissa's bonds with women are invested with desire in a way which has potential to threaten and bring disorder to both capitalist and heterosexual economies. However, it is the operation of the gift economy in this story that helps to realize Clarissa's subversive desires, desires which undermine capitalist and heterosexual economies. Her gift-giving wishes and fantasies signal her lesbian desires and an active subjectivity at odds with the implicitly heterosexual circuit of desire that Felski identifies, opening up the possibility of erotic bonds with women (65). She is an active subject, resisting the passive role for the female shopper engineered by masculine marketing, and acts on her own desires in her exchanges (of glances, touches, smiles and compliments) with women. It is Clarissa's gift-giving impulse that opens the way (as Still suggests about "the gift" in general) to "thinking the heterogeneous," and to a range of subversive possibilities in this story (12). Cixous argues that an open-ended text ("always endless, without ending" and determined by a "female libidinal economy") such as "Mrs. Dalloway in Bond Street" is one which, rather than providing a point of origin or closure, instead gives a "send-off . . . making a gift of departure" ("Castration" 53). Such writing passes on "an endless circulation of desire" which cuts across sexual and relational social norms (ibid). Woolf's story can surely be read as such a "gift" to her readers.

I'd like to thank Ruth Hoberman for kindly allowing me to make reference to her new work pre-publication, to Alison Johnson for her insightful suggestions, and to Mike Davis for his generosity in commenting on a draft of this essay

.

Works Cited

Abbott, Reginald. "What Miss Kilman's Petticoat Means: Virginia Woolf, Shopping, and Spectacle." *Modern Fiction Studies* 38.1 (Spring 1992): 193-214.

Abel, Elizabeth. *Virginia Woolf and the Fictions of Psychoanalysis*. Chicago and London: Uof Chicago P, 1989.

Adburgham, Alison. *Shops and Shopping 1800-1914: Where, and in What Manner the Well-dressed Englishwoman Bought Her Clothes*. London: Allen, 1964.

Barrett, Eileen and Patricia Cramer, eds. *Virginia Woolf: Lesbian Readings*. New York and London: New York U P, 1997.

Barrett, Eileen. "Unmasking Lesbian Passion: the Inverted World of *Mrs. Dalloway*." Barrett and Cramer: 146-64.

Blackmer, Corinne E. "Lesbian Modernism in the Shorter Fiction of Virginia Woolf and Gertrude Stein." Barrett and Cramer: 78-94.

Boone, Joseph Allen. *Libidinal Currents: Sexuality and the Shaping of Modernism*. Chicago and London: U of Chicago P, 1998.

Bowlby, Rachel. *Still Crazy After All These Years: Women, Writing and Psychoanalysis*. London and New York: Routledge, 1992.

Caughie, Pamela L. *Virginia Woolf and Postmodernism: Literature in Quest and Question of Itself*. Urbana and Chicago: U of Illinois P, 1991.

——. (ed).*Virginia Woolf in the Age of Mechanical Reproduction*. Ed. Pamela L. Caughie. New York and London: Garland Publishing, 2000.

Cixous, Hélène. "The Laugh of the Medusa." 1975. Translated by Keith Cohen and Paula Cohen. *New French Feminisms: An Anthology*. Ed. and Introductions by Elaine Marks and Isabelle de Courtivron. Hertfordshire: Harvester Wheatsheaf, 1981. 245-64.

———. "Castration or Decapitation?" 1976. Translated and Introduced by Annette Kuhn. *Signs: Journal of Women in Culture and Society*, 7.1, (1981): 36–55.

Conley, Verena Andermatt. *Hélène Cixous*, Interview. Nebraska and London: U of Nebraska P, 1991.

Delany, Paul. *Literature, Money and the Market: From Trollope to Amis*. Basingstoke: Palgrave, 2002.

DeSalvo, Louise and Mitchell A. Leaska (ed.). *The Letters of Vita Sackville-West to Virginia Woolf*. London: Virago, 1992.

Doan, Laura. *Fashioning Sapphism: The Origins of a Modern English Lesbian Culture*. New York and Chichester: Columbia U P, 2001.

Elliot, Bridget and Jo-Ann Wallace. *Women Artists and Writers: Modernist (Im)positionings*. London and New York: Routledge, 1994.

Felski, Rita. *The Gender of Modernity*. Massachusetts and London: Harvard U P, 1995.

Freedman, Jonathan. *Professions of Taste: Henry James, British Aestheticism, and Commodity Culture*. Stanford: Stanford U P, 1990.

Garrity, Jane. "Selling Culture to the 'Civilized': Bloomsbury, British *Vogue*, and the Marketing of National Identity." *Modernism/Modernity* 6.2 (1999): 29-58.

———. "Virginia Woolf, Intellectual Harlotry, and 1920s British *Vogue*." Caughie (*Mechanical*): 185 – 218.

Gaskell, Elizabeth. *Cranford*. London: Penguin, 1988.

Hankins, Leslie Kathleen. "Virginia Woolf and Walter Benjamin Selling Out(Siders)." Caughie (*Mechanical*): 3–35.

Herr, Cheryl. *Joyce's Anatomy of Culture*. U of Illinois P, 1982.

Hoberman, Ruth. "Collecting, Shopping and Reading: Virginia Woolf's Stories about Objects." *Trespassing Boundaries: Virginia Woolf's Short Fiction*. Ed. Kathryn N. Benzel and Hoberman. New York: Palgrave Macmillan, 2004. 81-98

Huyssen, Andreas. *After the Great Divide: Modernism, Mass Culture, Postmodernism*. Bloomington and Indianapolis: Indiana U P, 1986.

Hyde, Lewis. *The Gift: Imagination and the Erotic Life of Property*. London: Vintage, 1999.

Kirkpatrick, B.J. "Virginia Woolf: Unrecorded *Times Literary Supplement* Reviews." *Modern Fiction Studies* 38.1 (Spring 1992) 279–283.

Kershner, R.B. *Joyce, Bakhtin and Popular Literature*. Chapel Hill and London: U of North Carolina P, 1989.

Kucich, John. "Transgression and Sexual Difference in Elizabeth Gaskell's Novels." *Texas Studies in Literature and Language* 32.2 (1990): 187–213.

Majumdar, Robin and Allen McLaurin (ed.). *Virginia Woolf: The Critical Heritage*. London: Routledge and Kegan Paul Ltd., 1975.

Mansfield, Katherine. "The Little Governess." 1920. *Katherine Mansfield: Selected Stories*. Ed. D. M. Davin. Oxford: Oxford U P, 1981. 184–97.

Marcus, Laura. "Virginia Woolf and The Hogarth Press." Ian Willison, et al: 124-150.

McVicker, Jeanette. "'Six Essays on London Life': A History of Dispersal. Part 1." *Woolf Studies Annual* 9 (2003): 143–65.

Moretti, Franco. *Signs Taken for Wonders: Essays in the Sociology of Literary Forms*. Revised Edition. London: Verso, 1988.

Nicolson, Nigel. *Portrait of a Marriage*. London: Weidenfeld and Nicolson, 1990.

Rainey, Lawrence. *Institutions of Modernism: Literary Elites and Public Culture*. New Haven and London: Yale U P. 1998.

Raitt, Suzanne. *Vita and Virginia: The Work and Friendship of V. Sackville-West and Virginia Woolf*. Oxford: Oxford U P, 1993.

Rubin, Gayle. "The Traffic in Women: Notes on the 'Political Economy' of Sex." In *Literary Theory: An Anthology*. Ed Julie Rivkin and Michael Ryan. London: Blackwell, 1998: 533–560.

Simpson, Kathryn. "Pearl Diving: Inscriptions of Desire and Creativity in H.D. and Woolf." Forthcoming in *Journal of Modern Literature* 28.1 (2005).

Smith, Patricia Juliana. *Lesbian Panic: Homoeroticism in Modern British Women's Fiction*. New York: Columbia U P, 1997.

Snaith, Anna. *Virginia Woolf: Public and Private Negotiations*. Basingstoke and London: Macmillan Press, 2000.

Still, Judith. *Feminine Economies: Thinking Against the Market in the Enlightenment and the Late Twentieth Century*. Manchester and New York: Manchester U P, 1997.

Tratner, Michael. *Modernism and Mass Politics: Joyce, Woolf, Eliot and Yeats*. Stanford U P, 1995.

——. "Why Isn't *Between the Acts* a Movie?" Caughie (*Mechanical*): 115–34.

Walkowitz, Judith R. "The Making of an Outcast Group." *A Widening Sphere*. Ed. Martha Vicinus, 1977.

Wicke, Jennifer. *Advertising Fictions: Literature, Advertisement, and Social Reading*. New York: Columbia U P, 1988.

——. "Mrs. Dalloway goes to Market: Woolf, Keynes, and Modern Markets." *Novel: A Forum on Fiction* 28.1 (Fall 1994): 5-23.
Willison, Ian, Warwick Gould and Warren Chernaik (eds). *Modernist Writers and the Marketplace*. Basingstoke: Macmillan, 1996.
Woolf, Virginia. *The Voyage Out*. 1915. London: Penguin, 1992.
——. "Mrs. Dalloway in Bond Street." 1923. *Virginia Woolf: The Complete Shorter Fiction*. Ed. Susan Dick, London: Triad Grafton Books, 1991. 152–159.
——. *Mrs Dalloway*. 1925. London: Penguin, 1974.
——. "Street Haunting: A London Adventure." 1927. *The Essays of Virginia Woolf, Volume 4, 1925–28*. Ed Andrew McNellie. London: The Hogarth Press, 1994.
——. *Orlando: A Biography*. 1928. London: Grafton, 1989.
——. "Oxford Street Tide." 1932. *The London Scene: Five Essays by Virginia Woolf*. New York: Random House, 1975. 16-22.
——. *Three Guineas*. 1938. London: The Hogarth Press, 1991.
——. "The Duchess and the Jeweller." 1938. *Virginia Woolf: The Complete Shorter Fiction*. Ed. Susan Dick, London: Triad Grafton Books, 1991. 248-53.
——. *The Diary of Virginia Woolf, Volume 2, 1920–24*.1978. London: Penguin, 1981.
——. *The Diary of Virginia Woolf, Volume 3, 1925–30*. 1980. London: Penguin, 1982.

Aesthetic Taste, Kitsch, and *The Years*
Ruth Hoberman

The Years has always troubled Woolf's critics, much as its writing troubled Woolf herself. Categorized as a novel of "fact" rather than "vision," it was seen as a kind of step-child, an unnatural effort to create in a genre not her own. More recently, Woolf's talent for describing the "real world" has been better recognized, but *The Years* remains problematic, combining modernist complexity with a realistic treatment of setting that seems at once satirical and nostalgic. Crucial to this tonal complexity is the novel's depiction of physical objects—more particularly, its use of "kitsch" objects that appeal simultaneously to the reader's emotions and to her skepticism. In its embrace of kitsch, *The Years* sets itself in opposition to—or at least in conversation with—the aesthetics of Roger Fry, and ultimately asks us not to reject kitsch as bad art, but to read it carefully for its revelation, in this novel at least, of women's relationships and experiences.

My use of the term "kitsch" perhaps needs explaining. Most frequently, it has been used dismissively, to designate cheaply made, mass-produced goods that offer the "masses" shallow and entertaining images to distract them from their empty lives. But while Disney movies and Norman Rockwell paintings are Clement Greenberg's prime examples in his famous 1939 essay "Avant-garde and Kitsch," kitsch's roots stretch back to the nineteenth century—to romanticism's emphasis on emotion, on beauty, and on the democratization of aesthetic experience, and to the Victorian bourgeoisie, with its taste for sentiment, clutter, and incongruously conceived objects like flowers under glass globes and animal-shaped pen-wipes.[1] Most critics agree that all such objects share some kind of "*aesthetic inadequacy*" (Calinescu 236), though they differ on how to define it. Greenberg explains that inadequacy as "vicarious experience and faked sensations," formulaic and derivative (10); Tomas Kulka complains similarly that kitsch images depend parasitically for their emotional impact on the pathos of what they depict rather than on their formal qualities (78-80). Max Horkheimer and Theodor Adorno complain that the "culture industry" offers pre-digested experience that manipulates its viewers into passivity. Recently, however, as the whole notion of "aesthetic value" has become suspect, there has been an effort to read kitsch more sympathetically, as a culturally significant response to moder-

---

[1] Matei Calinescu includes in his description of kitsch the "pseudo-aristocratic aesthetic notions of the rich nineteenth-century bourgeois" (243), while Jacques Sternberg calls Sarah Bernhardt's 1900 salon exemplary (22).

nity. Susan Stewart, for example, writes that kitsch "offers a saturation of materiality, a saturation which takes place to such a degree that materiality is ironic, split into contrasting voices: past and present, mass production and individual subject, oblivion and reification" (167). Celeste Olalquiaga and Matei Calinescu see kitsch as resulting from middle-class angst in the face of modernity: in Calinescu's words, a middle class "reaction against the 'terror' of change and the meaninglessness of chronological time flowing from an unreal past into an equally unreal future" (248). Olalquiaga's paradigmatic kitsch object is a dead hermit crab under a glass globe, simultaneously a reminder of death and a transcendence of it. She reads the kitsch object, in fact, much as Walter Benjamin read the Paris Arcades, dialectically. Kitsch, she writes, "is the attempt to repossess the experience of intensity and immediacy through an object," an effort that inevitably fails, resulting in an object "whose decayed state exposes and deflects its utopian possibilities" (291).

Karen Jacobs, influenced like Olalquiaga by Benjamin, reads Woolf's *Between the Acts* as a project paralleling *The Arcades Project*;[2] I want to suggest that Benjamin's method is at least as useful in examining *The Years*, a novel in which things seem—as Benjamin's translators write of nineteenth-century Paris—"more entirely material than ever and, at the same time, more spectral and estranged" (Benjamin, *Arcades* xii). In "A Sketch of the Past," begun in April 1939, two years after the publication of *The Years*, Woolf wrote, "If I had the power to lift out a month of life as we lived it about 1900 I could extract a section of Victorian life, like one of those cases with glass covers in which one is shown ants or bees going about their affairs" (127). *The Years* is just such a terrarium: we get the sense that we are seeing life as it was, in all its material reality, but very much through that glass: distanced, ironized, but also resonant

---

[2] Jacobs writes of *The Arcades Project*, a massive collection of quotations and observations about the role of commodities in nineteenth-century Paris: "by providing images of the old amidst the new," the Arcades, if properly read, "create a flash of historical insight through which the present, in its relation to the past and future, could be illuminated" (207). The Arcades, according to Benjamin, displayed objects offering affordable luxury while obscuring "the class relations which stood behind their production" (Jacobs 206). I see Woolf's objects in similar terms, but add gender to the mix, looking for ways in which objects in *The Years* offer the solace of familiarity while obscuring both the class and gender relations underlying their production and use. In doing so, I am following through on Leslie Kathleen Hankins' essay juxtaposing Woolf and Benjamin, in which she points out the fascination for both of the "bourgeois *interieur*" (12). In their depictions of these interior spaces, she writes, they conveyed "both nostalgia for and repudiation of the past, providing that mix of attachment and loathing that gives the dialectical push to a new consciousness" (9).

with loss and longing, because, as the glass reminds us, it is a past populated by the dead. Leslie Hankins writes that both Benjamin and Woolf use "nostalgia to interrogate urban and class spaces in radical ways" (9). They read—and ask us to read—kitsch in complex terms: critically, as a symptom of the sentimentality with which the Victorian era disguised its exploitative gender and class relations; but also sympathetically, as expressing an understandable desire to hold onto the past—a past linked frequently, in the novel, to dead and marginalized women.

Why women? Kitsch, writes Ruth Barton, is often "associated with the feminine and with female consumption in so far as it was imitative, cheap and, above all, sentimental" (194). These objects are generally bought to decorate and serve the home, which, as Alan Bott suggests in *Our Mothers*, one of the books Woolf took notes from as she prepared to write *The Years*, was, during the Victorian period, intrinsically feminine: "The Victorian home, like the Victorian female body, was well covered, and like the Victorian female mind it was filled to overflowing with small superfluities" (60). Women serve as buyers or users or, in the case of paintings, as the subjects of, all the objects I discuss, and are the most scrupulous readers of these objects as well. While Digby and Martin, in *The Years*, tend to respond in aesthetic terms, labeling objects good or bad, Eleanor and Peggy contemplate and converse with their things, allowing them to emit revelatory, if contradictory associations that ask us, finally, to think about who used what, why, under what social and economic constraints. "Women," Woolf writes in *A Room of One's Own*, "have sat indoors all these millions of years, so that by this time the very walls are permeated by their creative force, which has, indeed, so overcharged the capacity of bricks and mortar that it must needs harness itself to pens and brushes and business and politics" (91). Objects in *The Years* contain the explosive energy of the women who have owned and used them. They work, in fact, much like Woolf's metaphor. By turning constricting rooms and walls into literal mortar and brick, Woolf makes it easier for us to imagine blowing them up. Unexamined, kitsch objects make the home (i.e., patriarchy and capitalism) feel safe, timeless, inevitable, the product of a series of freely determined purchases that imprint our personalities on our environment. Read carefully, however, these same objects reveal the way a patriarchal culture exploits and marginalizes women's experiences and labor and thus have an explosive power of their own.

Women, Sentimental Value, and Aesthetic Judgment

Haunting *The Years* from its starting point is the dying Mrs. Pargiter, whose picture hangs in the overcrowded drawing room on Abercorn Terrace: "a red-haired young woman in white muslin holding a basket of flowers on her lap" (10). The painting resembles the portrait of Kitty Lasswade, red-haired, wearing "white muslin" and "toying with a basket of roses" (256), which appears later in the novel hanging in her London house. Diane Gillespie calls that painting "a stereotypical rendition that suggests innocence as well as budding sensuality" and points out its resemblance to G. F. Watts's "Lillian" (209).[3] Its smiling young girl in white derives her appeal from these conventional qualities, reminding us of Kulka's definition of kitsch as work that derives its emotional impact from its referent rather than from its intrinsic design. Clearly not meant to be great art, the painting of Kitty is dismissed by Martin as a "horrid daub" (262). Equally mediocre, it is implied, is the picture of Mrs. Pargiter; in *The Pargiters*, in fact, the "novel-essay" Woolf wound up cutting from her novel, Eleanor explicitly dislikes the picture: "She was all in white: she held a posy: it was a silly simpering picture," in which her mother has been "refined into insipidity" (23).

In revising, however, Woolf deleted Eleanor's criticism. For in the finished version, while Martin judges paintings in aesthetic terms, the female members of his family respond more associatively. For them the painting of Rose Pargiter serves throughout the novel as a reminder of loss, of the passage of time (as it accumulates dirt), and of the powers of memory and imagination to reconstitute the past. More important than its quality is what it depicts: the Pargiters' dead mother. Thus Delia talks to the painting, Eleanor has it cleaned, and Peggy wonders about its subject and what it reveals about Peggy's own place within the family: "Was it like her?" she asks. Eleanor answers no, but goes on:

> "what's so interesting . . . is that what they thought ugly—red hair for instance—we think pretty; so that I often ask myself," she paused, puffing at her cheroot, "'What is pretty?'" "Yes," said Peggy. "That's what they were saying . . . . Is there any standard d'you think?" (326)

The question goes unanswered, for Eleanor's attention has already wandered, and in any case it is clear, the implied answer to the question "Is there any standard d'you think?" is no. The painting's value is in its history as a family artifact, in the story it tells of a generic young girl who married, had children, and died, and in the conversation it triggers, creating a web of connections among family members and between past and present.

The painting of Rose Pargiter is typical of the way objects work in *The Years*. A work of mediocre or indeterminate aesthetic value is described in a

---

[3] Woolf herself called Watts's 1905 posthumous exhibition "atrocious" (Gillespie 209).

way that emphasizes its physical materiality (frequently the object is dirty, decaying, or inconvenient). The object then recurs in a variety of contexts, allowing characters to find through it a sense of connectedness to each other and to the past. The object allows them to feel that to some extent they are transcending time: its stability amid their own changes is reassuring. Yet at the same time that very stability is alienating: its materiality casts it in opposition to their subjectivity. As a result, the illusion of connectedness is revealed to be just that: an illusion. Characters and readers are left with a sense of yearning and an object, to quote Olalquiaga again, "whose decayed state exposes and deflects its utopian possibilities" (291). As readers we are asked to identify with the characters' responsiveness to these objects, even as we recognize their sentimentality and detect the problematic social relations (Rose Pargiter trapped into playing "angel in the house") that the objects encode.[4]

Woolf's interest in objects in *The Years* is sentimental rather than aesthetic: standards of taste, as Peggy's conversation with Eleanor about the painting of Rose Pargiter suggests, are revealed to be subjective and even oppressive. Martin and Digby, the most aesthetically judgmental characters in the novel, wield their taste as an instrument of power, and while the narrator does occasionally seem dismissive—of Mira's or Lily Levy's bad taste for example—such judgments are more often undercut. The Robsons' house, like Mira's, includes "a small room, crowded with objects"(67). The "china was cheap with its florid red roses" (68), and on the wall is an "oily landscape in a heavy gilt frame" (70); in another room there are bamboo tables, "velvet books with brass hinges; marble gladiators askew on the mantel piece and innumerable pictures"(72), all, according to the narrator, "ugly" (70). And in a moment of discomfort, Kitty consoles herself, saying, "Anyhow their taste is awful" (69). Kitty's judgment is quickly undermined, however, when the objects' emotional context becomes clear: one picture is of the Yorkshire moor where Mrs. Robson grew up (and where Kitty herself has maternal roots and longs to be); another depicts Mr. Robson's mother, and a silver salver has been inscribed to Mr. Robson, the self-made scholar, by his students. Not only are the objects charged with emotional content; Kitty's comment is itself more motivated by her feeling of exclusion and frustrated desire (she would like Jo Robson to kiss her) than by her aesthetic taste. Ultimately, then, her judgment is undercut as the reader recognizes her failure to read the objects properly, in terms of their emotional context—their sentimental

---

[4] In T*he Pargiters*, the painting's explosive potential is more explicit; Eleanor says, looking at the picture of her mother, "I shouldn't live like this," i.e., amid upper middle class comfort and constraints (23).

value, linked most specifically to Mr. Robson's mother and his Yorkshire origins.[5] When Kitty returns home, she sees her own "tastefully" decorated home with new eyes: "She granted, as she looked round, the superiority of the Lodge china and silver; and the Japanese plates and the picture [at the Robsons'] had been hideous; but this dining-room with its hanging creepers and its vast cracked canvases was so dark" (76).

In any case no one's taste appears to be above reproach: Martin wonders if Kitty's Canaletto is genuine or merely from the "school of" (248) and dislikes her "little tables with photographs; ornate cabinets with vases of flowers; and panels of yellow brocade let into the walls" (262-3), while North critically contemplates Sara's lodging house room with its pot of pampas grass and cheap plates (313; 316). Even those who pride themselves on their taste may well be deluded; Kitty's mother shows off a "Gainsborough that was not quite certainly a Gainsborough" (72),[6] and Judge Curry collects chests of which Mr. Pargiter comments, "all shams I suspect" (105). North dismisses Nicholas as a "bounder" because of his fob (372). And when Edward tells North about Chipperfield, a porter's son who has grown rich off railroads and buys old masters, Eleanor interjects, "Shams, I should think?" (413). We never do find out if Maggie liked the cheap necklace Abel Pargiter gives her for her birthday (167). And when Kitty, in Yorkshire, reaches for a green and blue enamel cigarette case, she wonders what Martin would say of it: "Hideous? Vulgar? Possibly—but what did it matter what people said?" (275). The climax of this threat to aesthetic judgment comes with the performance of the caretaker's children at the novel's end, when the listeners find their incomprehensible song "so shrill, so discordant, and so meaningless" they don't know what to say. This "distorted" and "hideous" performance echoes one Roger Fry wrote about to Woolf in July 1931; listening to an "over-sweetened minor French composer's nonsense played very decidedly out of tune but with deep feeling," he writes, "my hatred of humanity in the mass is overpowering" (*Letters* 659). But Eleanor's response is less judgmental, and less certain, and in fact most critics read the children's song as potentially redemptive: "Beautiful?" Eleanor asks of Maggie, who responds

---

[5] In *The Pargiters* the wall display is linked explicitly not only to Mr. Robson's mother, but also to his wife: "it was her doing, framing his certificates & hanging them in the front room, together with the [*tea*] salver" (134).

[6] Martin, however, seems to assume it is genuine when he says to Kitty in the 1914 chapter, "Why have a picture like that"—he nodded his head at the portrait—"when they've a Gainsborough . . ." (263).

"Extraordinarily." But, we're told, "Eleanor was not sure that they were thinking of the same thing" (431).[7]

Roger Fry and Walter Sickert

The novel as a whole, in fact, seems part of a conversation with Roger Fry about aesthetics. Christopher Reed has pointed out two aspects of Fry's formalism that continued to pose problems for Bloomsbury thinkers: the relation of art to the "real world," and the subjectivity of aesthetic taste. Both are addressed in *The Years*, a book haunted as much by Fry as by Rose Pargiter. Woolf began thinking about *The Years* in 1931, the same year she went to Greece with Fry and his sister (Lee 632). She was working on the novel in 1933, when she wrote an essay about Walter Sickert, a painter Fry did not like, and in 1934, when Fry died—a death that, according to Grace Radin, shaped her depiction of Mrs. Pargiter's (27). Finally, she was still working on the novel in 1935, when she immersed herself in Fry's letters and publications in preparation for writing his biography. Frances Spalding, Diane Gillespie, Kate Benzel, Jane Goldman, and Panthea Reid (who writes also as Panthea Reid Broughton), as well as Reed, are among those chronicling the immense and complex impact Fry (as well as Vanessa and Clive Bell) had on Woolf's writing.[8] *The Years*, and Woolf's 1940 *Roger Fry* suggest Woolf continued to talk back to Fry after his death.

Fry was an early articulator of the values underlying the kitsch/high art distinction. Woolf's treatment of kitsch in *The Years* contrasts with Fry's complaints—increasingly urgent during the course of his career, according to her biography of him—about the bad taste of the British public. Especially after the demise of the Omega Workshop in 1919, according to Woolf's biography, Fry disliked the incurable sentimentality and literariness of the people he came

---

[7] Deletions Woolf made between early and later drafts of *The Years* suggest she paid increasing attention to how she was depicting aesthetic taste. Among the deleted material are a scene where Eleanor eats in a restaurant and thinks dismissively about the tasteless décor (Radin 124; Squier 163), and one where Kitty complains she would like to get rid of the ugly pictures in her London house but her husband will not let her (Radin appendix). The fact that Woolf moved some of Eleanor's critical comments about mass culture from her mouth to Peggy's (Radin 124) suggests she wanted to highlight the contrast between their responses to kitsch. The removal of Kitty's complaint undercuts the stability of judgments about taste; rather than having her agree with Martin's judgment of the pictures, Woolf leaves the issue of their quality undecided.

[8] Goldman, for example, argues that Woolf's aesthetics parted company with Fry's and Clive Bell's in part because of their isolation of art from its social impact; she suggests Vanessa Bell's emphasis on color provided an alternative, feminist aesthetics (130).

increasingly to call the "herd" (216; 238). Central to Fry's notion of good art, is its involvement in aesthetic as opposed to "social" emotions and "literary" associations. Fry begins his essay "Art and Life" with the negative example of an "old gentleman" with "deplorable" taste who surrounds himself with eighteenth-century French furniture; for him, "art was merely a help to an imagined dream life" (*Vision* 1). In "The Ottoman and the Whatnot," Fry elaborates on this idea that objects are sometimes admired because of the historical associations they conjure up; they can "affect our historical imagination through our social emotions," but this, he suggests, has nothing "to do with our aesthetic reactions to the objects as works of art" (*Vision* 29). And in "Art and Socialism," Fry complains that the British public has been "drugged by the sugared poison of pseudo-art," and values art mainly "as a symbol of social distinctions" (*Vision* 46). In Fry's 1926 *Art and Commerce*, published by Hogarth Press, Fry elaborates on the idea, derived from Thorstein Veblen, that most art objects—opifacts he calls them, to distinguish them from real art—are created and bought out of concern for social status.

This pseudo-art so sought after by social climbers is what we would call kitsch. What does it look like? In "Art and Socialism" there is a long description of a railroad refreshment room—a description quoted by Woolf in her biography of Fry, and in 1999 by Calinescu in his effort to define kitsch. The refreshment room is decorated with imitation thirteenth-century stained glass, carved moldings and medallions, imitation eighteenth-century satin brocade wallpaper, pots with India rubber plants (*Vision* 47-48). This kind of derivative clutter is evoked also in "The Ottoman and the Whatnot," where Fry writes of the recent vogue for Victorian "paper-weights, stuffed humming-birds and wax flowers" (*Vision* 30-31), calling the art objects of the period "a kind of bastard baroque passing at times into a flimsy caricature of rococo" (32), badly designed and badly made. Finally, in *Art and Commerce,* when he distinguishes real artists like Giotto, Giorgione, Poussin, and Daumier from opifact-producers, his example of an opifact is the statue of Edith Cavell that stands near Trafalgar Square in London (7). "We all know," he writes, "that the Edith Cavell sculpture is not at all the same kind of thing as the Medici tombs" (7).

Many of the objects described so meticulously in Woolf's novel fit Fry's various examples of bad art. The walrus pen-wipe, the portraits over mantels, Lucy Craddock's "cheap red villa," the décor of Mira's flat, of the Robsons' house, of Sara's apartment late in the novel, the necklace that Abel Pargiter gives his niece for her birthday, the Edith Cavell statue that Eleanor and Peggy drive by at the end, are all, to one degree or another, in "bad taste." The novel as a whole, in fact, could be read as elaborating on Fry's complaint that Victorian objects are in vogue because they evoke a deluded version of Victorian life, mak-

ing "a quite peculiar little earthly paradise out of the boredoms, the snobberies, the cruel repressions, the mean calculations and rapacious speculations of the mid-nineteenth century" (Fry, *Vision* 30). But while Woolf's novel does indeed expose the snobberies and repressions underlying Victorian life, she also allows her typically Victorian objects and interiors to turn up in chapter after chapter, losing their oppressiveness and taking on instead just the kind of sentimental value Fry dismisses as "narrative" or "social emotion." For while these objects have been—in Fry's terms—created and acquired because of conventional notions of status and appropriateness rather than for their aesthetic expressiveness, the novel gives them an emotive power that transcends their aesthetic limitations. The very "social" emotions and "literary" associations that make them bad art for Fry make them worth describing for Woolf.

In his discussion of Woolf's relation to Bloomsbury aesthetics, Christopher Reed points out a shift in her writing during the 1930s, away from formalism, toward a more politicized view of art (29).[9] Certainly Woolf's 1934 essay on

Walter Sickert suggests a move away from Fry. In November 1933, Woolf went to an exhibition of Sickert's work and wrote him to express her admiration (Lee 631). He asked her to write about it, and in December they had dinner together. Sickert, she wrote in her diary, told "great jokes about Roger" and announced, "I'm a literary painter, romantic—You are the only person who understands me" (*D*4 194). In her essay, Woolf emphasizes Sickert's "literary" qualities, praising his ability to tell stories through his depiction of figures in rooms, comparing him to Dickens, Balzac, and Gissing (*CE*2 238). This praise goes directly against Fry's dictum that art should work not through story-telling but through the interplay of shapes and colors. In a December 1933 letter Woolf recounts Fry's response to her Sickert essay in just these terms: "You wouldn't find any literature in my paintings," he told her (*L*5 256). Indeed, Panthea Reid suggests Woolf felt guilty about the essay when it came out just after Fry's death (366).[10]

Besides the narrative implied by Sickert's placement of his subjects, Woolf suggests, the very objects within his paintings tell stories. For the poor, she says, unlike the rich, "are very close to what they possess," and as a result their things take on an emotional coloration, a story-telling potential that trumps their aesthetic value. "Merely by process of use and fitness the cheap furniture has rubbed its varnish off; the grain shows through; it has the expressive quality that expensive furniture always lacks; one must call it beautiful, though outside the room in which it plays its part it would be hideous in the extreme" (*CE*2 239).

---

[9] Indeed Woolf's essay "The Artist and Politics," written for the *Daily Worker* in 1936, provides evidence for such a shift; there she writes that the contemporary writer, given the current political situation, must turn "from the private lives of his characters to their social surroundings" (*CE*2 230). Reed argues, however, that Fry too rethought formalism during this time, in his 1933 "The Double Nature of Painting" (31), which calls for a balance between form and content. Reed sees Fry's formalism as evolving simultaneously with Woolf's growing interest in it; but he suggests that Fry's influence on Woolf peaked in Woolf's 1927 *To the Lighthouse* (21) and declined during the 1930s. Broughton, in contrast, sees a separation of the ways earlier. For her, Woolf's 1920 "Solid Objects" indicated a turning point in her relation to Fry's theories, specifically his notion that art "appeals solely to the aesthetic faculties" ("Blasphemy" 56). Broughton contends that from then on Woolf integrated her interest in "pattern and design" with traditional narrative concerns like "character and conflict" (57).

[10] In contrast to Reid's emphasis on the Fry/Sickert contrast, Reed argues both Bell and Fry came to respect Sickert; Fry in 1920 felt he had underestimated his work, and in 1921, Clive Bell called Sickert behind the times but talented (30). Woolf's account of Fry's response to her essay on Sickert, however, suggests that the two painters had starkly contrasting responses to "literariness" in art.

Not only do Sickert's paintings tell stories, but the objects he depicts within them resonate a similar narrative potential.

As Hermione Lee has suggested, *The Years* has a Sickert-like atmosphere, with its detailed descriptions of interior spaces, its depiction of characters in terms of their possessions and décor, its vivid evocation of poverty (643).[11] Mira's lower middle-class identity is defined by her room with "too many little objects about"(7), while Lily Levy's vulgarity is signaled by her "finery"; she is "all covered with pearls and things" (31). Lucy Craddock lives in a "cheap red villa" and has an umbrella with a "parrot's head for a handle" (63).[12] The entire depiction of Abel Pargiter's relationship with Mira, in fact, is reminiscent of Sickert's "Ennui," a painting Woolf analyzes at length in her essay, in which a man and a woman gaze in opposite directions in a claustrophobically depicted room. On the wall is a painting; on the bureau, a glass globe containing "stuffed birds" according to Woolf (*CE2* 237). Woolf creates a context for them—he is a publican, and the woman too tired to serve their patrons—and even reads the glass globe, that classic kitsch item, much as I am reading the objects in her novel: as a hint of some "other world," where "beauty and order prevail" (237).[13]

Woolf's novel, then, works to undermine the reader's sense of aesthetic taste, inviting instead her participation in the story-telling process—a process that involves tracing the objects' associations and emotional impact through time and across relationships. Jane Goldman has described Woolf's fondness for a kind of promiscuous associativeness in which an idea (Athens, Queen Victoria) mentally accretes innumerable, apparently unrelated objects (41-2); in *The Years*, these objects are themselves read as accretions in which past moments and emotions still reside. Like Olalquiaga's hermit crab, the glass globe in Sickert's painting, and the painting of Rose Pargiter, they seem at once time-bound and

---

[11] Woolf's study of Sickert's paintings "infected her novel," Lee writes, calling Sickert "one of the great influences on *The Years*" (643). Simon Watney suggests similarly that Sickert's interest in ordinary people parallels Woolf's work in the 1930s (Goldman 142).

[12] Anna Snaith reads Miss Craddock's parrot's head umbrella as indicating the "originality of her situation" (108), but the decorative use of birds is actually quite common in the novel—Mira's screen has a kingfisher on it; Kitty embroiders a bird pecking fruit—linking the umbrella more to kitsch than eccentricity.

[13] For illuminating analyses of Woolf's essay on Sickert, see Benzel, and Goldman 113-15.

timeless, moving between, in Olalquiaga's terms, "partially retrieving a forfeited moment and immediately losing it again" (291).[14]

Crosby's Kitsch Still Life

Most often it is a woman whose presence objects seem both to evoke and lose. In the 1880 chapter, for example, as Rose Pargiter lies dying, Eleanor looks at her mother's writing table, "the silver candlestick, the miniature of her grandfather, tradesmen's books—one had a gilt cow stamped on it—and the spotted walrus with a brush on its back that Martin had given his mother on her last birthday" and thinks they will all be hers (34-5). In the 1891 chapter, Eleanor touches the "ink-corroded patch of bristle on the back of Martin's walrus" and thinks, "That solid object might survive them all. If she threw it away it would still exist somewhere or other. But she never had thrown it away because it was part of other things—her mother for example"(91). Eleanor's famous "dot with strokes raying round it" (91), which she draws on her blotting paper for the first time immediately after thinking about how Martin's walrus "was part of other things—her mother for example"—suggests this power of objects to radiate meanings, particularly in contexts associated with women's labor and affection.[15] Thus for Kitty, Lucy Craddock's villa is "haloed with romance" (63), and for Eleanor, a red chair with gilt claws "seemed to radiate out some warmth, some glamour," which she associates with Maggie's mother (287).[16] The chair, first seen at the Digby Pargiters' house, was apparently brought by Eugénie from Italy. Is it a thing of aesthetic value? We are never sure; Digby, we are told, is a connoisseur and never seems to approve of his wife's purchases. But that is not

---

[14] Rachel Bowlby also suggests that things in *The Years*, despite their apparent offer of stability over time, actually work more complexly. Because of their reappearance in differing contexts amid which characters must work to recognize them, she suggests, they actually destabilize our sense of the material world (102). Similarly, the picture of Rose Pargiter changes, as it becomes dirty and is then cleaned (108), undermining its apparent ability to transcend time.

[15] An alternative explanation of Woolf's depiction of objects is offered by Michael Whitworth, who links it to x-rays and "the Rutherford atom," both of which complicated popular perceptions of the material world. The "porous atom," Whitworth writes, "and the atom surrounded by a field of force" facilitate a view of people in terms of "interfusion and interdependency," a view he suggests would appeal to Woolf (152-153). In particular he links Eleanor's view of her teacup to the "porous" atom (155); in the light of Whitworth's essay, Eleanor's dot with rays could be read as the atom and its force field.

[16] In contrast, Mitchell A. Leaska suggests that the chair echoes Colonel Pargiter's claw-like hand, suggesting the "guilty claws" "of a crippling paternalistic world in which human values are subordinated to solemn and sterile abstractions" (185).

really the issue. What matters is, once again, the chair's recurrence, and its role as a memorial to a dead woman.

Besides associations gained through ownership, these objects radiate the labor involved in their use and upkeep. Eleanor and her sisters labor to make the water boil in the silver tea kettle; and Crosby labors to keep the house's many objects clean: "The whole room, with its carved chairs, oil paintings, the two daggers on the mantelpiece, and the handsome sideboard—all the solid objects that Crosby dusted and polished every day" (35). Woolf describes the Pargiters' dining room table, set by Crosby with newly polished silver, in language that echoes Eleanor's dot: the "[k]nives and forks rayed out round the table" (35). Later, as Eleanor prepares to leave Abercorn Terrace, she thinks about the fact that Crosby "had known every cupboard, flagstone, chair and table . . . not from five or six feet of distance as they had known it; but from her knees, as she scrubbed and polished; she had known every groove, stain, fork, knife, napkin and cupboard" (216). As Woolf writes in her essay on Sickert, the poor know objects differently, from closer up.

After her retirement, Crosby memorializes that labor by decorating her new home with all her salvaged objects: "Indian elephants, silver vases, the walrus that she had found in the waste-paper basket . . . She ranged them askew on the mantelpiece"(218). Crosby's mantel is a kind of still life memorializing not just Martin—as Joanna Lipking (143) and Susan Squier (150) have suggested—but also her own labor, through the objects she has seen, as Eleanor recognizes, from a uniquely intimate perspective. This intimacy is both literal and figurative; she has handled the objects, but she has also internalized them, as part of her emotional life. "What we used to call art," Benjamin writes in "Dream Kitsch," "begins at a distance of two meters from the body. But now, in kitsch, the world of things advances on the human being; it yields to his uncertain grasp and ultimately fashions its figures in his interior" (*Selected* 5). Such objects, for Benjamin, have colonized the human mind, creating a "creature who deserves the name of 'furnished man'" (5). Crosby is, in a sense, a "furnished woman": the objects she displays are "patched with cheap maxims," as Benjamin puts it (3): steeped in all the clichés of loyalty and love with which she has made sense of her role in life. But it is only when the mental "furniture" is put on display, when the mind is emptied of its bourgeois interior, that insight becomes possible.

As a kind of kitsch still life, Crosby's mantel complements in important ways the still life Woolf describes in her biography of Roger Fry—the still life arranged by Fry with the sign directed at his cleaning lady, Mrs. Filmer, saying "Do not touch." If Fry's art is defined, as Woolf suggests, by its separation from "real life" and the labor of Mrs. Filmer, Crosby's mantel is its underside, exposing how this separation of art from life marginalizes women's labor. In her biography of Fry, Woolf's summary of Fry's "Art and Life" provides a revealing contrast. Woolf sums up Fry's view: "Art and life are two rhythms . . . 'and in the main the two rhythms are distinct, and as often as not play against each other.'" There were, Woolf concludes, "Two rhythms in his own life. There was the hurried and distracted life; but there was also the still life" (214). But, she asks, "were they distinct?" Woolf argues that Fry in fact brought his aesthetics to bear on his life, when he made his studio a refuge from the war and within that studio created a literal "still life" which the cleaning lady was not to touch: "On the table, protected by its placard [reading "Do not touch"], was the still life—those symbols of detachment, those tokens of a spiritual reality immune from destruction, the immortal apples, the eternal eggs" (215). Fry's still life, in other words, was an attempt to create a reality immune to social disorder; Woolf, however, recognizes the inseparability of the two "rhythms": Fry defines his art in terms of its separation from real life and the labor of Mrs. Filmer, who, even as Fry paints his apples, is hard at work cleaning the rest of his house. When Woolf has Crosby rescue the walrus pen-wipe from the wastepaper basket and put it on display, she forces us to notice not only the object's materiality, but also its exposure of the class- and gender-bound hierarchies governing its cultural significance, and the sense of loss it both compensates for and memorializes (Mrs. Pargiter is dead, the house is sold, Crosby's job is gone, her labor lost).[17]

Fry himself talks about still lifes as wonderfully free of non-visual associations; "In still-life," he writes in his book on Cézanne, "the ideas and emotions associated with the objects represented are, for the most part, so utterly commonplace and insignificant that neither artist nor spectator need consider them" (39; qtd. Gillespie 278); the result is that the artist works solely in terms of aesthetic relationships. Descriptions of purely visual still lifes do turn up in *The Years*; Gillespie suggests, in fact, that such aesthetic contemplation is typical of Woolf's later work (238). Certainly Maggie's contemplation of Sara's mantel emphasizes its formal qualities: "there was the straight line of the mantelpiece with little black-and-white squares on it; and then three rods ending in soft yellow plumes. She ran her eye from thing to thing. In and out it went, collecting, gathering, summing up into one whole" (349; qtd. Gillespie 238). Gillespie

---

[17] Woolf, of course, had a long-standing interest in maids: they appear in many of her novels, and in *Three Guineas*, she bemoans the absence of maids from the *Dictionary of National Biography* (166). Most relevantly, in her biography of Fry, Woolf suggests that Fry was egalitarian in that he felt aesthetic sensibility was distributed throughout the populace—"one's housemaid 'by a mere haphazard gift of providence' might surpass one"—but only in terms of an initial responsiveness, not analytical ability (161).

astutely points out the passage's resemblance to Vanessa Bell's paintings, specifically *Still Life on Corner of a Mantelpiece* (1914) (238). But while Gillespie takes this aesthetic viewpoint to be typical of the novel's treatment of objects—"Solid objects," she writes, " . . . are freed from quotidian associations and viewed as shapes and colors that, juxtaposed, make pleasing wholes" (242)—I see it as atypical; indeed, Maggie recontextualizes her formalist vision before leaving when she looks again at the "cheap lodging-house room" and notes the "pampas grass in its terra-cotta pot; the green vase with the crinkled lip" (350). The objects move back and forth between being patches of color and symptoms of a particular social environment.

Crosby's mantel is also illuminated by Nancy Armstrong's recent discussion of modernist "iconophobia," which cites William Stieglitz's photography as a typically modernist rejection of a pictorialism and sentimentality culturally coded as "feminine." Stieglitz, she writes, sought to "renounce the rhetoric of the perfect copy, an image that derives meaning from its subject matter. He made [his photographs] testify to the originality of the copy instead" (55). Images, Armstrong writes, lose their aesthetic value when they "happened to be stuck to other images already charged with meaning" (50). This distrust of representationalism resembles Fry's insistence on formal relationships and rejection of "literary" painting, and Kulka's definition of kitsch as depending parasitically on its referent—rather than its design—for its emotional charge. To avoid the contamination of referentiality, Stieglitz's photographs of household objects decontextualize them, stripping them of the feminine associations they would otherwise have (54).

Clive Bell writes of the role of objects in still life in similar terms: the object's function is irrelevant; the coal-scuttle, he writes (yet another object linked to women's labor), is "an end in itself, as a significant form related on terms of equality with other significant forms. Thus have all great artists regarded objects" (qtd. Goldman 132). Bell's "significant form," Goldman points out, "smooths over the cultural and political implications of such images" (132), a move she detects also in Fry's rejection of "associated ideas" in the analysis of art (134; see also Fry, *Cézanne* 51). If Woolf's novel as a whole seems to share Crosby's iconophilia, it is perhaps to subvert this modernist obscuring of the feminine in the name of high art.[18]

---

[18] Jane Marcus has an alternative but relevant reading of Crosby's role; she links Crosby's cleaning to a larger movement in the novel between "dirt and cleanliness": this dialectic, she writes, "mimics both the artist making order out of chaos and the fundamental rhythm of women's lives," creating a "metaphor of the artist as charwoman to the world" (56).

Reading Kitsch

Objects in *The Years* are insistently embedded in the texture of everyday life; they also recur, providing reassurance through their familiarity and endurance over time. According to Sam Binkley, these are two defining qualities of kitsch, which he reads as unproblematically reassuring, celebrating "repetition and conventionality as a value in itself" (133). But as described by Woolf in *The Years*, they also have a third quality, that "saturation of materiality" mentioned by Stewart, that invites us to read them dialectically—critically as well as sympathetically, for their contradictions as well as for their sentimental value. The tea cups with roses, for example, connect the various people who use them, but they are also meaningless matter, undercutting their comfortable familiarity and even subverting Eleanor's reading of the spiritual Renan: "What was it made of?" Eleanor asks of a cup. "Atoms? And what were atoms, and how did they stick together? The smooth hard surface of the china with its red flowers seemed to her for a second a marvellous mystery" (155).

To the extent that kitsch objects are incongruously conceived—the walrus pen-wipe for example—or do not work, or decay, or get dirty, they draw attention to their existence as matter. They take on what Bill Brown calls "misuse value": displaced from their ordinary function, they become visible as material things in their own right, resistant to human needs, reminders of an indifferent, non-anthropomorphic world. Once visible as recalcitrant matter, the human labor objects require becomes visible as well. Thus in *The Years*, the Robsons' hen shed needs repairing, as do Mira's roof and Eleanor's flats; the tea kettle will not boil, forcing Eleanor to use her hairpin to fray the wick; Whiteley's sends the wrong sheets, forcing Milly to return them (13). The walrus has a decayed spot, the Digby Pargiters' mirror is spotted, the laundry needs washing, and the sunflower plaques designating Eleanor's building are cracked. Collectively, objects in *The Years* reassure, through their reappearance, but they also draw attention to their own inadequacy, to the mismatch between our needs and their reality, and to the economic relations underlying their existence and upkeep.

When kitsch is read carefully, this mismatch emerges forcefully, revealing complex and counterproductive power-relations involving women. Take, for example, the ducks Rose wants at Lamley's. As *The Years* opens, Mrs. Pargiter is dying while her daughter is venturing on a shopping trip, where she is traumatized by her encounter with a masturbating man. The incident suggests the contradictory position of late-nineteenth-century women, whose role as consumers collides with their already contradictory roles as domestic angels and objects of male desire. The male-like agency Rose embraces in leaving for the store late in the day in search of a grail-like duck offers her a kind of freedom, but it is a freedom already qualified by the store display that made her want the ducks in the first place and then qualified still more by the trauma she endures. And Mrs. Lamley's duck-like waddle as she ponders her "two-penny watches, cards of tools, toy boats and boxes of cheap stationery" (28) suggest her own reification by the selling process. As for the duck itself, so desperately desired that Rose is willing to sneak out of the house with all the care of a woman secretly meeting a lover, it is never mentioned again; solid yet fleeting, the duck is a "wish symbol" containing, besides itself, both "its origin and its decline" (Benjamin, *Arcades* 911).

Objects thus have the potential not only to radiate sentimental associations but also to expose the uneven power relationships they seem to disguise. This dialectical response to kitsch is offered most neatly by the contrasting characters of hopeful Eleanor and satirical Peggy. As they approach the theatre district in the book's "present day," they have a chance to notice the mass culture around them: "Advertisements popped in and out. Here was a bottle of beer: it poured: then stopped: then poured again" (336). Later, at Delia's party, sounding a lot like Adorno, Peggy will remember the "faces mobbed at the door of a picture palace; apathetic, passive faces; the faces of people drugged with cheap pleasures" (388). Then they pass a statue of Edith Cavell, and Peggy, perhaps conditioned by the ads she has just seen, comments, "Always reminds me of an advertisement of sanitary towels" (336). As a national monument appealing to conventional emotions like patriotism, maternity, and self-sacrifice, the statue is nothing if not kitsch.[19] But its very conventionality and materiality open it to multiple readings. Eleanor, ignoring the statue's patriotic iconography, focuses on its all but invisible inscription, "Patriotism is not enough," evoking her sense of underlying unity and hope. Peggy, in contrast, satirically emphasizes the familiarity of the image and its use by those invested in manipulating women's bodies—in times of war, asking women to supply soldiers and serve as symbols of British womanhood, and in peace, as consumers of products, whose desires for objects must somehow be fanned and facilitated. Cavell herself, figured in the statue as nurse, soldier (she was executed for her service to British soldiers during World War I), and advertisement (for war, country, and sanitary napkins) offers a kind of fulfillment

---

[19] A monument becomes kitsch, according to Gillo Dorfles, when it is an "empty incarnation of a non-authentic sentiment" (82).

of young Rose Pargiter's desires at the start of her book: to expand women's roles, to be a soldier, to buy a duck.[20] Eleanor and Peggy's dual reading allows us to tease out the economic and social forces encoded in the statue, with its suggestion that women's hopes for social change have been co-opted by jingoism and capitalism.

What matters finally about kitsch in *The Years* is not whether it is good or bad art, genuine or "sham," but how it is read. Kitsch domesticates experience, processes the new in terms of the old, turns feelings of loss into the familiar pleasures of nostalgia. But it never quite works. Crosby's décor, with its "Indian elephants, silver vases," and walrus, makes her new flat "quite like home" (218), i.e., not quite home. The objects encode their own failure, their very inadequacy drawing the reader beyond identification toward analysis and insight.

So, too, does the novel's ending, where kitsch seems to escape from the world of objects into the narrative itself. The novel's final lines depict a couple getting out of a taxi, Eleanor's response to them as she watches from a window ("There!"), her question as she turns back to the room ("And now?"), and a sunrise: "The sun had risen, and the sky above the houses wore an air of extraordinary beauty, simplicity and peace" (434-35). The two images, of taxi-couple and sunrise, are familiar: the taxi-couple from Woolf's own *A Room of One's Own*, where a similar couple symbolizes the androgynous mind of the artist; the sunrise an obvious cliché. We might wonder, along with Peggy, how to pinpoint Eleanor's sensibility: "'Sentimental' was it? Or, on the contrary, was it good to feel like that . . . natural . . . right?" (334). Finally, it seems to me, the novel's closing lines express a utopian desire all the more poignant for the inad-

---

[20] Jane Marcus also links the statue to Rose's expedition, calling the statue one of three key moments characterized by a "fusion of sexual and political meanings" (41).

equacy of its vehicle.[21] The sunrise echoes Eleanor's cracked sunflower plaque, emblem of her effort to improve workers' housing. Eleanor's "there" gestures toward a future she cannot know. And with her "and now?" it is as if Woolf has removed one wall from her terrarium; the past has been juxtaposed with a "present day" as yet unformed.

In *The Arcades Project* Benjamin writes, "The belief in progress—in an infinite perfectibility understood as an infinite ethical task—and the representation of eternal return are complementary. They are the indissoluble antinomies in the face of which the dialectical conception of historical time must be developed" (119). The conventional language of kitsch is a kind of eternal return often mindlessly conflated with a sense of progress. The sunrise is, in this sense, the ultimate kitsch image, hackneyed and repetitive, suggesting both eternal return— Annie's "The sun'll come out tomorrow"—and hope for the future—Scarlett O'Hara's "Tomorrow is another day." But Woolf allows us no such mindless conflation. In the skepticism hinted at by the narrator's deflating "wore an air of," in the inarticulate gesture of Eleanor's "there" and the uncertainty of her "and now?" the inadequacy of these images is revealed. By recycling a past charged with nostalgia and yearning, kitsch paradoxically offers the possibility of insight and movement toward an uncharted future.[22]

The Edith Cavell statue, Crosby's mantel with its walrus pen-wipe, the Robsons' sitting room, the paintings of Rose Pargiter and of Kitty, the novel's closing sunrise evoke sentimental responses—patriotism, loyalty, nostalgia, maternal love, hope—associated in one way or another with women's experiences and labor. As depicted in *The Years*, however, they do not lull the reader into the smug emotional solipsism generally associated with kitsch. Read care-

---

[21] In his fragmented notes, "Materials for the Exposé of 1935," Benjamin refers to a "dialectic of sentimentality" which he relates to kitsch (*Arcades* 909); the term aptly describes the tension between sentiment and skepticism that characterizes the final pages of *The Years*.

[22] A similar tension is detected by Jacobs in *Between the Acts*, which, she says, sets up "a dialectic between a model of history as eternal recurrence based on natural cycles— what might be called natural history—and of a mythos of eternal progress based on the unfolding of unique events—what we might call human history" (224). Critics of *The Years*, however, have tended to read its ending as either negative or positive. In contrast to my reading, for example, Victoria Middleton sees the ending of *The Years* as part of a series of repetitions that go nowhere. She points out the recurrence of words and actions, suggesting that characters gain no insight and the final sunrise should be taken literally and anticlimactically as a sign of entrapment in repeated patterns (169). Other critics read the sunrise more optimistically, linking it to Dante's vision of paradise as a glowing white rose (Leaska 210; Lipking 145).

fully, through the double vision of Eleanor and Peggy, these objects ask the reader to go beyond sentiment into analysis, to ask, "What insights can I gain by scrutinizing the way this object has triggered my emotional identification?" In its final pages, as *The Years* moves from all-night party into daylight, the reader, like a dreamer waking up, can feel for a moment both the pull of the phantasm and the skepticism of consciousness. "The side which things turn toward the dream is kitsch," Benjamin writes (*Selected* 3). Woolf's dream-infused objects, like Benjamin's Paris Arcades, draw us, through their very sentimentality, into a deeper understanding of the world she depicts.

I would like to thank Karen Whisler, Sue Abel, and Bev Cruse of Eastern Illinois University for their help in obtaining research materials, and the College of Arts and Humanities for funding travel connected to this project. I am grateful also to Tim Wallis for granting permission to reproduce his picture of the Edith Cavell statue at Trafalgar Square.

Works Cited

Armstrong, Nancy. "Modernism's Iconophobia and What It Did to Gender." *Modernism/Modernity* 5 (April 1998): 47-75

Barton, Ruth. "Kitsch as Authenticity: Irish Cinema and the Challenge to Romanticism." *Irish Studies Review* 9 (August 2001): 193-202.

Benjamin, Walter. *The Arcades Project*. Transl. Howard Eiland and Kevin McLauglin. Cambridge: Belknap P of Harvard UP, 1999.

———. *Selected Writings. Vol. 2 1927-1934*. Transl. Rodney Livingstone and Others. Cambridge: Belknap P of Harvard UP, 1999.

Benzel, Kathryn N. "Modern In(ter)vention: Reading the Visual." *Visual Resources.* 19.4 (Fall 2003): 321-338.

Binkley, Sam. "Kitsch as a Repetitive System: A Problem for Theory of Taste Hierarchy." *Journal of Material Culture* 5 (July 2000): 131-52.

Bott, Alan, ed. and Irene Clephane. *Our Mothers: A Cavalcade in Pictures, Quotation and Description of Late Victorian Women 1870-1900*. London: Victor Gollancz, 1932.

Bowlby, Rachel. *Feminist Destinations and Further Essays on Virginia Woolf.* Edinburgh: Edinburgh UP, 1997. Broughton, Panthea Reid. "The Blasphemy of Art: Fry's Aesthetics and Woolf's Non-'Literary' Stories." *The Multiple Muses of Virginia Woolf.* Ed. Diane F. Gillespie. Columbia: U of Missouri P, 1993. 36-57.

Broughton, Panthea Reid. "The Blasphemy of Art: Fry's Aesthetics and Woolf's Non- 'Literary' Stories." *The Multiple Muses of Virginia Woolf.* Ed. Diane F. Gillespie. Columbia: U of Missouri P, 1993. 36-57.

Brown, Bill. "The Secret Life of Things: Virginia Woolf and the Matter of Modernism." *Modernism/Modernity* 6 (April 1999): 1-28.

Calinescu, Matei. *Five Faces of Modernity.* Durham: Duke UP, 1987.

Dorfles, Gillo. *Kitsch: The World of Bad Taste.* NY: Universe Books, 1969.

Fry, Roger. *Art and Commerce.* London: Hogarth P, 1926.

———. *Cézanne: A Study of His Development.* 1927. Chicago: U of Chicago P, 1989.

———. *Vision and Design.* NY: Oxford UP, 1981.

———. *The Letters of Roger Fry.* Ed. Denys Sutton. NY: Random House, 1972.

Gillespie, Diane Filby. *The Sisters' Arts: The Writing and Painting of Virginia Woolf and Vanessa Bell.* NY: Syracuse UP, 1988.

Goldman, Jane. *The Feminist Aesthetics of Virginia Woolf.* Cambridge: Cambridge UP, 2001.

Greenberg, Clement. "Avant-garde and Kitsch." *Art and Culture: Critical Essays.* Boston: Beacon, 1965.

Hankins, Leslie Kathleen. "Virginia Woolf and Walter Benjamin Selling Out(Siders)." In Pamela L. Caughie, *Virginia Woolf in the Age of Mechanical Reproduction.* NY: Garland, 2000. 3-36.

Horkheimer, Max and Theodor W. Adorno. *Dialectic of Enlightenment.* Transl. John Cumming. Freiburg: Herder and Herder, 1972.

Jacobs, Karen. *The Eye's Mind: Literary Modernism and Visual Culture.* Ithaca: Cornell UP, 2001.

Kulka, Tomas. *Kitsch and Art.* University Park: Pennsylvania State UP, 1996.

Leaska, Mitchell. "Virginia Woolf, the Pargiter: A Reading of *The Years.*" *Bulletin of the NY Public Library* 80 (Winter 1977): 172-210.

Lee, Hermione. *Virginia Woolf.* NY: Knopf, 1998.

Lipking, Joanna. "Looking at the Monuments: Woolf's Satiric Eye." *Bulletin of the NY Public Library* 80 (Winter 1977): 141-45.

Marcus, Jane, ed. *Virginia Woolf and the Languages of Patriarchy.* Bloomington: Indiana UP, 1987.

Middleton, Victoria. "*The Years*: 'A Deliberate Failure.'" *Bulletin of the NY Public Library* 80 (Winter 1977): 158-71.

Olalquiaga, Celeste. *The Artificial Kingdom: A Treasure of the Kitsch Experience.* NY: Pantheon, 1998.

Radin, Grace. *Virginia Woolf's "The Years": The Evolution of a Novel.* Knoxville: U of Tennessee P, 1981.

Reed, Christopher. "Through Formalism: Feminism and Virginia Woolf's
    Relation to Bloomsbury Aesthetics." *The Multiple Muses of Virginia
    Woolf.* Ed. Diane F. Gillespie. Columbia: U of Missouri P, 1993. 11-35.
Reid, Panthea. *Art and Affection: A Life of Virginia Woolf.* NY: Oxford UP,
    1996.
Snaith, Anna. *Virginia Woolf: Public and Private Negotiations.* NY: Palgrave,
    2003.
Spalding, Frances. *Roger Fry: Art and Life.* Berkeley: U of California P, 1980.
———. "When are words not enough? Roger Fry and Virginia Woolf." Woolf in
    the Real World: Thirteenth Annual Conference on Virginia Woolf.
    Northampton, MA, June 2003.
Squier, Susan. *Virginia Woolf and London: The Sexual Politics of the City.*
    Chapel Hill: U of North Carolina P, 1985.
Sternberg, Jacques. *Kitsch.* Ed. Marina Henderson. NY: St. Martin's P, 1972.
Stewart, Susan. *On Longing: Narratives of the Miniature, the Gigantic, the
    Souvenir, the Collection.* Durham: Duke UP, 1993.
Whitworth, Michael. "Porous Objects: Self, Community, and the Nature of
    Matter." In Jessica Berman and Jane Goldman, eds. *Virginia Woolf Out
    of Bounds: Selected Papers from the Tenth Annual Conference on
    Virginia Woolf.* NY: Pace UP, 2001: 151-56.
Woolf, Virginia. *Collected Essays.* 4 Vols. Ed. Leonard Woolf. NY: Harcourt,
    Brace and World, 1967.
———. *The Diary of Virginia Woolf.* 5 Vols. Ed. Anne Olivier Bell and Andrew
    McNeillie. NY: Harcourt Brace Jovanovich, 1977-1984.
———. *The Letters of Virginia Woolf.* 6 vols. Ed. Nigel Nicolson and Joanne
    Trautmann. NY: Harcourt Brace Jovanovich, 1975-80.
———. *Moments of Being.* NY: Harcourt Brace Jovanovich, 1976.
———. *The Pargiters: The Novel-Essay Portion of* "The Years." Ed. Mitchell
    A. Leaska. NY: Harcourt/Harvest, 1977.
———. *Roger Fry: A Biography.* 1940. NY: Harcourt Brace Jovanovich,
    1976.
———. *A Room of One's Own.* 1929. NY: Harcourt, Brace and World, 1957.
———. *Three Guineas.* 1938. NY: Harcourt Brace Jovanovich, 1966.
———. The Years. 1937. NY: Harcourt, Brace and World, 1965.

"Mixed Virginia": Reconciling the "Stigma of Nationality" and the Sting of Nostalgia in Virginia Woolf's Later Fiction

Helen Southworth

> *"For,"* the outsider will say, *"in fact, as a woman, I have no country. As a woman I want no country. As a woman my country is the whole world."* And if, when reason has said its say, still some obstinate emotion remains, some love of England dropped into a child's ears by the cawing of rooks in an elm tree, by the splash of waves on a beach, or by English voices murmuring nursery rhymes, this drop of pure, if irrational, emotion she will make serve her to give to England first what she desires of peace and freedom for the whole world.
> Virginia Woolf, *Three Guineas*

An analysis of foreignness in the work of Virginia Woolf is complicated by the ambivalent feelings about home that one finds there. As my epigraph suggests, Woolf was torn between a desire to escape the restrictions of home, which she saw become increasingly repressive in the years spanning the two world wars, and a deep-seated, visceral attachment to it. While she celebrates the denial to women in *Three Guineas* of what she provocatively terms "the full stigma of nationality," the sting of nostalgia haunts her resolve (82).[1] Soft pastoral images of England flutter about the hard edges of her fierce, condemnatory statements about the barbarism of war and the repression of women at home, in so doing forming a "knot in the smooth skein of her argument" (*O* 155).[2]

Further complicating Woolf's ambivalence about England were contradictory ideas about the alternatives, ideas which manifest themselves in the mixed treatment of foreignness in her work. Thus, one finds twisted together in Woolf's

---

[1] "The law of England sees to it that we do not inherit great possessions; the law of England denies us, and let us hope will continue to deny us, the full stigma of nationality" (*TG* 82).

[2] Gillian Beer notes this contradiction in slightly different terms: "Virginia Woolf was chary of the 'we' of patriotism, and of the self-gratifying claims of male writers to speak in universals which cover (in many senses) the experience also of women. Her reaction in writing to social communities was sceptical and wary; she needed to find ways of maintaining difference as well as constellation, lest clusters become ordered as hierarchies. Yet her writing emphasises communality and the body" (*Virginia Woolf: The Common Ground* 50). In her recent book, *Step-daughters of England*, Jane Garrity raises a similar

work remnants of a stereotypical nineteenth century romanticization of a certain foreignness in figures like *Mrs. Dalloway*'s young Sally Seton and *The Years*' Eugénie Pargiter, and an early twentieth century hostility, directed by what Linden Peach calls "a postwar 'conservative nationalism'" (116), to an alien presence in England informing figures such as *Mrs. Dalloway*'s Doris Kilman, Elizabeth Dalloway's governess of German descent, and Rezia Warren Smith, Italian wife of Septimus, of the same novel. One notes in Woolf's work the nostalgia for the colonies of the repatriated colonial patriarchs Old Parry of *Mrs. Dalloway*, Abel Pargiter of *The Years* and Bart Oliver of *Between the Acts*, in their responses to characters such as *Mrs. Dalloway*'s Sally, *The Years*' Eugénie and *Between the Acts*' Mrs. Manresa.[3] And alongside it, one sees colonialism's negative legacy among women at home in their conception of the New World embodied by the same putatively Tasmanian born Mrs. Manresa and her nouveau riche Jewish husband Ralph, *Mrs. Dalloway*'s Peter Walsh's Anglo-Indian bride ("silly, pretty, flimsy nincompoops," for Clarissa [8]) and *The Years*' American Mrs. Fripp. Up against these imperialistic views of the colonies, one finds also the intrigue and fascination for these same places—now places where one might escape the strictures of England, rather than reproduce them—among the younger generations. This is represented by a defrocked Ambassador Extraordinary Orlando who finds, at least initially, respite from the restrictions of home among the Turkish gypsies, and by many of *The Years*' women, among them, the young Kitty Malone, who longs to visit America, and Eleanor Pargiter, who rejects the insularity of England and Englishness in favor of Italy and India.[4]

---

question: "Seeking continually both to disavow and to reify their Englishness, these women [Virginia Woolf, Mary Butts, Sylvia Warner, and Dorothy Richardson] adopt a series of complex, ambivalent, and experimental literary strategies of identification and disidentification in locating themselves as national subjects" (2-3). Woolf would have also found her anxieties echoed in the work of writers such as archaeologist Jane Harrison, a figure influential for Woolf, who, in the closing essay of her *Alpha and Omega*, addressing the contradictions of the university's involvement in the war, condemns patriotism.

[3] Mrs. Manresa "restores [Bart] to his spice island" (*BTA* 41). In *The Years*, in a related example, Old Chuffy, the great Dr. Andrews, is charmed by the American Mrs. Fripp: "she was small and vivacious and Chuffy liked ladies to be small and vivacious" (57).

[4] While Kathy Phillips argues that the Pargiters' relationship with the colonies is purely a negative one, I perceive a more positive note to the approach of characters such as Eleanor to the foreign. "[*The Years*] counterpoints emptiness in England against constant references to the British Empire. Many of the Pargiters have been to the colonies, spreading their civilization. Yet the family's hypocrisy, loneliness and dullness, typical of a

This paper sets out to better understand this tangle of ideas centered around the concepts of nostalgia and nationality via a closer look at representations of foreignness in Woolf's later works. How does the contradiction between love and hate for England, a love of country and a love of universal freedoms, "a troubled half-love for England," as Jed Esty has recently termed it (93), inform and complicate the representation of foreign characters and foreign landscapes in Woolf's later fiction? What might an analysis of the relationship between Englishness and foreignness, home and away, tell us about Woolf's evolving ideas concerning nationality and nostalgia and the strains to which these concepts were subject as a second world war loomed? How does an engagement with the foreign enable Woolf to reconcile the contradictions of what Tuzyline Jita Allan calls her "double status as woman and English" (119) and as "both a product of and rebel against her culture" (125)? And lastly, in what sense does an engagement with the foreign provide Woolf with a means to counter a wartime jingoism, which relied on a coherent image of nation, and with a way to balance a remembered, intact "English" past with a fractured (foreign) present?

In *The Future of Nostalgia*, Svetlana Boym underscores nostalgia's impossibility. She describes nostalgia "(from [the Greek] *nostos*—return home, and *algia*—longing)" as "a rebellion against the modern idea of time, the time of history and progress" (xiii, xv). "The nostalgic," she argues, "desires to obliterate history and turn it into private or collective mythology, *to revisit time like space*, refusing to surrender to the irreversibility of time that plagues the human condition" (my emphasis; xv). In this sense, as Linda Hutcheon has suggested, "nostalgia is fundamentally conservative in its praxis, for it wants to keep things as they were—or, more accurately, as they are imagined to have been" (199). Indeed, the line dividing nostalgia from chauvinism, especially when national borders are threatened, is a fine one, a fact of which Woolf is acutely aware in *Three Guineas*.

Woolf's redirection of the nostalgic impulse in *Three Guineas* toward the future, her attempt to recuperate nostalgia from a chauvinism which she associates with patriotism, however, would seem to run counter to Boym's definition.[5]

---

whole society, represent nothing worth exporting. Repressed sexuality and emotion become distorted into money lust and militarism, turning the eminently 'nice' Pargiters into the perpetrators of an unjust Empire" ("Woolf's Criticism" 30).

[5] "'Englishmen are proud of England. For those who have been trained in English schools and universities, and who have done the work of their lives in England, there are few loves stronger than the love we have for our country […]' But the educated man's sister—what does 'patriotism' mean to her? Has she the same reasons for being proud of England, for loving England, for defending England? Has she been 'greatly blessed' in

While she recognizes the irrationality of a woman's love of a country in which she is relegated to the status of second class citizen, she acknowledges nostalgia's potential as a weapon: "this drop of pure, if irrational, emotion she will make serve her to give to England first what she desires of peace and freedom for the whole world" (109). For Woolf, nostalgia *can* push on the parameters of time and space and take on a utopian quality. It can produce "*a new space of time*" (my emphasis; *TY* 297)—love of country will serve England and the rest of the world in the future.[6] The fact that an advocating for a new kind of nostalgia follows on a call for the destruction of national boundaries and that it opens up to "the whole world," and the fact that Woolf considers women's disenfranchisement in terms of citizenship or lack thereof in *Three Guineas*, suggests the implication of the foreign in its process.[7] How does Woolf use the foreign to change the stakes and the terms of nostalgia in her work?

Many critics, among them Herbert Marder and most recently Jeanette McVicker, argue that Woolf's life experiences during the 1930s, including her greater engagement with social issues, her writing of *Three Guineas*, *The Pargiters*, which would become *The Years*, and her "Six Essays on London Life," on which McVicker focuses her analysis, mark a major shift in her work. McVicker suggests that Woolf "turns the imperial metaphorics of center/periphery on its head in [the] series of texts [she writes between 1928 and 1931, *Orlando*, *A Room of One's Own* and *The Waves*,] demonstrating with mocking irony that the imperial center is filled with garbage, tombs and carrion" (159). Marder, whose biography *The Measure of Life* covers Woolf's later years, "the enlightened Virginia of the 1930s" (10), argues that "under [the] stress" (9) associated with the interwar period in Britain and the personal ghosts with which she wrestled at this same time, Woolf began to "[create] chronicles *without nostalgia*—juxtaposing Victorian and modern times, observing that the domestic tyranny of the former led to the political fanaticism of the latter" (my emphasis; 6). My analysis tests the neatness of this hypothesis about the evolution of

---

England? History and biography when questioned would seem to show that her position in the home of freedom has been different from her brother's; and psychology would seem to hint that history is not without its effects upon mind and body. Therefore her interpretation of the word 'patriotism' may well differ from his" (*TG* 9).

[6] Not, however, the utopian quality confined to the past or to a "sideways" movement that Boym acknowledges as a frequent characteristic of nostalgia (Boym xiv).

[7] As Allan has argued, highlighting Woolf's relevance to postcolonial theory, "[t]his eruption of what might be called 'bound-less desire' [on the part of the "incontrovertibly English" Woolf] is clearly a postcolonial act that bears prophetic witness to the imminent demise of Empire and prefigures the transnationalism of postimperial society" (118).

Woolf's thinking. Do Woolf's ideas about nostalgia and nationality, Englishness and foreignness develop from novel to novel or are they rather dictated by the particular circumstances in which she is writing?

To that end, it is worth noting, even if only briefly here, the degree to which the terms invoked in this paper, such as race, nation, nationalism, nationality, foreignness and citizenship, were at issue in Woolf's life time. These were urgent questions for England as it faced what Leonard Woolf defined as "two vast, oecumenical problems [...] first, the prevention of [a second world] war and the development of international government; [and] secondly, the dissolution of the empires of European states in Asia and Africa" (*Downhill All the Way* 195-6). Questions of nationalism and citizenship in the context of imperialism were being debated by thinkers such as Trinidadian Trotskyite C.L.R. James[8] and J.A. Hobson,[9] both Hogarth Press authors, by Leonard Woolf's fellow Fabian Clement Attlee, a figure instrumental in defining England's relationship with India, first as a member of the Indian Statutory Commission in 1927, then as British Prime Minister (1945-1951),[10] by Italian socialist Antonio Gramsci (although his *Prison Writings* did not appear until after World War Two and therefore after Woolf's death in 1941), and indeed by Leonard Woolf himself, who wrote extensively on empire, his *Imperialism and Civilization* appearing alongside Woolf's *Orlando* in 1928.[11] At the time Woolf was writing, race and

---

[8] In his *The Case for West-Indian Self Government*, published as part of the Day to Day Pamphlet series by the Hogarth Press in 1933, James addresses among other things the dynamics of British patriotism: "What at home is the greatest virtue becomes in the colonies the greatest crime" (12). See also James' *World Revolution 1917-1936*. The Woolfs' Hogarth Press published a series of essays treating contemporary political and social problems between 1924-1926 and then in 1930, in the Day to Day Pamphlets series, published alongside James' work Mussolini's *The Political and Social Doctrine of Fascism*, John Maynard Keynes' *The Economic Consequences of Mr. Churchill* and Maurice Dobb's *Russia Today and Tomorrow* (Leonard Woolf 161-2).

[9] Hobson's titles include: *Imperialism* (1902), and *The Psychology of Jingoism* (1901). The Hogarth Press published his essay *Notes on Law and Order* in 1926 and his *From Capitalism to Socialism* as part of the Day to Day Pamphlets series in 1932

[10] See Attlee's autobiography, *As It Happened* (1954).

[11] See Jane Marcus' chapter entitled "A Very Fine Negress" in her *Hearts of Darkness: White Women Write Race* for a discussion of Leonard Woolf's work on imperialism and Woolf's involvement with it. Beginning with Woolf's comment in *A Room of One's Own* ("It is one of the great advantages of being a woman that one can pass even a very fine negress without wishing to make an Englishwoman of her") Marcus conceives of the black woman's relationship with Woolf in similar terms to those employed here in terms of the foreign woman. "[S]he is [...] the embodiment of Woolf's own anxiety about the limits of her double narrative of female emancipation and the history of women artists in England" (24).

heredity were central concerns for her many friends and associates who advocated eugenics—a movement which became a source of embarrassment for many of its surprisingly liberal supporters when in the 1930s and 1940s it became the justification for Nazi extermination of Jews and homosexuals.[12] The eugenicists' ideas were informed by the work of figures such as Francis Galton, who coined the term in the 1880s, Charles Darwin and the sexologist Havelock Ellis.[13] Legislation and popular political movements also complicate Woolf's consideration of questions of national identity and race: instances include the jingoism stirred up by the Aliens Act of 1905 and the Defense of the Realm Acts or DORA of 1914 and 1915 and the xenophobia promoted in the 1930s by former Labour Party politician Oswald Mosley and his British Union of Fascists.[14]

Adding yet another layer to the complexity of Woolf's understanding of these difficult concepts was a growing sense of her own foreignness—the "mixed"-ness (both national and sexual) to which she herself refers in the phrase of my title[15]—combined with and encouraged by her personal experiences with the foreignness of family and friends. Among her many foreign friends Woolf counted fellow writers such as Russian S.S. Koteliansky (Kot) who was Jewish,[16] New Zealander Katherine Mansfield, and Americans Tom and

---

[12] Hitler's Nazism was informed by the ideas of Joseph Arthur Comte de Gobineau's *The Inequality of Human Races* (1853-1855). See Donald Childs' *Modernism and Eugenics*.

[13] For a discussion of the degree to which eugenics was an issue for Woolf, see David Bradshaw's response to Childs' work on Woolf, T.S. Eliot and W.B.Yeats ("Eugenics: 'They should certainly be killed'" 49-53). In his first chapter on Woolf, Childs lists her eugenics associates: Sidney and Beatrice Webb, and closer to home John Maynard Keynes, Ottoline Morrell and Goldsworthy Lowes Dickinson. See also Doyle on Woolf and eugenics.

[14] See Marwick's *The Deluge* (36).

[15] Woolf wrote to her friend composer, writer and suffragist, Ethel Smyth: "I must cook dinner—macaroni cheese with a bacon fry. But, perversely I long for the Ivy [restaurant] and champagne. Too many souls and bodies to be satisfied: the Puritan and the Harlot. Mixed marriages result in this mixed Virginia" (*L6* 309). In another letter to Smyth, Woolf boasts of her descent from a suitor of Marie Antoinette: "If you want to know where I get my (ahem!) charm, read Herbert Fisher's autobiography. Marie Antoinette loved my ancestor: hence he was exiled; hence the Pattles, the barrel that burst, and finally Virginia" (*L6* 461). Hermione Lee explains the link: "James Pattle of Calcutta made a romantic marriage to a French aristocrat, Adeline de l'Etang, the daughter of the Chevalier de l'Etang, who had been a page—possibly a lover—to Marie-Antoinette and an officer of the Garde du Corps of Louis XVI, and had married the Indian-born Thérèse Blin de Grincourt (not, as the family legend had it, one of the Queen's maids of honour)" (88).

[16] For details on Kot's relationship with the Woolfs, see J.H. Willis, *Leonard and Virginia Woolf as Publishers: The Hogarth Press, 1917-41* (80-101).

Vivienne Eliot, D.H. Lawrence's German wife Frieda, John Maynard Keynes' Russian ballet dancer wife Lydia Lopokova, and perhaps closest to home her husband Leonard Woolf and his family, who were also Jewish. Many of these figures and many of the ideas espoused by the philosophical thinkers and political figures listed above are revealed by Woolf and cited by scholars as possible sources for her foreign characters.

Woolf's foreigners are mainly secondary characters. While they have individually received critical attention, they are rarely considered in relation to each other as foreigners.[17] Due to the contradictory nature of their foreignness—among the most "out of place," and perhaps intentionally so, are Elizabeth Dalloway's oriental mystery and Lily Briscoe's Chinese eyes[18]—this is a feature that is often ignored in favor of other aspects which set these characters (interestingly they are mainly women[19]) apart and tie them together, such as their sexual orientation or their class.[20] Thus, in her analysis of the racialization of the mother figure in Woolf's work, Laura Doyle sets aside questions of nationality, in the sense in which I understand it here, when she asserts that "no obviously mixed-race characters appear in [Woolf's] novels; in fact, very few non-Anglo-Saxons can be found in her work" (139), and Terry Eagleton overlooks Woolf's

---

[17] See, for example, Karen Levenback, Elizabeth Primamore and Reginald Abbott on Miss Kilman, Roberta Rubenstein on Sasha, Diane Gillespie and Jane Marcus on Miss La Trobe, Hermione Lee on Renny, and Elizabeth Abel on Rezia.

[18] Two very different interpretations of what Lily's Chinese eyes and Elizabeth's oriental mystery represent are offered by Patricia Laurence and Donald Childs. Laurence suggests that, via Lily, Woolf "presents [...] an artist enriched by the 'foreign,' or, more specifically, Chinese discernment. Lily's 'Chinese eyes' suggest not the Empire's forging glance toward the distant lands of China and India for trade and gain, but the new aesthetic voyaging in the East during the modernist period. A new space unfolds before Lily, the English artist with postmodern yearnings for 'a hundred pairs of eyes to see with'" (9-10). Childs suggests that "[a]gainst the background of [*Mrs. Dalloway*'s] question about the biological origins of such features [as Elizabeth's], and against the background of Woolf's longstanding personal concern about the heritability of mental instability, [...] this passage can be seen as a freighted allusion to mongolism—a mysterious condition (today known as Down's Syndrome) that Woolf indirectly invokes as a figure for the eugenical anxieties about her own fertility" (50).

[19] In her thesis entitled *Channel Crossings* on the critical reception of Virginia Woolf's work in France, Barbara Kneubuhl suggests that Woolf saw the foreign in three forms, via her mother (distant heredity), via her sister (who lived abroad), and via Vita (who spoke fluent French, lived in France as a child and had a Spanish grandmother named Pepita). Kneubuhl's observations suggest that the foreign was in many ways feminine for Woolf.

[20] In terms of class, see, for example, Alex Zwerdling's "*Mrs. Dalloway* and the Social System," in *Virginia Woolf and the Real World.*

foreign characters in his reading of *Mrs. Dalloway* in his book about literal and social expatriates, *Exiles and Émigrés: Studies in Modern Literature*.[21] While Rachel Bowlby acknowledges the presence of foreign women in Woolf's *Mrs. Dalloway*, she includes them under the broader category of exiles to whom she concedes, citing the most exiled of the exiled, the female vagrant in *Mrs. Dalloway*, the privilege of "'speculat[ing] boldly'" (95). In the same way, Leena Kore Schröder buries a suggestion that foreignness, and specifically a female strain thereof, in *Mrs. Dalloway* represents a "resistance to British imperialism," one more covert than that of the shell shocked Septimus Smith, in an essay also focused on the female vagrant in Woolf's work (339).

Similarly, Woolf's use of foreign landscapes, and foreignness in her work, while studied quite extensively by critics is rarely analyzed in a general sense.[22] Here I will develop questions raised by Peach who, noting commonalities in the treatment of foreignness across Woolf's works, suggests that "Woolf uses foreignness, the perception of foreigners, or those who have been out of the country for some time, to challenge the myths of homogeneity and of origins which underpinned post-war notions of Englishness" (102). I will expand the comments of Sonita Sarker, who notes the pervasiveness in Woolf's work of what she calls a "multifaceted Englishness":[23]

---

[21] In his *Exiles and Émigrés*, Eagleton opens his chapter on "Evelyn Waugh and The Upper-Class Novel" with a critique of Woolf's *Mrs. Dalloway*. He begins first with Peter Walsh—labeling him an outsider, "a rootless expatriate in a wilderness of London drawing-rooms" (34)—identifying him as "the means—the only means, indeed, in the novel—whereby a trenchant social criticism can be effectively focused on the shimmering futility of the upper-class world of which Clarissa [Dalloway] is symbol" (33).
Eagleton argues that the novel as a whole does to some degree endorse this criticism (33): Clarissa for all her engagement in the upper-class world, concedes Eagleton, does recognize its emptiness. However, Walsh's critique is ultimately hampered, Eagleton contends, by the manner in which he is handled in the novel: he is portrayed as "a 'bookish' ex-socialist, and so is easily categorisable as the kind of intellectual for whom it is wise, in an honoured upper-class tradition, to reserve a slight, pitying contempt" (35). Eagleton does mention Sally Seton. However, he omits references to the young Sally, descended from Marie Antoinette, who reads William Morris and rides her bicycle around the parapet at Bourton, and instead analyzes her in her capacity as provincial matriarch. In his reading of *Mrs. Dalloway*, Eagleton makes no mention of Miss Kilman, Elizabeth Dalloway, or Rezia Warren Smith, all of whom, like Peter, are foreigners in one capacity or another. Septimus is similarly absent from Eagleton's discussion.

[22] See Rowena Fowler on Greece, Natalya Reinhold and Rubenstein on Russia, for example.

[23] Sarker's essay focuses on Woolf's "The London Scene" articles, a series originally written for *Good Housekeeping* magazine.

> [T]he entirety of Woolf's oeuvre projects a multifaceted Englishness. Her early reviews of travel writing in *Nation and Athenaeum* and the *Times Literary Supplement* emphasize the difference between insiders' and outsiders' views of English culture; her first published novel, *The Voyage Out* (1915) studies English people abroad; *Orlando* (1928) follows an English (wo)man on travels through exotic lands; *The Waves* (1931) analyzes legacies of empire-building; and *Three Guineas* registers Woolf's fierce protest against jingoistic Englishness which becomes louder in her last novel, *Between the Acts* (1941) (5).

Susan Stanford Friedman's work on Woolf's exploitation of what she calls "the geopolitical," developed very recently by McVicker, the former in a reading of Woolf's *To the Lighthouse*, the latter, like Sarker, of her London essays, also informs my analysis. Advocating that the feminist reader think spatially and geographically, as well as temporally and historically (130), Friedman asserts that "[t]he geopolitical Woolf goes beyond the psychopolitics of intimacy to show how the local is never purely local, but always belongs to 'a regional/national/global nexus,' to echo James Clifford" (125). Highlighting the degree to which gender inflects questions of nationality and vice versa, Friedman argues that Woolf's life and work provides material for "a case study for internationalizing feminism 'at home,' for developing strategies to interpret the geopolitical axis of difference that threads itself throughout her work, always mediated by other axes of difference like gender, sexuality and class" (115). Reflecting this inevitable "imbrication," to borrow Friedman's term, gender, although not the primary focus of this essay, is at issue throughout.

While, as Sarker's comments suggest, the question of foreignness is dealt with in Woolf's earlier as well as in her later writing, I have chosen here to focus on a selection of the novels she produced in the interwar years, a period when, as Alison Light has eloquently suggested, "the dialectic between old and new, between past and present, between holding on and letting go, between conserving and moving on" was complicated by the sense of dislocation resulting from World War One (19). I begin with *Mrs. Dalloway*, where the juxtaposition of Bourton and London provides a neat backdrop for an exploration of the tension between two Englands, an old insular one, nostalgically reconstructed by Clarissa, and a new racially and socially hybrid one, continually intruding on this outdated fantasy. Next I consider Woolf's more humorous approach to the same set of questions in *Orlando*. And finally, in *The Years* and *Between the Acts*, Woolf's last novels, which in some senses might be read as a division in two and expansion of *Mrs. Dalloway* (and there are interesting resonances involving former titles, *The Hours*, the former *Mrs. Dalloway* title, becomes *The Years*, Bourton becomes *Pointz Hall*, the original title of *Between the Acts*) I explore how Woolf first puts the fiction of nostalgia to bed in the capital and then resurrects it in a new form in the heart of the English countryside. While *To the Lighthouse* is a natural choice for an exploration of questions of nostalgia, its focus on the maternal figure as object of nostalgia puts it outside the purview of this essay.[24]

Ponies, Cricket Bats . . . Lawns and Pitches: *Mrs. Dalloway*

The lines which emanate from a central Clarissa Dalloway in *Mrs. Dalloway*, the chimes of Big Ben, the glinting facets of a diamond, might be understood as lines of longitude and latitude on a map of the world. Set as a counterpoint to Clarissa's ordered world—a London which consists of Westminster, Big Ben, Victoria Street, "ponies [...] cricket bats: Lords, Ascot, Ranelagh" (5), "lawns and pitches," "laughing girls in their transparent muslins" (5), the Fleet, the Admiralty (7), old Uncle William (11) and Buckingham Palace—and buried at its center Bourton, the pastoral paradise of Clarissa's youth, is a society in flux (racially, socially and culturally). This is a new chaotic world peopled by the exiled Italian Rezia and the rejected Briton of mixed descent Miss Kilman. It is the world of Britain's colonial legacy embodied by the returning disenchanted misfit Peter Walsh, whose India contrasts sharply with that of Clarissa's father Old Parry, and the shell shocked Septimus Smith. It is a world which looks outwards and forwards, not, as does Clarissa, nostalgically backwards.[25]

That this heterogeneity represents a change that Clarissa resists is suggested by her reluctance to come to terms with the foreign in the novel. Clarissa, whose geographical knowledge is scant ("ask her what the Equator was, and she did not know" [*MD* 122]), appears to deliberately resist the foreign. She blankets or freezes out difference, as in her oft cited confusion of Richard Dalloway's Armenians and Albanians, for whom, she candidly admits, she "[feels] nothing"

---

[24] See Rubenstein's chapter on Woolf and Doris Lessing in *Home Matters: Longing and Belonging, Nostalgia and Mourning in Women's Fiction* (13-33). See also Friedman's analysis of *To the Lighthouse* in *Mappings* (114-31) and Doyle's analysis of *The Voyage Out/Melymbrosia* and *To the Lighthouse* in *Bordering on the Body* (139-73).

[25] Peter too suffers from nostalgia in a manner he himself cannot explain (but it's lightly mocked, and perhaps somewhat sympathized with, by Woolf): "Coming as he did from a respectable Anglo-Indian family which for at least three generations had administered the affairs of a continent (it's strange, he thought, what a sentiment I have about that, disliking India, and empire, and army as he did), there were moments when civilization, even of this sort, seemed dear to him as a personal possession; moments of pride in England; in butlers; chow dogs; girls in their security" (*MD* 55).

(120). Clarissa's somewhat incongruous romantic admiration for and desire to emulate the stereotypically foreign-identified Lady Bexborough, who is "dark [...] with a skin of crumpled leather and beautiful eyes" (10), and "who opened a bazaar, they said, with the telegram in her hand, John, her favourite, killed" (5), highlights her focus on home and her refusal to acknowledge the harsh realities of the recent war and its ramifications for English society. Lady Bexborough's foreignness is neatly contained, like an unusual gem stone, in a conservative English setting: she is "slow and stately; rather large; interested in politics like a man; with a country house, very dignified, very sincere" (10).

However, the integrity of Clarissa's chauvinistic nostalgia is continually threatened in *Mrs. Dalloway*. Her romanticization of Bourton—whose foreigners are a singing German, Joseph Breitkopf,[26] and a rebellious Sally Seton, the exoticism of whom consists of an incongruous amalgam of Marie Antoinette, William Morris, Monte Carlo and an implicit bisexuality, and for whom a melodramatic Clarissa, herself appropriately named for Richardson's tragic heroine, foresees "some awful tragedy; her death; her martyrdom" (182)[27]—is undercut when contrasted with her dismay at the end of the novel at Sally's provincialism. Married to a midlands industrialist, "a bald man with a big buttonhole," the mother of five boys, Sally has lost much of her former charm for Clarissa (182). Similarly, Peter Walsh's unfortunate, to Clarissa's mind, choice of an Anglo-Indian bride highlights the flimsiness of Clarissa's nostalgia: this Peter is not Bourton's Peter. Underscoring the insularity of Clarissa's world, acts involving a redefinition of Britain's boundaries, both positive and negative, are represented as in some sense undertaken in defiance of Clarissa. She is not invited to the lunch at which (a militantly imperialistic[28]) Lady Bruton enlists Richard's and Hugh's help in her efforts to promote emigration; and the foreign-looking Elizabeth Dalloway's ("her eyes were fine, Chinese, oriental" [135]) thoughts are with Miss Kilman, not her mother, as she contemplates her future atop the bus on

---

[26] Breitkopf talks about Wagner with Peter Walsh, and sings Brahms without any voice (*MD* 35).

[27] It is thought that Woolf based Sally Seton on her cousin's wife Madge Vaughan. Vaughan spent time as a child in the Alps, hence the French connections ascribed to Sally.

[28] See Phillips on the implications of Lady Bruton's name (*Virginia Woolf Against Empire* 9). Although space precludes consideration of them here, Lady Bruton's and Milly Brush's ties to South Africa might be pursued in terms of Woolf's representation of the foreign and, in the case of Lady Bruton, its tie to questions of sexuality.

the Strand.[29] Clarissa's brand of nostalgia cannot survive the onslaught of change taking place in post World War One England.

The fact that Elizabeth looks to Miss Kilman, not Mrs. Dalloway, as she contemplates her future conforms with the oppositional role Miss Kilman plays in the novel with regard to Clarissa. Miss Kilman challenges Clarissa as she highlights difference, national, sexual and in terms of class. According to Clarissa: "she was never in the room five minutes without making you feel her superiority, your inferiority; how poor she was; how rich you were [...]" (12). Based, critics suggest, on the born again Christian, Jean Thomas,[30] the proprietor of the convalescent home Burley where Woolf stayed on four occasions, or on Louise Ernestine Matthaei, a fellow and Director of Studies at Newnham, (perhaps the source of Miss Kilman's foreignness), who was forced to resign her post during World War One because her father was German, both of whom are singled out by Woolf for their unflinching conviction, Miss Kilman is resolute where Clarissa waivers (Trombley 277; Levenback 80).[31] The fact that Miss

---

[29] "Was it that some Mongol had been wrecked on the coast of Norfolk (as Mrs. Hilbery said), had mixed with the Dalloway ladies, perhaps, a hundred years ago? For the Dalloways, in general, were fair-haired; blue eyed; Elizabeth, on the contrary was dark; had Chinese eyes in a pale face; an Oriental mystery; was gentle, considerate, still" (*MD* 122-3).

[30] According to Stephen Trombley, Thomas was a born again Christian, like Miss Kilman; also like Miss Kilman, her conversion appears to have taken place in a bovaresque fashion. Childs reminds us that Thomas was a Christian eugenicist. Peach reads the literal meaning in Miss Kilman's name—she becomes an idea for Peach as she is for Clarissa—suggesting that "Doris Kilman's name and her German origins—a reference to the German sex psychologists of the 1890s—suggest that she is not simply a character but an illustration of how hostile discourses about same-sex relationships can affect an individual's emotional and psychic development" (95). Kilman's name also resembles in its negative resonances that of Dr. Slaughter, a renowned eugenicist (see Bradshaw "Eugenics" 39-40). See also Eileen Barrett on *Mrs. Dalloway*, Miss Kilman and contemporary sexology.

[31] Karen Levenback (in *VWM* 37:4) suggests Louise Ernestine Matthaei as a possible model for Miss Kilman. Matthaei was forced to resign her post during World War I because her father was German, recalling Kilman's being let go by the school where she had secured a post because of her sympathies for the Germans. Just as Miss Kilman is hired by Richard Dalloway to instruct his daughter Elizabeth in history in *Mrs. Dalloway*, so Matthaei worked for Leonard Woolf as assistant editor on the *International Review* and the *Contemporary Review* (Hussey 155). Woolf describes Matthaei in her diary on April 9, 1918: "I remember her at Newnham. She has left, we understand, 'under a cloud.' It is easy to see from her limp, apologetic attitude that the cloud has sapped her powers of resistance. We skirted round the war, but she edged away from it, & it seemed altogether odious that anyone should be afraid to declare her opinions—as if a dog used to

Kilman has refused to deny the German heritage that hampers and hinders her, and that has cost her her livelihood ("It was true that the family was of German origin; spelt the name Kiehlman in the eighteenth century; but her brother had been killed. They turned her out because she would not pretend that the Germans were all villains—when she had German friends, when the only happy days of her life had been spent in Germany!" [*Mrs. Dalloway* 123-4]), highlights the shallowness of Clarissa's commitment to England, a commitment which by contrast costs her nothing ("this woman [Clarissa] did nothing, believed nothing," according to Miss Kilman [125]). Miss Kilman's relegation to the peripheries, the landings and doorways, of the Dalloway household and her exclusion from the central event of the novel, Clarissa's party, parallel in spatial terms the incompatibility of "the foreign" Miss Kilman and Clarissa's England, Clarissa's failure to find a place for Miss Kilman and all that she represents at home. Miss Kilman's assertive occupation of the peripheries, however, cements her definitive role in terms of Clarissa's understanding of self.

Also outside Clarissa's world is the Italian Rezia Warren Smith (one of Woolf's few fully foreign characters). Rezia is assimilated to some degree into *Mrs. Dalloway*'s London—as a result of her mixed marriage her Italian last name is swallowed up, to a point where she becomes the most English of Englishwomen, Mrs. Smith. However, she appears to deliberately resist conformity and homogeneity. Little is known about Rezia. "[Her] history, like her name," suggests Elizabeth Abel, "is abbreviated" (34). The youngest daughter of a Milanese innkeeper, Rezia's move to England in the company of (an already ailing) Septimus, whom she married when he was billeted with her family at the end of the war, is not elaborated upon in the novel ("so simple, so impulsive, only twenty-four, without friends in England, who had left Italy for his [Septimus's] sake" [16]). Like Miss Kilman, Rezia highlights the negative ramifications of the war on the home front.[32]

---

excessive beating, dreaded even the raising of a hand. She and L. discussed their business, which has to do with W[ar]. & P[eace]. & may result in an offer to her of a place on the staff. She has to earn her living. 'I must tell you one thing, she said, when the talk was over, my father was a German. I find it makes a good deal of difference—it is a distinct hindrance commercially.' L. agreed that it was. She is a lanky, gawky unattractive woman, about 35, with a complexion that blotches red & shiny suddenly; dressed in her best, which was inconceivably stiff & ugly. But she has a quick mind, & is an enthusiast; said she loved writing" (*D1* 135-6).

[32] See Levenback's discussion of Miss Kilman and Rezia in her *Virginia Woolf and the Great War* (44-82).

In her capacity as (literal, rather than social) exile, Rezia's vision of London, like Miss Kilman's conception of England, runs up against that of Clarissa: "She had given up her home. She had come to live here, in this awful city" (66). In the same way, Rezia's nostalgia for her home country and family challenges that of Clarissa.[33] This challenge is highlighted when the two characters come together figuratively in the novel as Rezia has a vision of bursting, Bourton Clarissa-like, through "long windows" after drinking a tonic meant to calm her after Septimus' suicide (perhaps Dr. Holmes' effort to promote love of home) (150). She imagines that "she was opening long windows, stepping out into some garden" (150), recalling Clarissa's recollection of "[bursting] open the French windows and [plunging] at Bourton into the open air" (3).

> [Rezia] put on her hat, and ran through a cornfield—where could it have been?—on to some hill, somewhere near the sea, for there were ships, gulls, butterflies, they sat on a cliff. In London too, there they sat, and, half dreaming, came to her through the bedroom door, rain falling, whisperings, stirrings among dry corn, the caress of the sea, as it seemed to her, hollowing them in its arched shell and murmuring to her laid on shore, strewn she felt, like flying flowers over some tomb. (150)

Rezia's dreams appear to range at this point in the work from Italy to England. Her nostalgia is dislocated: "where could it have been?" she asks herself. Her "in London too" suggests an erasure of boundaries (between city and country, England and Italy). This confusion highlights the complexity of nostalgia, of mixed marriage and (dual) nationality, and of exile and assimilation central to *Mrs. Dalloway*.[34] In a broad sense, Rezia's refusal of containment runs counter to the homogeneity of hegemonic nation-state discourses.

---

[33] Elizabeth Abel makes a similar argument, suggesting that Rezia, like Clarissa, is "plucked by marriage from an Edenic female world with which she preserves no contact" (qtd in Hussey 177).

[34] That these were issues that Woolf explored in terms of Rezia might be supported by the fact that she did so in terms of Rezia's avowed real life model, John Maynard Keynes' wife, Russian ballet dancer Lydia Lopokova. Woolf was explicit about her use of Lopokova as "a type" (distinct here from a model), for Rezia. Woolf frequently gossiped about this mixed union. Her comments about Lopokova are especially condescending—and focus in particular on Lopokova's abandonment of her own identity and her life prior to Maynard Keynes, as a dancer and as a Russian, and her embracing of her role as English wife and mother. Lopokova's broodiness exasperated Woolf. In her letter, Woolf mimics Lopokova's accent and mocks her efforts to assimilate, targeting her attempts to read Shakespeare and to speak like an English woman: "Lydia is now going on stage, as Rosalind or Ophelia: though she speaks English like a parrokeet" (*L5* 209).

Anticipating Woolf's focus in *Three Guineas*, both Miss Kilman and Rezia celebrate, and at once warn of, the implications of woman's statelessness, her lack of full citizenship, as they reveal their own. In this way, neither Miss Kilman nor Rezia conform to Clarissa's romantic, nostalgic conception of the foreign. Their foreignness, their discomfort in England, and their alternative (national) affiliations—and in the case of Miss Kilman at least, her alternative sexuality, reminding us how inextricably questions of sexuality and nationality are tangled together, a tie that is complicated further in *Orlando*—challenge Clarissa's attempts to preserve a safe old England. The choice of German and Italian specifically for her foreign characters' national affiliations in *Mrs. Dalloway*—the one nation an ongoing threat, the other a potential threat as she wrote—is complicated by the fact that Woolf chose to cast both as women.

Wild Panoramas: *Orlando*

In *Orlando*, Woolf takes a much more spacious and expansive (in terms of textual geography and also in terms of the fantastical quality of the work), and a more humorous look at the question of nostalgia and nationality. Concerns about empire appear to shape these questions in *Orlando*, as opposed to the more predominant anxieties about war in *Mrs. Dalloway*. More open to change than Clarissa, Orlando's vacillation between love of country and recognition of the limitations of that same country captures the ambivalence voiced more explicitly ten years later in Woolf's *Three Guineas*.[35] These questions and the shift in Woolf's understanding of them are informed at this point in large part by the dedicatee of the work, Woolf's model for Orlando, Vita Sackville-West, an avid traveler and a figure who did much to complicate Woolf's conceptions of foreignness and alternative sexualities.[36] Shot through Sackville-West's own life

---

[35] *Orlando* anticipates the sentiment of *Three Guineas* illustrated in the epigraph: "'What a phantasmagoria the mind is and meeting-place of dissemblables. At one moment we deplore our birth and state and aspire to an ascetic exultation; the next we are overcome by the smell of some old garden path and weep to hear the thrushes sing'" (*O* 176).

[36] Foreignness figures prominently in Sackville-West's writings, in works such as *Challenge* and *Heritage* and in her book based on her Spanish maternal grandmother, the dancer Pepita. It is also central to her relationships, particularly that which she shared with Violet Trefusis. As Woolf became closer to Vita Sackville-West, she began to toy more and more seriously with the idea of her own foreignness—an aspect of her personality, based on somewhat tenuous grounds (a French great-grandmother), that she associated with a certain romanticism. This was an identification that Sackville-West encouraged and appreciated in Woolf. As Bradshaw reminds us, quoting Suzanne Raitt, Sackville-West was an "unashamed eugenicist" ("Eugenics" 49).

and work is this same tension between nostalgia for England—a very specific traditional, hierarchical England and ironically one which prevented her from inheriting her family home, Knole, on the basis of her sex and one which Woolf, quite vindictively I would argue, mocks in *Orlando*, the novel written as Woolf's relationship with Sackville-West cooled[37]—and a draw to the foreign.[38]

The fluidity characteristic of Orlando's gender so central to the novel also characterizes somewhat his nationality and his capacity to cross national boundaries, to pass for a foreigner. As Lisa Carstens has noted, in *Orlando* "[s]exual multiplicity is then just one aspect of the multiply-rooted self" (43). When with the gypsies in Turkey, "[Orlando's] dark hair and dark complexion bore out the belief that she was, by birth, one of them and had been snatched by an English Duke from a nut tree when she was a baby and taken to that barbarous land where people live in houses because they are too feeble and diseased to stand the open air" (141-2). We find this same fluidity of nationality signaled by Woolf's choice to have Angelica Bell, her niece, pose for the photograph of the Russian

---

[37] *Orlando* forms part of a network of texts in its capacity as response to Sackville-West's *Challenge*, based on the author's relationship with Trefusis, and as anticipatory of Trefusis' own vengeful *Broderie Anglaise*. In this latter text the character based on Trefusis herself, Anne, and that based on Woolf, Alexa, ultimately become allies in their struggle against John, Sackville-West's character.

[38] Further inspiration for Woolf's treatment of nostalgia and the foreign in *Orlando* might be found in the first *Common Reader*, published the same year as *Mrs. Dalloway*, in which Woolf explored in depth the differences between Russian and English literature and, in terms again of Russian literature and ancient Greek literature (in "On Not Knowing Greek"), the difficulties of mutual comprehension among nationalities. In "Modern Fiction," Woolf lauds Russian fiction, characterizing (perhaps in anticipation of Orlando's failed bid for the hand of Sasha in *Orlando*—and several critics have tied the two together [Rubenstein 109]) the Russian mind as "inconclusive": "It is the sense that there is no answer," writes Woolf, "that if honestly examined life presents *question after question* which must be left to sound on and on after the story is over in hopeless interrogation that fills us with a deep, and finally it may be with a resentful, despair." The English mind, by contrast, Woolf argues, has been bred to "enjoy and fight rather than to suffer and understand." It is more bounded, grounded: "English fiction from Sterne to Meredith," Woolf goes on, "bears witness to our natural delight in humour and comedy, in the beauty of the earth, in the activities of the intellect, and in the splendour of the body" (*CR*1 158). In the same volume, in her essay entitled "The Russian Point of View," again anticipating themes raised in *Orlando*, Woolf highlights the divide between the native and the foreigner in terms of each one's ability to understand those among whom they dwell: "A special acuteness and detachment, a sharp angle of vision the foreigner will often achieve; but not that absence of self-consciousness, that ease and fellowship and sense of common values which make for intimacy, and sanity, and the quick give and take of familiar intercourse" (*CR1* 176).

Sasha which accompanies the novel.[39] Like Orlando, she is an Englishwoman masquerading as a foreign woman.

Based in part on Sackville-West's lover the English/Dutch Francophile Violet Trefusis adding multiple layers to Bell's masquerade, the Russian Princess Sasha ("the foreign Princess" [70]), who enters early into the text, is the first to complicate Orlando's bounded vision of the world.[40] Sasha's heritage, like that of *Mrs. Dalloway*'s Rezia, is vague, obscured in large part by her own reserve on the subject for "seldom would she talk about her past life" (53-4). Having outlined his own family history in hyperbolic terms, "[Orlando] would pause and ask [Sasha], Where was her own house? What was her father? Had she brothers? Why was she here alone with her uncle? Then, somehow, though she answered readily enough, an awkwardness would come between them" (48). From his own house Orlando surveys England, its landmarks the houses of his aunts and uncles. Sasha, whose physical and verbal mobility contrasts sharply with that of her English hosts—a point perhaps best illustrated when she rejects the court for the mob, reversing the terms for each as she goes (43, 55-6)—draws no such lines.[41] Recalling comments made in Woolf's *Common Reader* essay "The Russian Point of View," while home consists for Orlando of the calm and order suggested by "pleasant country ways of sport and tree planting" (50), marriage and elopement with Sasha promises a change of place and a change of pace: he will be forced to forfeit hunting rabbits for reindeer and drinking canary (wine) for vodka (50).

Just as the foreign woman upsets Orlando's neatly conceived ideas about home, so does the foreign landscape. In Constantinople, to where the jilted Orlando, newly appointed Ambassador Extraordinary, flees memories of Sasha, he finds a landscape as antithetical to home as the Russian had promised to be: "Nothing [...] could well be less like the counties of Surrey and Kent or the towns of London and Tunbridge Wells [...] [P]arsonage there was none, nor

---

[39] See Talia Schaffer's detailed analysis of the photographs in *Orlando*.
[40] Woolf, as is well known, based Orlando's lover, the whimsical Russian princess, on the writer Violet Trefusis, a rival of Woolf's for the affections of Vita Sackville-West (Orlando's model), with whom Violet had had a torrid affair and had fled to France in the early 1920s. As she did with Rezia, Woolf switches Trefusis' nationality, providing a thin veil of anonymity. Violet's Dutch ancestry, her assumed Frenchness, becomes Sasha's Russianness (allying her with Miss La Trobe of *Between the Acts*), perhaps in response to Vita's nickname of Lushka for Violet, and Violet's of Mitya for Vita, and Violet's husband's flight as a young man to Russia. In Sackville-West's *Knole and the Sackvilles*, there is a mention of a portrait of a Madame Muscovita at Knole (169).
[41] Recalling Woolf's remark from "The Russian Point of View," that "it is not the samovar but the teapot that rules in England; time is limited; space crowded; the influence of other points of view, of other books, even of other ages, makes itself felt" (*CR1* 184).

manor house, nor cottage, nor oak, elm, violet, ivy, or wild eglantine" (120-1). Orlando marvels in the pleasure that he, as one who is English to the core, takes in this new landscape. His whimsical contemplation of the possibility of his own foreignness highlights nostalgia's mythical quality:

> That he, who was English root and fibre, should yet exult to the depths of his heart in this wild panorama [...] surprised him [...] He wondered if, in the seasons of the Crusades, one of his ancestors had taken up with a Circassian peasant woman; thought it possible; fancied a certain darkness in his complexion and going indoors again [...] (121).

Orlando's subsequent stay among the gypsies in Turkey after revolution, marriage to Pepita Rosina and change of sex in Constantinople, provide Woolf with an opportunity to turn a sharply critical eye back on England and on Orlando's attachment to it. Heritage, class privilege, snobbery, the exclusivity, the materialism and the sexism of English society are resoundingly condemned by the gypsies, who class nostalgia as a disease. However, in time, Orlando's nostalgia gets the better of her and she forfeits the freedom she had enjoyed in Turkey for home. The absence of ink and writing paper, the lack of respect for wealth or class—"neither reverence for the Talbots, nor respect for a multiplicity of bedrooms"—renders Turkey intolerable to Orlando (150). Nature conspires to draw her home. It "played her a trick or worked a miracle" as an English landscape erupts in the "bald [Turkish] mountain-side" (150):

> [A] great park-like space opened in the flank of the hill. Within, she could see an undulating and grassy lawn; she could see oak trees dotted here and there; she could see the thrushes hopping among the branches. She could see the deer stepping delicately from shade to shade, and could even hear the hum of insects and the gentle sighs and shivers of a summer's day in England (150-1).

While nostalgia wins out, the ramifications of its victory become almost immediately clear to the homecoming protagonist. Orlando's increasing femaleness, which builds as she travels home via the Italian coast (159), and the dismay with which it is accompanied, is paralleled by a realization of the strictures of England and "the full stigma of nationality," especially those to which she is subject as a woman. While she marvels at the "urban glories" of a changed London (165), which contrast sharply with the savages and nature she has most recently left behind, and while she looks forward, rather ironically of course, to the "comfort," "opulence," "consequence and state," that will be hers on her return to her native land, she sees clearly how her return home will limit her: "it meant conventionality, meant slavery, meant deceit, meant denying her love, fettering her limbs, pursing her lips, and restraining her tongue" (163). She'll not be able to swear an oath, "crack a man over the head, or tell him he lies in his teeth, or draw my sword and run him through the body, or sit among my peers, or wear a coronet [...]. All I can do, once I set foot on English soil," Orlando laments, "is to pour out tea, and ask my lords how they like it" (158). The promise of nostalgia is undermined by the realities of second-class citizenship at home.

The broad temporal scope of *Orlando*, which stretches from the Elizabethan period to the twentieth century, allows Woolf to consider how conceptions of nostalgia and nationality change. Orlando's early nostalgia underscores his/her blindness to the negatives of a rigid class structure in England. England is divided between those who have and have not, those who live upstairs and those who live downstairs (one notes the large numbers of servants mentioned in *Orlando*). However this is a distinction that Orlando sees change in the twentieth century in figures such as the struggling seventeenth century writer Nick Greene, who once enjoyed Orlando's patronage, and who has lately become "the most influential critic of the Victorian age" (277). Orlando even encounters Sasha once again, shopping at Messrs. Marshall & Snelgrove—now a fixture in a more racially diverse England, appropriately bereft, as was Sally Seton of *Mrs. Dalloway*, of her earlier romanticism. Exploding Orlando's nostalgia, Sasha's exoticism is commodified and artificial: she's now "a fat, furred woman, marvellously well preserved, seductive, diademed, a Grand Duke's mistress; she who, leaning over the banks of the Volga, eating sandwiches, had watched men drown" (303).

In the same way, again suggesting an end to nostalgia, Orlando's family estate becomes an artifact—it's a museum, a monument, no longer home. "The house was no longer hers entirely, she sighed. It belonged to time now; to history; was past the touch and control of the living" (318). Further, when Orlando returns to the oak tree (323-6), the one thing which has stood firm and indeed flourished across the ages (it provides the backbone to the work, as does the text of the same name), her survey of England has changed; she looks further afield first, beyond England at Snowdon's crags and Scottish hills, then at her land, now no longer her own (as a woman?). As she does so, a wild Turkish landscape emerges—mirroring the emergence of the English landscape amid the Turkish during her stay with the gypsies—and old Rustum appears to remind Orlando of the dangers of nostalgia, the proportions included in his question suggesting the absurdity of Orlando's attachment to the trappings of the English nobility: "'What is your antiquity and your race, and your possessions compared with this? What do you need with four hundred bedrooms and silver lids on all the dishes, and housemaids dusting?'" (326).

A New Space of Time: *The Years*

Rustum's question anticipates further speculation around the questions of nationality and nostalgia in *The Years*. In this penultimate novel, written in conjunction with *Three Guineas*,[42] the modest cleft made in the landscape of *Orlando* broadens to encompass England across its length and breadth. Like the narrative itself, in terms of its flow, which Woolf herself characterized as—"a curiously uneven time sequence—a series of great balloons, linked by straight narrow passages of narrative" (*D4* 142), Englishness is fractured in *The Years*. Significantly, among its earlier titles, suggesting an end to an attachment to home and the past, were *Other People's Houses, Here & Now* and *The Caravan* (Anne Olivier Bell qtd in Hussey 387). Homelessness and dislocation dominate after the sale of the family homes, the Pargiters' Abercorn Terrace house and the house of Digby and Eugénie Pargiter and their daughters Sara and Maggie (147-8). The houses' contents, like their inhabitants, the children, are scattered haphazardly across London, across England and across the world. India, China, Africa, Australia, France and Italy are all evoked as destinations for *The Years'* characters. Like the plates at Maggie's house which Eleanor recognizes from the cabinet at Eugénie and Digby's home, the family heirlooms are now in use and being broken, Renny tells her, at a rate of one per week (284). However, this is a fracturing on which the Pargiters thrive.

Thus, when Eleanor, fresh from a trip to Spain and Greece, visits her brother Morris and his wife in Wittering, Dorset, she contemplates English village life in terms of the Mediterranean landscape from whence she has recently returned: "Like everything English, she thought, laying down her umbrella on the refectory table beside the china bowl, with dried rose leaves in it, the past seemed near, domestic, friendly" whereas in Greece "one was always going back two thousand years" (196). England's narrowness disappoints Eleanor: "it was small; it was pretty; she felt no affection for her native land—none whatever" (199). Signaling England's shift away from the center as a world power, Woolf prefaces this episode with a sweep across the South of France, following the sun across the English channel to London (192).

Although encouraged by her brother and his wife to settle down in the country, Eleanor ultimately rejects home in favor of travel—she envisions a ship, a train:

---

[42] Radin provides a detailed analysis of how the material that Woolf excised from *The Pargiters* became the basis for *Three Guineas*.

> When I've pensioned Crosby off, when . . . Should she take another house? Should she travel? Should she go to India, at last? Sir William was getting into bed next door, his life was over; hers was beginning. No, I don't mean to take another house, not another house, she thought, looking at the stain on the ceiling. Again the sense came to her of a ship padding softly through the waves; of a train swinging from side to side down a railway-line (213).

Thus, Eleanor, tying together the spatial and the temporal, opts for something beyond the confines of a family estate, beyond the parameters of the here and now: "Things pass, things change, she thought, looking up at the ceiling. And where are we going? Where? Where?" (213). As Sir William Whatney retires to bed along with England's imperial aspirations—"'He was in India, you know. Now he's retired [...]'" Celia tells Eleanor (205)—Eleanor embarks "at last" on her journey abroad.

In a related episode, which parallels Orlando's re-visioning of the land towards the close of *Orlando*, late in *The Years* Kitty Lasswade (Kitty Malone) lingers in the gardens and contemplates nostalgically the house and the landscape she shares with her husband: "the Castle looked grey and stately [. . .] Very noble it looked, and ancient, and enduring" (277), the repetition of "and" here suggesting the way in which this particular idea of England stretches back into the past. However Kitty's nostalgia is undercut rather abruptly in the novel—this last sentence is followed by "Then she went on into the woods," suggesting that she is entering a period of confusion represented by the density of the trees—by the fact that this landscape is not hers: "[n]othing of this belonged to her; her son would inherit; his wife would walk here after her" (277). Kitty, however, again recalling *Orlando* and echoing Eleanor, looks beyond this discrepancy, beyond the boundaries of her husband's (and her son's) property and celebrates the liberty this restriction affords her.

> She broke off a twig; she picked a flower and put it to her lips. But she was in the prime of life; she was vigorous. She strode on. The ground rose sharply; her muscles felt strong and flexible as she pressed her thick-soled shoes to the ground. She threw away her flower. The trees thinned as she strode higher and higher. Suddenly she saw the sky between two striped tree trunks extraordinarily blue. She came out on the top. The wind ceased; the country spread wide all around her. Her body seemed to shrink; her eyes to widen. She threw herself on the ground, and looked over the billowing land that went rising and falling, away and away, until somewhere far off it reached the sea. Uncultivated, uninhabited, existing by itself, for itself, without towns or houses it looked from this height. Dark wedges of shadow, bright breadths of light lay side by side. Then, as she watched, light moved and dark moved; light and shadow went travelling over the hills and over the valleys. A deep murmur sang in her ears—*the land itself, singing to itself, a chorus, alone. She lay there listening. She was happy completely. Time had ceased* (my emphasis; 277-8).

Kitty's engagement with the land—confident (she "strides"), victorious (she "comes out on the top"), and yet humble and reverential (her body shrinks and is enveloped by the countryside; her eyes widen)—suggests the advent of a new kind of relationship to home. Her celebration of borderlessness, her look beyond the parameters imposed on her by virtue of English tradition and her status as a woman, recall her encounter as a young woman with one of the four central foreign characters in *The Years*. The American Mrs. Fripp highlights, as does Mrs. Manresa in *Between the Acts*, the narrow-mindedness of the English, here specifically the Oxford ladies. Mrs. Fripp is "small and vivacious" with a "queer nasal voice" (57). She's "extraordinarily pretty and gay," "in the fashion," according to Kitty, and all of the women, Kitty notes, including herself, look dowdy and dumpy beside her, with the exception of her mother (57). While others sneer and raise their eyebrows at Mrs. Fripp's "American phrases," however, Kitty admires them in their difference from her own (58). In Mrs. Fripp's company, Kitty thumbs her nose at Oxford tradition, eating ices when she should have been showing her guest around the Bodleian (59). However, when the neatly coiffed Mrs. Fripp kisses Kitty, a kiss which echoes Sally's kiss of Clarissa in *Mrs. Dalloway*, and invites her to visit America (a country which, incidentally, Woolf never visited), suggesting the complications of such a venture, Kitty pulls a comb with difficulty through her very English hair, "which was like a fuzz bush" (61).

A second foreigner is the southern European Eugénie Pargiter, aunt by marriage to Eleanor and her brothers and sisters. Eugénie is a stereotypically romanticized character reminiscent of the young Sally Seton. She introduces, according to Radin, "an exotic strain to the prosaic Pargiter line," one which she passes onto her daughters, Sara and Maggie, in terms of their artistic streak (39). Abel Pargiter, recalling Old Parry's confusion in *Mrs. Dalloway*, is reminded on contemplating Eugénie of "the east," of India, ("so women sat in hot countries in their doorways in the sun" [119]). Eugénie's solidity, her dramatic nature, her "feminine effusiveness" (125), her ambiguity (127), highlights the insubstantiality, the plainness, the orderliness of the Englishwoman: she is "a fine large woman, growing ample, [Abel] noted as he shook hands; but it suited her," a type he admired "more than the pink-and-white pretty Englishwoman" (119). While she embraces her role as object of Abel's nostalgia—when Abel hands Eugénie the camelia it is his custom to bring her, she "put the stalk between her lips" (119) charming Abel—a certain discomfort marks her presence in prewar England, highlighted especially by her apparently difficult marriage with Abel's brother, Digby Pargiter. Remarked for "her indolent Southern manner" (122), her exact origins remain unspecified across the length of the work, endowing her with a broad claim to a number of different countries: Italy, Spain, Southern France.[43] Woolf highlights Eugénie's freedom from borders in physical terms: "Her eyes, her large dark eyes, were ambiguous" (127); "[H]er body seemed to become indolent and suave. The heavy lids lowered themselves slightly over her large dark eyes" (142); and when Eleanor reminisces about Eugénie with Maggie she sees her aunt "not sitting but in movement. '. . . dancing,' she added" (287). Suspected sexual transgressions, although, again, somewhat stereotypical—her nephew Martin wonders "What had her private life been [...]—her love affairs? She must have had them—obviously, obviously" (153)—suggest she breaks free of the propriety which grips so many of the other characters in *The Years*.

A third foreign figure somewhat less stereotypical than Eugénie or Mrs. Fripp is Eugénie's French son-in-law René, called Renny by the English characters in the work. Perhaps modeled, Hermione Lee suggests, on French painter Jacques Raverat, "Neo-Pagan" husband of Gwen Darwin (and indeed, he bears a physical resemblance to Raverat: "his thin cheek, his big nose" [386]), René, like Raverat, spends a period of time during the novel living in England with his wife and children and a period living in France (Raverat died of multiple sclerosis in Vence in 1925).[44] René's presence in the work complicates Eleanor's relationship with England. During the 1917 segment of the novel, as Eleanor recalls how she had been "overcome by an absurd but vehement desire to protect those [English] hills" on first hearing about the war (286), she looks across "at the foreigner [Renny or Nicholas] opposite" (286). When Eleanor asserts, somewhat uncertainly, that it is natural to want to protect one's home country when it is under threat of invasion, Renny appears angry or pained, Eleanor cannot tell which, and he cryptically asserts "'I help them to make shells,'" suggesting the dangers implicit in Eleanor's national sentiment and the ease with which one becomes implicated in a project one despises (286). Woolf's sympathetic portrait of Renny, her only French character—he's forthright, decent and Eleanor is a little in love with him—conforms not only with Woolf's warm feelings for Raverat, but also her passion for France and the French language, voiced on many occasions, among them in her essay "On Not Knowing French."

The origins and identity of the fourth *Years*' foreigner, René's friend Nicholas Pomjalovsky, also known as Brown—perhaps an effort to nominally assimilate him as the Pargiters do Renny or perhaps, as David Bradshaw has sug-

---

[43] Radin says that Eugénie is half-Spanish (39). Physical descriptions of Eugénie suggest possible ties to Ottoline Morrell.

[44] See the letters exchanged by Woolf and the Raverats, recently collected under the title *Virginia Woolf and the Raverats: A Different Kind of Friendship* (Clear Books, 2003), edited by Raverat's grandson William Pryor.

gested, a reference to the term "brown hat," upper-middle-class slang for a homosexual in the 1930s (186) (Nicholas loves "the other sex," Sara tells Eleanor [297])—remain obscure across the length of the work, highlighted by the recurrence of the question of his nationality (282, 368, 418).[45] Our knowledge of Nicholas, whom Avrom Fleishman has tied to Woolf's Russian friend and co-translator Koteliansky, is fragmentary, the stuff of legends (Radin 67). Is he "Russian, Polish, Jewish," Eleanor wonders (282)? "'He's an American,' [said Renny,] nodding at Nicholas. "'No [...], I'm a Pole,'" asserts Nicholas (287).[46] His mother, they repeat, was a Princess. He discusses Napoleon and "the psychology of great men" with Renny (280-1) and he lectures about the soul. Sara mockingly characterizes him as "'the professor preaching his little sermon'" (370). His "rather ill-assorted dress-clothes, [...] and his swarthy wrinkled face" remind Eleanor "of some loose-skinned, furry animal, savage to others but kind to herself" (368-9). For North, he's "one of those voluble foreigners with a theory about everything [...] he gave off an aroma; a whirr" (323). His failure to conform to national, sexual and socio-cultural norms, and his auguring of a New World inspire Eleanor to turn away from her past: "He seemed to have released something in her; she felt not only *a new space of time*, but new powers, something unknown within her" (my emphasis; 297).

A fifth minor foreign figure who has prompted debate among Woolf scholars is Sara's Jewish neighbor, Abrahamson, with whom she shares a bathroom and about whose bathing habits she has a strange conversation, replete with anti-Semitic remarks, with her nephew North (338-343). While Phyllis Lassner has condemned Woolf's portrait, others, like Radin, have excused it as not unusual for its day. In response to these arguments, Bradshaw asserts that a broader look at the novel in terms of its Jewishness suggests that this scene is meant to reflect the anti-Semitism of Woolf's day (not Woolf's own feelings towards Jews) and that it is just one aspect of her "[anatomization of] the 'deformed' culture of which she was both a product and a victim" ("Hyams Place" 179). Bradshaw reads Sara's comments about Abrahamson alongside other moments in the work which suggest, he contends, that Jews have a right to be in Britain, such as references to blue and white and the imaginary names chosen for two important locations in the work: Hyams Place and Milton Street ("Hyams Place" 179).[47]

---

[45] Radin adds that Eleanor's supplying of words to Nicholas reflects the translation collaboration relationship of Woolf and Koteliansky. Koteliansky, she adds, was, like Nicholas, a utopian (Radin 67).

[46] Radin notes that Nicholas is half-Jewish in the holograph (95).

[47] See also Lassner and recently Leena Kore Schröder's "Tales of Abjection and Miscegenation: Virginia Woolf's and Leonard Woolf's Jewish Stories." Both look at Woolf's short story "The Duchess and the Jeweller," among other pieces.

My analysis of the other foreigners in *The Years* would seem to support Bradshaw's contention.

As Radin's careful analysis of *The Pargiters*, *The Years* and various typescripts demonstrates, Woolf excised much of the discussion on issues such as war, patriotism and sexuality from the final version of *The Years*. Thus, Sara's (called Elvira in *The Pargiters*) and Maggie's difficulty understanding patriotism, having been raised outside England, does not make it into *The Years* in any explicit way (Radin 51-52, 68-69, 76-77). Similarly, while the earlier versions offer a clearer exposition of Renny's involvement in the manufacture of shells and his ultimate decision to stop doing so (Radin 99) and include Sara's decision to continue sharing her bath with her Jewish neighbor (Radin 102), these details are not included in the final version. Radin attributes the decision to omit some of these scenes to Woolf's fear that her criticism of patriotism and her espousal of unorthodox ideas would be poorly received on the eve of a second World War. "Both Leonard and Virginia Woolf," writes Radin, "were struggling in those years to reconcile their commitment to peaceful solutions with their growing horror of fascism" (84). What these omissions do demonstrate, however, is first, Woolf's profound engagement with questions of nationalism and nostalgia, one which found its vehicle in *Three Guineas*; and second, the degree to which historical circumstances shaped, and in fact in this case, hindered a discussion of these questions—a situation which problematizes somewhat the assertion with which we began that Woolf's ideas evolved from novel to novel. The very number of foreigners in *The Years* and the often cryptic and varied responses to them suggests an uneasiness on the part of its author which is not rationally articulated.

Foreignness, in terms of both character and landscape, then, functions in *The Years* to unsettle English tradition. The wartime setting of certain segments of the novel and the centrality to the work of questions of empire allows Woolf to interrogate the attraction of nostalgia in its various forms (Abel's, Kitty's, Eleanor's, René's), to highlight its increasing inappropriateness and to look forward to an alternative. Thus, Abel Pargiter's condescending imperialistic admiration of the foreign Eugénie contrasts sharply with Eleanor's and Sara's forward-looking love of Nicholas.

England Forgot Her Lines: *Between the Acts*

When one considers Eleanor's rejection of the narrow-mindedness of rural England in *The Years* and the general openness of that novel, it seems odd that

Woolf chose to follow it with the pastoral *Between the Acts*.[48] Woolf's choice to locate this novel, written on the verge of a second World War, "in the heart of England," however, suggests that it might be read as a response to Eleanor's question of one's relation to home in *The Years*, one which essentially echoes *Three Guineas*' dilemma on which this paper opened. How can one reconcile a desire to protect the country one cherishes when faced with the threat of war with a recognition that that same country provides little protection for many of its so called citizens? How can one square one's love of country with the knowledge that that same love is at the root of the war that will cost so many people their lives?[49] What kind of nostalgic tribute is appropriate to a heterogeneous Englishness that has been misleadingly nourished on "myths of homogeneity"? As she fashions her own version of English history via Miss La Trobe's play, Woolf suggests how nostalgia might "serve [the woman writer] to give to England first what she desires of peace and freedom for the whole world" (*TG* 109).

In *Between the Acts*, set in the pastoral haven of the appropriately fractured family home of the Olivers, Pointz Hall, foreignness does not involve the invocation of foreign landscapes as it does so often in *Mrs. Dalloway*, *Orlando* and *The Years*. With the exception of the patriarch, Old Bart Oliver, reminiscing about India, the characters' few references to travel abroad are colored by their anxiety over the impending war. Suggesting its greater proximity, foreignness, and here it is significantly one as much imagined as real, enters the text instead via two central female figures, Miss La Trobe and Mrs. Manresa. Miss La Trobe is "suspected" of having foreign blood by Mrs. Bingham: "With that name she wasn't presumably pure English. From the Channel Island perhaps? Only her eyes and something about her always made Mrs. Bingham suspect that she had Russian blood in her: "'Those deep-set eyes; that very square jaw' reminded

---

[48] When *The Years*' Eleanor visits her brother and sister-in-law in Dorset, a village fair (similar to *Between the Acts*' pageant) has just ended.

[49] In 1927, comments made during a conversation with Harold Nicolson, seem to confirm this hypothesis. When Nicolson praises British imperialism, Woolf asks "'But why not grow, change?' [...] Also, I said, recalling the aeroplanes that had flown over us, while the portable wireless played dance music on the terrace, 'can't you see that nationality is over? All divisions are now rubbed out, or are about to be'" (*D3* 145). The planes flying overhead and the sound of the gramophone in *Between the Acts* suggest that Woolf perhaps considered this conversation when writing her last novel.

her—not that she had been to Russia—of the Tartars" (37);[50] Mrs. Manresa is reputed to have been born in Tasmania: "She had been born, but it was only gossip said so, in Tasmania: her grandfather had been exported for some hanky-panky mid-Victorian scandal; malversation of trusts was it?" (26). Compounding both women's foreignness is a suspicious sexual history, echoing the entanglement of nationality and sexuality in Woolf's earlier work. Miss La Trobe is rumored to be a lesbian,[51] Mrs. Manresa, promiscuous.

An evolved Miss Kilman in many regards, Miss La Trobe is no longer exiled to the peripheries of the house, although to some degree she chooses to locate herself there. Unlike Miss Kilman, who engages in a dialogue with Clarissa in *Mrs. Dalloway*, Miss La Trobe maintains her distance from the gossip of which she is frequently the object, suggesting a more peaceful coexistence of difference. The self-loathing which was characteristic of Miss Kilman does not infect

---

[50] Marcus suggests that Miss La Trobe of *Between the Acts* is partly modeled on Ethel Smyth, as was Rose Pargiter of *The Years* (*Art and Anger* 99). Also, according to Marcus: "Woolf [...] saw part of herself as Miss La Trobe, the lonely artist, preserver of culture, allied with people who keep history and art alive while the upper classes ignore or destroy civilization. In *Between the Acts*, Miss La Trobe leaves bits of her property at the big house, where they care about such things, but she takes her lonely, misunderstood, awkward, visionary self down to the local pub. The view of the alienated artist allied with ordinary people to educate the middle and upper classes is consistent with Woolf's view of herself as an 'outsider,' a feminist, socialist, artist, and worker" (*Art and Anger* 121). Miss La Trobe, Marcus also tells us, was the name of an important abolitionist mentioned in the *Life of Wilberforce* which Woolf was reading in order to trace her blood ties to Octavia Wilberforce via her great-grandfather's marriage (*Languages of Patriarchy* 167). Marcus has also suggested Edith Craig, daughter of Ellen Terry as a possible model for La Trobe ("Some Sources"). Abel suggests that: "[t]he role of France as lost maternal origin [France fell to Germany in 1940 as Woolf wrote *Between the Acts*] is implied in the novel by the exiled Miss La Trobe, whose name suggests a French origin of feminine gender. In the historical context of the pageant, France replaces the sea as a figure of the mother, and Germany becomes a figure of the overriding father" (n. 28, 171). Gillespie ties Miss La Trobe to a prominent nineteenth century family of the same name in England, although not originally English. Although Gillespie feels that this link is in some senses mock-heroic, she sees Miss La Trobe tied to these musicians and clergymen in her capacity as an artist, as "evangelical in her efforts to communicate, and while in England, not of it" ("Virginia Woolf's Miss La Trobe" 43).

[51] "Rumour said that she had kept a tea shop at Winchester; that had failed. She had been an actress. That had failed. She had bought a four-roomed cottage and shared it with an actress. They had quarrelled. Very little was actually known about her. Outwardly she was swarthy, sturdy and thick set; strode about the fields in a smock frock; sometimes with a cigarette in her mouth; often with a whip in her hand; and used rather strong language—perhaps, then, she wasn't altogether a lady? At any rate, she had a passion for getting things up" (*BTA* 37).

Miss La Trobe. Rather, she conceives of herself as a Magus of sorts: "one who seethes wandering bodies and floating voices in a cauldron, and makes rise up from its amorphous mass a *re-created world*" (my emphasis; 92). Indeed, in the course of her play, Miss La Trobe rewrites England's master narratives, nostalgia's script, as does Woolf in the course of the novel. As the play opens, England forgets her lines . . . the plot no longer matters; "it didn't matter what the words were or who sang what" (58). Miss La Trobe "cut[s] the knot in the centre," as she parodies English history (highlighting its heterogeneity with a cacophony of literary allusions ranging from Shakespeare to Aphra Behn, William Blake and T.S. Eliot) (56).[52] Again recalling our *Three Guineas* epigraph, to the two emotions "love; and hate" which shape the play, a third is added to the "ply of human life": that of "peace" (56-7).

Mrs. Manresa, appropriately based in part, critics contend, on Woolf's New Zealander rival Katherine Mansfield who settled in England, or the pseudo-foreign Sackville-West, is complicit in Miss La Trobe's reworking of England's script.[53] Her saucy interjections, her bawdy nursery rhymes (the very stuff of nostalgia, according to Woolf in *Three Guineas*), cover the embarrassments of forgotten lines and round out Miss La Trobe's alternative history. Recalling Miss La Trobe's cauldron, Mrs. Manresa stirs cream and sugar into her coffee as she adds spice to the pageant's plot: "She took the little silver cream jug and let the smooth fluid curl luxuriously into her coffee, to which she added a shovel full of brown sugar candy. Sensuously, rhythmically, she stirred the mixture round and round" (35). She makes her words/the pageant seem "ripe like the apricot into which the wasps were burrowing" (36). Mrs. Manresa rewrites the lines dividing the classes. Her preference for teaching the village women how to weave

---

[52] The figure of the knot and of tangling and untangling recurs across the length of the play: "from the distaff of life's tangled skein, unloose her hands" (57).

[53] While Mrs. Manresa is rumored to have been born in Tasmania, Mansfield was a New Zealander by birth. According to Evelyn Haller, Mansfield lived "one block west of Manresa Street" in London when Woolf met her (qtd in Hussey 154). There is an ambivalence in Woolf's vision of Mrs. Manresa that matches the ambivalence of her relationship with Mansfield. Mansfield died following a haemorrhage at age 33 in 1923, many years prior to Woolf's writing of *Between the Acts*. Thus, Woolf could write about her with impunity. Peach suggests that Manresa's name "ironically associates her with arousing or teasing men" (206). Beer tells us that "Manresa is the name of a street in Chelsea; the generic name of many Jesuit novice-houses like the one at Roehampton where Gerald Manley Hopkins lived; and—here—also a pun on 'man-raiser'" (n.32, *BTA*, Penguin annotated edition). Another possible source for the character of Mrs. Manresa is contemporary British novelist Berta Ruck (see Gillespie on Ruck). Mitchell Leaska ties Manresa to Sackville-West (12-3).

"frivolous baskets out of coloured straw" rather than pickling and preserving, reflects her own addition of color to the pageant, and to village life: "Pleasure's what they want, she said. You often heard her, if you called, yodelling among the hollyhocks 'Hoity te doity te ray do . . .'" (28).

In contrast to Miss Kilman, Mrs. Manresa exploits her obscurity. Like a number of her foreign predecessors in Woolf's novels, Mrs. Manresa creates her own autobiographical fictions. Mrs. Manresa offers only "a sample of her life; a few gobbets of gossip; mere trash; but she gave it for what it was worth" (27). Her husband's initials, R.M, on her silver plated car are twisted in such a way "to look at a distance like a coronet," suggesting Mrs. Manresa's distortion of the truth of her identity and that of her husband (30).[54] Available on the outside, her private life is inaccessible, obscure, unknown:

> Her hat, her rings, her finger nails red as roses, smooth as shells, were there for all to see. But not her life history. That was only scraps and fragments to all of them, excluding perhaps William Dodge, whom she called 'Bill' publicly—a sign perhaps that he knew more than they did. Some of the things that he knew—that she strolled the garden at midnight in silk pyjamas, had the loud speaker playing jazz, and a cocktail bar, of course they knew also. But nothing private; no strict biographical facts (26).

Many critics have explored the implications of Woolf's deployment in *Between the Acts* of the traditional pageant form as a means, paradoxically, to undermine tradition and patriotism and its attendant nostalgia in ways which parallel my argument about the foreign in this same novel. Vanessa Manhire, for example, contends that Woolf counters the conservative, nationalistic purpose of the English Folk Revival—a movement which sought to promote folk culture in part in an effort to counter "perceived threats to English racial and cultural superiority" (Boyes qtd in Manhire 237) and a movement for which the pageant was an important form—by making the urban central to her rural pageant in *Between the Acts* and by substituting in this novel and other works a mobile, "contami-

---

[54] "Sometimes she referred to an uncle, a Bishop," but "he was thought to have been a Colonial Bishop only [...] Also it was said her diamonds and rubies had been dug out of the earth with his own hands by a 'husband' who was not Ralph Manresa. Ralph, a Jew, got up to look the very spit and image of the landed gentry, supplied from directing City companies—that was certain—tons of money; and they had no child" (*BTA* 26). In her article, "'The Milk of Our Mother's Kindness has Ceased to Flow': Virginia Woolf, Stevie Smith, and the Representation of the Jew," Lassner treats xenophobia and anti-Semitism in *Between the Acts*, focusing on Ralph Manresa. She ties Isa Oliver to Isidore Oliver, one of several earlier names for the jeweller Oliver Bacon from Woolf's controversial short story "The Duchess and the Jeweller."

nated" figure (a foreign figure of sorts) for "the specter of 'pure Mother Earth' which stands in for the dubious authenticity of invented tradition" (241). Edward Barnaby, looking at the metahistorical aspects of *Between the Acts*, and by extension the social function of the novel as a genre, discusses the capacity of the novel, and the pageant within the novel, to support or undermine historical accuracy, to contain or to liberate its audience. And most recently, Esty argues that Woolf, like T.S. Eliot (*The Rock*) and E.M. Forster (*Abinger Pageant, England's Pleasant Land*), "experiments with pageantry in an effort to reestablish the nationalism of shared experiences (pastoral memory) as against the nationalism of shared goals (imperial mission)" (90).

The Reverend's closing attempts to explain the "message" of the pageant in *Between the Acts*, a question the by this point "invisible" authoress refuses to answer for herself, sanctions the role of foreigners/outsiders Miss La Trobe and Mrs. Manresa in its production: "'we were shown different groups'" he suggests haltingly, "'To me at least it was indicated that we are members one of another. Each is part of the whole [...] We act different parts; but are the same'" (114). In this last novel, Woolf unties the knot, as does Miss La Trobe, that is the contradiction between a love of country and a recognition of the restrictive nature of that same country by rewriting national boundaries and stories of nationhood to include other voices. Like the Reverend, Woolf suggests in this novel, written on the eve of World War Two, the benefit, if not the necessity, of a peaceful coexistence of difference in England. As Beer has argued, highlighting the forward-looking nature of Woolf's love of country, the hybridity of which she considers an asset, in *Between the Acts*, "Woolf sought to produce another idea of England, one which might survive, but survive without portentousness—as mixture and common place" (*Virginia Woolf* 147). Stripping nostalgia of its chauvinistic aspect by implicating the foreign in its process, highlighting the role of the other in the creation of the identity of the same, the foreigner in the shaping of Englishness, Woolf reconciles a love of country with a love of freedom.

Following McVicker, Marder et al. one can argue then for progress in Woolf's conception of foreignness and nationality. The demystification of the foreign in *Between the Acts* heralds a new kind of nostalgia, an alternative vision of home. A look at foreignness *in general* suggests a drive to create a different breed of patriotism, one which admits a mixedness and one which distinguishes itself with increasing urgency from jingoism. This study highlights the potential of further work on the specific political ramifications of Woolf's foreigners, on the impact of Woolf's many foreign ties on her work and on the implications of the entanglement of nationality and gender which one finds throughout her later fiction.[55]

Works Cited

Abbott, Reginald. "What Miss Kilman's Petticoat Means: Virginia Woolf, Shopping, and Spectacle." *MFS: Modern Fiction Studies* 38.1 (1992 Spring): 193-216.

Abel, Elizabeth. "Narrative Structure(s) and Female Development: The Case of *Mrs. Dalloway*." In *Virginia Woolf: A Collection of Critical Essays*. Ed. Margaret Homans. Englewood Cliffs, N.J.: Prentice Hall, 1993.

Allan, Tuzyline Jita. "Civilization and its Pretexts in Virginia Woolf's Imagination." *Virginia Woolf and Communities. Selected Papers from the Eighth Annual Conference on Virginia Woolf*. Eds. Jeanette McVicker and Laura Davis. New York: Pace UP, 1999: 117-127.

Barnaby, Edward. "Visualizing the Spectacle: Virginia Woolf's Metahistory Lesson in *Between the Acts*." *Virginia Woolf: Turning the Centuries. Selected Papers from the Ninth Annual Conference on Virginia Woolf*. Eds. Ann Ardis and Bonnie Kime Scott. New York: Pace UP, 2000: 311-317.

Barrett, Eileen. "Unmasking Lesbian Passion: The Inverted World of *Mrs. Dalloway*." *Virginia Woolf: Lesbian Readings*. Eds. Eileen Barrett and Patricia Cramer. New York: New York UP, 1997: 146-164.

Beer, Gillian. *Virginia Woolf: The Common Ground*. Ann Arbor: U of Michigan P, 1996.

——. "Notes." *Between the Acts*. (1941) London: Penguin, 1992.

Bowlby, Rachel. *Virginia Woolf: Feminist Destinations*. Oxford: Basil Blackwell, 1988.

Boym, Svetlana. *The Future of Nostalgia*. New York: Basic Books, 2001.

Bradshaw, David. "Hyams Place: *The Years*, the Jews and the British Union of Fascists." *Women Writers of the 1930s: Gender, Politics, History*. Ed. Maroula Joannou. Edinburgh: Edinburgh UP, 1999: 179-191.

---

[55] I am grateful to Caleb Southworth, Mark Hussey and the two anonymous *WSA* reviewers for their insightful recommendations as I revised this paper. I would also like to thank those who made comments during and subsequent to my presentation of a very early version of this paper at the 12th Annual Conference on Virginia Woolf at Sonoma State University, Rohnert Park, in 2002, including Vara Neverow, Elizabeth Shih and Nick Smart.

——. "Eugenics: 'They should certainly be killed.'" *A Concise Companion to Modernism*. Ed. David Bradshaw. Malden, MA: Blackwell Publishing, 2003.

Carstens, Lisa. "The Science of Sex and the Art of Self-Materializing in *Orlando*." *Virginia Woolf Out of Bounds: Selected Papers from the Tenth Annual Conference on Virginia Woolf*. Eds. Jessica Berman and Jane Goldman. New York, NY: Pace UP, 2001.

Childs, Donald. *Modernism and Eugenics: Woolf, Eliot, Yeats, and the Culture of Degeneration.* Cambridge: Cambridge UP, 2001.

Doyle, Laura. *Bordering on the Body: The Racial Matrix of Modern Fiction and Culture*. Oxford: Oxford UP, 1994.

Eagleton, Terry. *Exiles and Émigrés: Studies in Modern Literature*. New York: Schocken Books, 1970.

Esty, Jed. *A Shrinking Island: Modernism and National Culture in England.* Princeton: Princeton UP, 2004.

Fowler, Rowena. "Moments and Metamorphoses: Virginia Woolf's Greece." *Comparative Literature* 51. 3 (Summer 1999): 217-42.

Friedman, Susan Stanford. *Mappings: Feminism and the Cultural Geographies of Encounter*. Princeton: Princeton UP, 1988.

Garrity, Jane. *Step-daughters of England: British Women Modernists and the National Imaginary*. Manchester: Manchester UP, 2003.

Gillespie, Diane Filby. "Virginia Woolf's Miss La Trobe: The Artist's Last Struggle Against Masculine Values." *Women & Literature* 1 (1977): 38-46.

——. "Virginia Woolf and the Curious Case of Berta Ruck." *Woolf Studies Annual* 10 (2003): 109-38.

Hussey, Mark. *Virginia Woolf A to Z*. New York: Facts on File, Inc., 1995.

Hutcheon, Linda. "Irony, Nostalgia and the Postmodern." In *Methods for the Study of Literature as Cultural Memory*. Eds. Raymond Vervliet and Annemarie Estor. Amsterdam: Rodopi, 2000.

Kneubuhl, Barbara. *Channel Crossings: Virginia Woolf in France, 1920-1977.* PhD. Dissertation. University of Michigan, 1979.

James, C.L.R. *The Case for West-Indian Self Government*. London: Hogarth Press, 1933.

Lassner, Phyllis. "'The Milk of Our Mother's Kindness Has Ceased to Flow': Virginia Woolf, Stevie Smith, and the Representation of the Jew." *Between "Race" and Culture: Representations of "the Jew" in English and American Literature*. Ed. Bryan Cheyette. Stanford: Stanford UP, 1996.

Laurence, Patricia. *Lily Briscoe's Chinese Eyes: Bloomsbury, Modernism and China*. Columbia: U of South Carolina P, 2003.
Leaska, Mitchell A. *Pointz Hall : The Earlier and Later Typescripts of Between the Acts*. New York: University Publications, 1983.
Lee, Hermione. *Virginia Woolf*. New York: Knopf, 1997.
Levenback, Karen L. *Virginia Woolf and the Great War*. Syracuse: Syracuse UP, 1999.
———. "Clarissa Dalloway, Doris Kilman and the Great War." *Virginia Woolf Miscellany* 37 (Fall 1991): 3-4.
Light, Alison. *Forever England: Femininity, Literature and Conservatism Between the Wars*. London: Routledge, 1991.
Manhire, Vanessa. "'The Lady's Gone A-Roving': Woolf and the English Folk Revival." *Virginia Woolf Out of Bounds: Selected Papers from the Tenth Annual Conference on Virginia Woolf*. Eds. Jessica Berman and Jane Goldman. New York: Pace UP, 2001.
Marcus, Jane. *Hearts of Darkness: White Women Write Race*. New Brunswick: Rutgers UP, 2004.
———. *Art and Anger: Reading Like a Woman*. Columbus: Ohio State UP, 1988.
———. *Virginia Woolf and the Languages of Patriarchy*. Bloomington: Indiana UP, 1987.
———. "Some Sources for *Between the Acts*." *Virginia Woolf Miscellany* 6, 1977: 1-3.
Marder, Herbert. *The Measure of Life: Virginia Woolf's Last Years*. Ithaca: Cornell UP, 2000.
Marwick, Arthur. *The Deluge: British Society and the First World War*. New York: W.W. Norton & Company, 1965.
McVicker, Jeanette. "'Six Essays on London Life': A History of Dispersal Part I." *Woolf Studies Annual* 9 (2003): 143-65.
Peach, Linden. *Virginia Woolf*. New York: St Martin's, 2000.
Phillips, Kathy. "Woolf's Criticism of the British Empire in *The Years*." *Virginia Woolf Miscellanies: Proceedings of the First Annual Conference on Virginia Woolf*. Eds. Mark Hussey and Vara Neverow-Turk. New York: Pace UP 30-31.
———. *Virginia Woolf Against Empire*. Knoxville: U of Tennessee P, 1994.
Primamore, Elizabeth. "A Don, Virginia Woolf, the Masses, and the Case of Miss Kilman." *Lit: Literature Interpretation Theory* 9.2 (Oct 1998): 121-37.
Radin, Grace. *Virginia Woolf's The Years: The Evolution of a Novel*. Knoxville: U of Tennessee P, 1981.
Rubenstein, Roberta. "Virginia Woolf and the Russian Point of View." *Comparative Literature Studies* 9 (1972): 196-206

———. "*Orlando*: Virginia Woolf's Improvisations on a Russian Theme." *Forum for Modern Language Studies* 9 (1973): 166-69.
———. *Home Matters: Longing and Belonging, Nostalgia and Mourning in Women's Fiction*. New York: Palgrave, 2001.
Sackville-West, Vita. *Challenge*. London, Collins, 1974.
———. *Heritage*. (1919) London: Futura Publications, 1975.
———. *Knole and the Sackvilles*. London: L. Drummond, 1949.
Sarker, Sonita. "Locating a Native Englishness in Virginia Woolf's 'The London Scene'" *NWSA Journal* 13.2 (Summer 2001).
Schaffer, Talia. "Posing Orlando." In *Sexual Artifice: Persons, Images, Politics*. Eds. Ann Kibbey, Kayann Short, Abouali Farmanfarmaian. New York: New York UP, 1994: 26-63
Schröder, Leena Kore. "*Mrs. Dalloway* and the Female Vagrant." *Essays in Criticism: A Quarterly Journal of Literary Criticism* 45.4 (Oct 1995): 324-46
———. "Tales of Abjection and Miscegenation: Virginia Woolf's and Leonard Woolf's 'Jewish' Stories." *Twentieth Century Literature: A Scholarly and Critical Journal* 49.3 (Fall 2003): 298-327.
Trombley, Stephen. *All that Summer She was Mad: Virginia Woolf, Female Victim of Male Medicine*. New York: Continuum, 1982.
Willis, J. H. *Leonard and Virginia Woolf as Publishers: The Hogarth Press 1917-41*. Charlottesville: U P of Virginia, 1992.
Woolf, Leonard. *Downhill All the Way: An Autobiography of the Years 1919-1939*. NY: Harcourt, Brace & World, Inc, 1967.
Woolf, Virginia. *Between The Acts*. 1941. London: Penguin, 1992.
———. *The Common Reader*. 1925. New York: Harvest, 1953.
Mrs. Dalloway. 1925. San Diego: Harvest/HBJ, 1981.
———. *The Diary of Virginia Woolf*. Eds. Anne Olivier Bell and Andrew McNeillie. San Diego: HBJ, 1978. 5 volumes.
The Letters of Virginia Woolf Editor, Nigel Nicolson, assistant editor, Joanne Trautmann. New York: Harcourt Brace Jovanovich, 1975-1980. 6 volumes.
———. "Modern Fiction." In *The Common Reader*. New York: Harvest, 1953.
———. "On Not Knowing French." *The New Republic*, Feb. 13, 1929.
———. *Orlando*. 1928. San Diego: Harvest/HBJ, 1956.
———. *Three Guineas*. 1938. San Diego: Harvest/HBJ, 1966.
———. *To the Lighthouse*. 1927. San Diego: Harvest/HBJ, 1981.
———. *The Years*. 1937. San Diego: Harvest/HBJ, 1965.
Zwerdling, Alex. *Virginia Woolf and the Real World*. Berkeley: U of California P, 1986.

Listening for "Found Sound" Samples in the Novels of Virginia Woolf

Angela Frattarola

> *[T]here is a music in the air for which we are always straining our ears*
> —Virginia Woolf, "Street Music"
> *When we read to ourselves, our ears hear nothing.*
> *When we read, however, we listen.*
> —Garrett Stewart, *Reading Voices: Literature and the Phonotext*

The musical undercurrents and aural quality of Woolf's later fiction prompts Garrett Stewart in *Reading Voices: Literature and the Phonotext* to claim that through her "poetic resonance" and "stray reverberations," Woolf performs the "vocal writing" that Roland Barthes valorizes in *The Pleasure of the Text* as necessary though not practiced by most writers (261, Barthes qtd. in Stewart 279).[1] While Stewart's analysis focuses on the verbal play and phonic elements of *The Waves*, I will focus this article on a more overt example of Woolf's performance of "vocal writing": her representation of sound. In order to discuss Woolf's inclusion of real-world sound, which progresses with each of her succeeding novels until it culminates in her last work, *Between the Acts*, I will make use of the musical term "found sound" sampling—the art of recording sounds from the real world such as sirens, rain, cars, street conversations, and using those sounds in an original musical composition.[2] The term "found sound" sampling allows us to account for not only the onomatopoetic sounds of "chuff" and "tick" mixed throughout *Between the Acts*, but also the street hawkers' cries, which intrude repeatedly in *The Years*, and the song of the old woman on the street heard in

---

[1] Though Barthes claims that there is a lack of writers who practice "vocal writing," Stewart asserts: "On the contrary, I think we can find it in a unique and allusive concentration, on almost every page of Woolf's late fictional prose—find it as a writing that amounts to a virtual rereading of the whole literary tradition, its sensuist impulses and its missed chances" (279).

[2] In a larger work in progress, I argue that the term sampling, when appropriated from music into literary criticism, presents a way to explore resonances in the novel that are uncannily familiar, though not traceable to a specific original text (like one would expect in allusion). Genre sampling and inter/intra-textual sampling, along with "found sound" sampling, are examples of what I call nonspecific sampling. Since we already have a vocabulary with which to address sound in poetry, sampling is a term I reserve for the often-overlooked aurality of the twentieth-century novel.

Mrs. Dalloway. This article will demonstrate how Woolf's use of "found sound" sampling forces a heightened sense of the aural into her narrative, which is sounded out by the "reading voice" of her reader. By examining Woolf's preoccupation with sound representation and the aural dimension of her fiction, moreover, we can gather a more complex sense of her modern notions of community and individuality, whereby her characters are momentarily united, as if in a chorus, through their shared aural experiences, though they are simultaneously separate, individual, isolated.

Modernism and the Beginnings of "Found Sound" Sampling

While it is often assumed that musical sampling is only a digital phenomenon, for the purposes of this project, I propose that any recording technology that enables the reuse of a sound in a new composition is, in essence, sampling.[3] With the growing usage of the phonograph and gramophone, invented by Edison in 1877 and improved by Emile Berliner with the replacement of records for cylinders in 1887, composers began to experiment with the art of sampling in the early 1900s. Since the first marketed phonographs were not advanced enough to play music, they were advertised as devices that could record and replay an assortment of sounds, heralding a new fascination with noise. For instance, an advertisement for the Edison phonograph from *The Illustrated London News* on February 3, 1900 assured readers that they could hear "the HUMAN VOICE, the

---

[3] Music critics Tricia Rose, Houston A. Baker, Jeremy J. Beadle, and Chris Cutler, assume that sampling is digital because their studies are primarily concerned with hip-hop and contemporary uses of sampling that are enabled through such technological advances. However, in its most basic sense, sampling is the process of recording, storing, and replaying sound in a new context. See Martin Russ, *Sound Synthesis and Sampling*: "the distinguishing feature of the sampler is its ability to record sounds" (196). Russ concludes that "a wide range of equipment" such as tape recorders, cassette recorders, and video recorders can "be classified as being samplers" (196). I expand this definition further in considering the phonograph and gramophone as the earliest samplers. In general studies of rap and hip-hop, such as Baker's *Black Studies, Rap, and the Academy*, which categorizes rap and sampling as postmodern and hybrid, and Rose's *Black Noise: Rap Music and Black Culture in Contemporary America*, which sees sampling in rap as "a process of cultural literacy and intertextual reference" (89), the concern is not specifically with sampling or "found sound" sampling, but rather the larger context of hip-hop and rap. Thus, there is a lack of theorization on the art of sampling itself, a point discussed in Joseph Glenn Schloss's dissertation, "Making Beats: The Art of Sample-Based Hip-Hop" (U of Washington, 2000). Schloss's study explores the aesthetics of sampling production through a number of interviews with music producers, though it does not analyze the effects of sampling upon a listener, which is the central concern of my study.

NOISE OF THE CATARACT, the BOOM OF THE GUN, the VOICES OF BIRDS AND ANIMALS" (qtd. in Morton 224).

One of the first composers to explore the use of everyday noises and sounds as musical components was the Futurist painter turned composer, Luigi Russolo, who used the real-world sounds of whistles, engine motors, and hissing in his 1913 performances of *Awakening of a City* and *Meeting of Automobiles and Airplanes*—compositions performed with Russolo's hand-made noise instruments, *intonarumori*. As early as the 1920s, the French composer Darius Milhaud changed the speeds of phonograph recordings to manipulate the sounds for musical compositions, and the Italian composer Ottorino Respighi used the phonograph to include the songs of nightingales in his orchestral composition, *Pines of Rome* (Ernst 7). George Antheil, an American composer who worked with James Joyce on an adaptation of his Cyclops Episode entitled "Opéra Méchanique," was notorious for his composition *Ballet Méchanique*, which included car horns, airplane propellers, saws and anvils.[4] Joyce himself attended the 1923 performance of *Ballet Méchanique*, and remarked that parts of the composition sounded "like Mozart" (Ellmann 557).

In 1937, John Cage, the composer of *Imaginary Landscape No. 1* (1939), an orchestration of the Victor test recordings played at different speeds on phonographs, began a talk with: "Wherever we are, what we hear is mostly noise. When we ignore it, it disturbs us. When we listen to it, we find it fascinating. The sound of a truck at fifty miles per hour. Static between the stations. Rain. We want to capture and control these sounds, to use them not as sound effects but as musical instruments" (3). In music, a listener's attention is provoked by a sampled "found sound," which is defamiliarized and thus perceived in a more self-conscious and interested way than if it were in its mundane context.[5] "Found sound" samples can seem random: a cry in the street that was recorded by chance

---

[4] This adaptation of Joyce's work was never finished. For more on Antheil's relationship with Joyce and the literary scene of Paris, see Paul Martin's essay in *Bronze by Gold: The Music of Joyce* (NY: Garland Publishing, 1999) and Antheil's autobiography, *Bad Boy of Music* (NY: Doubleday, Doran & Company, 1945). Also of interest is Ezra Pound's *Antheil and the Treatise on Harmony with Supplementary Notes* (1924), in which he praises Antheil's work. Like the "ballet" *Parade*, presented by Erik Satie and Jean Cocteau (with sets by Picasso) in 1917 in France, which used typewriter pounding, steamship whistles, a siren, and airplane motor, Antheil's work became infamous for inciting riots in audiences (Holmes 115).

[5] I use the term defamiliarization here as it is elucidated by Victor Shklovsky in "Art as Technique": "The technique of art is to make objects 'unfamiliar,' to make forms difficult, to increase the difficulty and length of perception" (12).

or a chain falling to the ground.[6] Yet "found sounds," once they are made into art become intentionally and formally manipulated by an artist while still maintaining their randomness and common, real-world quality. By sampling and reassembling raw fragments of sound from everyday life, an artist can jolt a listener out of her absent-minded reception, causing that listener to become apperceptively aware of how she hears sounds. Indeed, hearing the quotidian debris of cultural noise *captured* and *controlled* in an aesthetic form, as Cage suggests, allows listeners to hear the world anew.

First built by a Dutch inventor in 1898, the tape recorder was perfected throughout World War II, opening the door for *musique concrète*, the art of splicing magnetic tapes of recorded sounds pioneered by Pierre Schaeffer in the Paris radio station *Radio Television Français* (RTF) in the late 1940s.[7] Similar to the use of "found objects" in the collage work of Dadaism and Surrealism, this French radio technician appropriated the everyday sounds of trains, toys, and bells from the real world and placed them into a new context which aestheticized them. Though they were not labeled "found sound" sampling, these early examples of musicians incorporating real-world sounds into their compositions point to a growing inclination in the arts that was doubtlessly influenced by modernization and technology; the noises of urban experience, nature, and overheard fragments of speech seeped into the music and literature of the time, as artists sought to defamiliarize a soundscape that was otherwise received absent-mindedly.

Exemplary of this compulsion to include sound in literature is the Futurist poet F. T. Marinetti, a financial and artistic supporter of Russolo, who incorpo-

---

[6] For example, in 1965, the American composer Steve Reich, renowned for his minimalist works, composed "It's Gonna Rain," which consists solely of tracks of a modified "found sound" sample of "a young black Pentecostal preacher who called himself Brother Walker." Reich comments in the liner notes for this piece, "I recorded him along with the pigeons and traffic one Sunday afternoon in Union Square in downtown San Francisco" (*Steve Reich: Early Works*).

[7] The following examples are presented to give a better idea of the range and development of "found sound" sampling. In 1948, Schaeffer composed "Etude aux chemins de fer," which is based on sound-effects recordings of locomotives, and "Etude aux tourniquets," which is a mix of a xylophone, bells, toy whistling tops, and variable-speed phonographs (Ernst 10). "Found sound" tape splicing was further advanced and popularized in the musical performances of the 1958 Brussels World Fair, where the Greek architect and composer Iannis Xenakis composed "Concrete P-H," which piped the manipulated sounds of smoldering charcoal through four hundred loud speakers, and the French composer Edgar Varèse exhibited a light show, which accompanied his piece "Poem Electronique," a tape composition of electric sounds, church bells, organ chords, and sirens, among other sounds (Ernst 13, 17).

rated noise and real-world sound into his poetry through extensive use of onomatopoeia, claiming in his *Futurist Manifesto* (1913) that such sound representation "vivifies lyricism with crude and brutal elements of reality" (519). Marinetti begins this same manifesto with a catalogue of technological innovations, which changed the fabric of existence for an early twentieth-century society:

> People today make use of the telegraph, the telephone, the phonograph, the train, the bicycle, the motorcycle, the automobile, the ocean liner, the dirigible, the aeroplane, the cinema, the great newspaper (synthesis of a day in the world's life) without realizing that these various means of communication, transportation and information have a decisive influence on their psyches. (516)

In mixing the sounds of new technologies with human and natural sounds, Marinetti, along with the composers mentioned above, attempted to reflect the influence and pervasiveness of sound technology and industrial noise in everyday modern experience. The fragmentation inherent to such sampling techniques, moreover, gestures toward a modernist aesthetic of multi-perspectival and destabilized representations of reality.

The relation between technological advancements and early twentieth-century culture and art, a relation that consumes much of Marinetti and Russolo's Futurist manifestos, has become central to contemporary studies of modernist literature and culture. Sara Darius, focusing on the high modernist works of Thomas Mann, Marcel Proust, and Joyce, holds that "technology is in a specific sense *constitutive* of high-modernist aesthetics" (3). More specifically, the emerging auditory technologies of the telephone (1876), phonograph (1877), wireless telegraph (1899), and radio (1906), which became popularized throughout the early twentieth century, radically changed the ways in which people experienced and perceived sound.[8] Steven Connor, in an essay titled "The Modern Auditory I," convincingly argues that a newfound auditory sense of self is reflected in the literature of twentieth-century writers like Marinetti, Woolf, Joyce, and Samuel Beckett. These writers, as Connor shows, often include representations of sound technologies in their work, and consistently depict

---

[8] For more on the development of sound technologies and their influence, see Jonathan Sterne's *The Audible Past: Cultural Origins of Sound Reproduction* (Duke, 2003), Fredrich A. Kittler's *Gramophone, Film, Typewriter* (Stanford, 1999), Lisa Gitelman's *Scripts, Grooves, and Writing Machines: Representing Technology in the Edison Era* (Stanford, 1999), and John M. Picker's *Victorian Soundscapes* (Oxford, 2003).

characters listening to sounds.[9] In addition to literary characters listening to the sounds of industry and war highlighted by Connor, however, modernist and twentieth-century writers, I would argue, sought to present, rather than just abstractly describe, the sounds of the real world in their art through the technique of "found sound" sampling. Though I see this technique exemplified in Woolf's developing representation of sound, "found sound" sampling is also heard in the "Mkgnao!" and "Jingle" of Joyce's *Ulysses*, as well as in Beckett's Trilogy and short prose piece, "Ping."

Descriptions of Sound in Woolf's Novels: A Burgeoning Aesthetic

Woolf's "found sound" sampling reflects her recognition of the significance of sound in modern sensibilities and experience, and it is one of her many contributions to the development of the modernist novel. Though Woolf begins to place value on the sounds of the real world as early as *Jacob's Room*, *Mrs. Dalloway*, and, to a lesser extent, *To the Lighthouse*, her attention to sound becomes more distinct in *The Waves* and *The Years*, and reaches a climax, both formally and thematically, in *Between the Acts*.[10] Such a survey of Woolf's fiction reveals a development in her representation of sound, which progresses from descriptions of sounds to "found sound" sampling. Though *Jacob's Room* and *Mrs. Dalloway* contain some "found sound" samples, these novels primarily describe sounds, such as Big Ben striking out the hour, rather than representing the sounds themselves on the page. For example, in these passages from *Jacob's Room*, the sound of the clock is merely written about: "The worn voices of clocks repeated the fact of the hour all night long"; and again, "The frail waves of sound broke among the stiff gorse and the hawthorn twigs as the church clock divided time into quarters" (99, 133). *Mrs. Dalloway* also describes rather than replicates Big Ben and St. Margaret's church bell: "There! Out it boomed. First a warning, musical; then the hour, irrevocable. The leaden circles dissolved in the air" (2). This last sentence is repeated four times through the novel, and these repetitions arguably become a repeating sound in themselves (2, 51, 102, 203); however, while this recurring sentence enacts the repetition of the bell, it still only describes the sound conceptually rather than represents the sound itself through a "found sound" sample like the "ding, dong" heard in *Between the Acts* (199, 200, 201).

---

[9] For a summary of critics who have focused on Woolf and sound, particularly in her later work, see Rishona Zimring's "Suggestions of Other Worlds: The Art of Sound in *The Years*" (131).

[10] While *The Voyage Out* and *Night and Day* refer to sound conceptually in descriptions of scenes, they do not exhibit "found sound" sampling.

That presenting a sense of the sounds of the real world was an essential part of Woolf's concept of the novel is shown through the rhythms and phonetic repetitions with which she imbued her fiction, particularly *The Waves*. Though there are few "found sound" samples in *The Waves*, the text has an aural quality, as sound is conveyed through the texture and cadence of the words themselves.[11] Upon starting her most experimental novel, Woolf questioned, "Could one not get the waves to be heard all through? Or the farmyard noises? Some odd irrelevant noises" (*D3* 236). Woolf achieves this as her sentences, especially in the opening italicized sections, lull and lap, and the reader gets a sense of the movement of the repeatedly described waves: "*Gradually as the sky whitened a dark line lay on the horizon dividing the sea from the sky and the grey cloth became barred with thick strokes moving, one after another, beneath the surface, following each other, pursuing each other, perpetually*" (179). When she finished *The Waves*, Woolf wrote in her diary, "Thus I hope to have kept the sound of the sea & the birds, dawn & garden subconsciously present, doing their work under ground" (*D4* 11). Though these are examples of rhetorical devices other than "found sound" sampling, they affirm that Woolf sought to import sound itself into the experience of reading her novels, purposefully manipulating words that would "work" to suggest real-world sounds.

These descriptions of sound in Woolf's novels are instructive: they ask readers to be attentive to sound and to consider the ways in which sounds are absent-mindedly consumed. Woolf, in fact, declares that for the "modern novel" to flourish, writers need to put aside the convention of grand plots and a "materialist" depiction of reality, and focus on the frequently overlooked details of life: "Let us not take it for granted that life exists more fully in what is commonly thought big than in what is commonly thought small" ("Modern Fiction" 150). Woolf's inclusion of sound in her novels serves to accentuate the subtle auditory perceptions that make up daily life, and are too often disregarded as only background noise. Lecturing on Woolf's fiction after her death, E. M. Forster praises her novels for being "not about something" but that "something" itself (7). For Woolf, as with other modernist writers, representing how the senses are affected by experience, even the most ordinary experience, is generally more important than plot and character development. Woolf makes her novels *be* something, rather than just *describe* something by presenting the sounds of the

---

[11] In *Reading Voices: Literature and the Phonotext*, Garrett Stewart performs an excellent analysis of poetic resonance in *The Waves*. He holds that Woolf is able to resist "the high style of the fathers" of the English canon through "textual resistance, a thickening or impedance of syntax, an intrusion of the phonic into the scriptive" (261).

real world, along with showing how her characters perceive and are influenced by those sounds. By presenting soundscapes in her fiction, Woolf is able to portray a more full sense of the world of her characters—what Patricia Laurence discerns in *Between the Acts*, Woolf's most aural novel, as "a tonal sense of reality" (210). Yet, Woolf's various attempts to represent the sounds of the real world through "found sound" samples do not only affirm a modernist inclination to *present* rather than *describe* the reality of experience. Repeated "found sound" samples become infused with an aural resonance, which causes Woolf's prose to take on a poetic, almost musical, quality.

"Found sound" sampling in literature defamiliarizes the prose of the novel, and aesthetically renders common real-world sound.[12] As "found sounds" are mediated through literary language, the reader's attention is drawn to the texture and acoustics of the words themselves, creating a cadence and rhythmic repetition, which is layered into the narrative. For instance, the "found sound" samples, "tick, tick, tick" and "chuff, chuff, chuff," interspersed throughout the pageant of *Between the Acts* are read primarily for their sound rather than their meaning; they disrupt syntax and fail to signify for the reader in familiar ways. The effect of this sampling technique is that it heightens the aurality of Woolf's prose, while acknowledging the limits of representation. Gillian Beer makes a similar claim about Woolf's "nonce words," "scurred" and "scrurred," in *Between the Acts*: "the mimesis comes close, and falls pleasurably short, encouraging the reader to try the sounds out with the inner ear, yet acknowledging also that we are reading words" (131). Woolf's "found sound" samples not only play with the inner ear of the reader, but also bring the common and poetic into her prose by signifying the common sounds of everyday life, while simultaneously defamiliarizing the usual flow of narrative. Woolf herself proposes such a merger when she prophesizes that the novel of the future would "have something of the exaltation of poetry, but much of the ordinariness of prose" ("The Narrow Bridge of Art" 224).

In this next section, I will draw primarily upon Woolf's diary entries about World War II, her last essay, "Anon," and her final novel, *Between the Acts*, all of which display a noticeable attention to sound. I connect these texts to make

---

[12] A possible tangential argument here is that in order to defamiliarize the language of the novel, which through its artistic form should always already be defamiliarized, modernist writers had to invent new defamiliarization techniques. In other words, the art form of the novel was no longer enough to produce an effect of defamiliarization, and new ways to defamiliarize the prose of the novel had to be imagined to get the same slowed and heightened experience, which Shklovsky valorizes as the purpose of art.

the case that as Woolf anxiously shares the aural experiences of war with her community, she, in turn, begins to use "found sound" samples within her fiction to negotiate the relationship between the separate individual and his or her community, which is variably lamented as being too distant or too close throughout her work.

Shared Aural Experiences: Air Raids, Bird Chirping, and the Gramophone

In the same diary entries in which Woolf outlines her ideas for her last fragments of writing—what she calls her "common history book"—she devotes even more attention to the sounds of air raids in and around London during World War II. Far from the chirps of birds Woolf cites as perhaps spurring the first attempts at song and literature, she records in her diary the "pop pop pop" of guns, sirens, the "roar" and "drone" of planes flying low, and bombs dropping (*D5* 285, 313). Woolf meticulously describes the sound of the planes in her diary: "The sound was like someone sawing in the air just above us. [. . .] Hum and saw and buzz all round us. A horse neighed in the marsh"; "The air saws: the wasps drone; the siren"; "we hear the sinister sawing noise [. . .] which loudens and fades; then a pause; then another comes" (*D5* 311, 313, 318).[13] Her diary paints a picture of her and Leonard Woolf anxiously waiting to hear the proximity of planes, bombs and guns, wondering if the Germans had landed and if they should "go to bed at midday," a euphemism for going to their garage to commit suicide together (*D5* 293).[14]

Though I would not argue a simple causal relationship, it is certain that the sounds of World War II encroaching upon her own world, as shown through her diary entries and the role the war plays in her last novel, *Between the Acts*, forced

---

[13] Woolf also writes in her essay "Thoughts on Peace in an Air Raid": "It is a queer experience, lying in the dark and listening to the zoom of a hornet, which may at any moment sting you to death. It is a sound that interrupts cool and consecutive thinking about peace. Yet it is a sound—far more than prayers and anthems—that should compel one to think about peace. [. . .] Let us think what we can do to create the only efficient air-raid shelter [peace] while the guns on the hill go pop pop pop and the searchlights finger the clouds and now and then, sometimes close at hand, sometimes far away, a bomb drops" (173).

[14] The fact that two of Woolf's homes (at 37 Mecklenburgh Square and 52 Tavistock Square), in addition to Vanessa Bell's studio, were bombed between 1940 and 1941, verifies the extent to which the war personally touched Woolf's life.

Woolf to become more conscious of sound later in her life.[15] The sounds of bombs dropping became a signal of the rising death toll and destruction, heightening one's perception of the minutiae of daily individual life, while at the same time uniting one more closely with the community sharing such life threatening experiences. Woolf's sense of "community feeling"—the "us" and "we" of the above diary entries—was strengthened by the war, as she declares in her diary entry of April 15, 1939: "all England thinking the same thing—this horror of war—at the same moment. Never felt it so strong before. Then the lull & one lapses again into private separation" (*D5* 215). The sounds of bombs, air raids, and airplanes are one manifestation of the communal feeling Woolf sensed during WWII; and as the English listened together to these sounds, they shared the experience of war.

Yet Woolf's ambivalence and constant self analysis during the war reveals her wariness of the communal feelings inspired by war: "I don[']t like any of the feelings war breeds: patriotism; communal &c, all sentimental & emotional parodies of our real feelings. But then, we're in for it. Every day we have our raids [. . .]. I open my window when I hear the Germans [. . .]. Then the drone buzz booms away, rather like a dentist[']s drill" (*D5* 302). Written in July of 1940, this diary entry oscillates between "I" and "we," illustrating Woolf's persistent notion of "private separation" in the midst of communal experience. A month later, Woolf writes, "When the 12 planes went over, out to sea, to fight, last evening, I had I think an individual, not communal BBC dictated feeling. I almost instinctively wished them luck" (*D5* 306). The hesitancy of this sentence and the trepidation with which Woolf approaches her mild patriotism, once again suggests her ambivalence. Though Woolf affirms that her feelings are individual, these very feelings make her instinctively sense a connection with her community, as she wishes the pilots luck. By extension, the paradox of Woolf's artistic drive to be popular and communicate with the masses through her fiction and her repulsion from being identified with the masses is exemplified and solved, I would argue, in her use of real-world sounds. "Found sound" samples interrupt Woolf's narrative momentarily with the common, evoking the communal; these

---

[15] Woolf notes in her essay "The Leaning Tower" that because of technology and proximity, the war cannot be ignored by twentieth-century writers as it could for nineteenth-century writers. "Today we hear the gunfire in the Channel. We turn on the wireless; we hear an airman telling us how this afternoon he shot down a raider [. . .]. Scott never saw the sailors drowning at Trafalgar; Jane Austen never heard the cannon roar at Waterloo. Neither of them heard Napoleon's voice as we hear Hitler's voice as we sit at home of an evening" (131).

shared sounds, however, are also defamiliarized and particularized through the aesthetic form of her novels, preserving individuality.

It seems no coincidence that while listening for the "drone buzz booms" of war, Woolf is writing her most sound-oriented novel, *Between the Acts*, and her posthumously published essay, "Anon," both of which reflect a growing preoccupation with the relationship of the dramatist and audience, whereby a "common life still unites them; but there are moments of separation" ("Anon" 398). In what was intended to be the opening essay of her "Common History book," "Anon," Woolf posits a theory about the first experiences of the English with song and literature (*D5* 318). Woolf imagines a prehistoric England with a lush forest housing "innumerable birds" singing, which is heard by only "a few skin clad hunters" ("Anon" 382). Connecting these bird songs with the first human endeavors at song, Woolf wonders: "Did the desire to sing come to one of those huntsmen because he heard the birds sing, and so rested his axe against the tree for a moment?" (382).[16] Though Woolf deduces that the hunters did not have the leisure to create songs and poetry, she proposes that the "voice that broke the silence of the forest was the voice of Anon," the first poet who "is the common voice singing out of doors. [. . .] lifting a song or a story from other peoples lips, and letting the audience join in the chorus" (382). The voice of this anonymous poet, like the birds chirping, inspires participation and communes with the common audience, drawing them together in a chorus as they collectively listen to and identify with the voice of Anon. Indeed, because the audience "shared in the emotion [. . .] and supplied the story" for Anon's poetry and songs, they are always already a part of the chorus (382). In the end of her essay, Woolf laments that Anon is dead because of the birth of the printing press and the separation of the now silent audience and the isolated individual writer.[17] I suggest, however, that Woolf is momentarily able to revive Anon in her own novels through her "found sound" sampling, which brings her characters temporarily

---

[16] It is interesting to note that Woolf reportedly heard birds speaking Greek in one of her bouts of madness (For an analysis of this, see Hermione Lee's *Virginia Woolf*, 195-97). In addition, birds often appear throughout Woolf's novels, playing significant parts in *The Waves* and *Between the Acts*. Woolf's associations among birds singing, English literature, and the role of the chorus are also approached in "On Not Knowing Greek" in *The Common Reader: First Series*.

[17] In her commentary on "Anon" and "The Reader," Brenda R. Silver astutely remarks, "In both the notes and the essays themselves, not to mention her recent novel [*Between the Acts*], Woolf contrasts the communal aspects of early literature with the isolation of the individual writer who emerged in the Renaissance, and who was struggling in 1940 and 1941 to remain creative in a world where silence and emptiness were the norm" (360).

together in a chorus through shared aural experiences. Though Woolf concludes that the playwright and audience have been replaced by the novelist and reader, she combats the condition of the modern isolated artist—a condition that she in a seeming paradox attempts both to preserve and disturb—by incorporating sounds that embody the anonymous "impersonality" and "generality" associated with the voice of Anon (397). While maintaining her individual artistic vision, Woolf uses "found sound" samples to sound out common aural experiences, which rouse her characters to feel momentarily part of a chorus.

The role of the chorus figures as both a thematic and formal motif in *The Waves*, a novel in which Woolf makes consistent reference to the sounds of the real world. Aside from the form of the novel, in which the characters are loosely arranged as if in a chorus of voices, there are also moments in which characters listen to and are called to participate in the chorus of the world. Bernard, since he brings the rest of the characters together in the last section of the novel, is usually the only one who names the chorus as such. As a child, he relates, "'I hear [. . .] the chorus beginning; wheels; dogs; men shouting; church bells; the chorus beginning'" (193); and later, at boarding school, he "'lingers'" to "'listen'" to the "'rollicking chorus'" of boys playing (237). In the last section of the novel, Bernard listens to and unites the chorus of characters, as he repeats parts from each of their roles within it: "'And I am so made, that, while I hear one or two distinct melodies, such as Louis sings, or Neville, I am also drawn irresistibly to the sound of the chorus chanting its old, chanting its almost wordless, almost senseless song that comes across courts at night'" (347). The birds of the opening italicized sections often sing in chorus, though equally important is the "roar of London," the modern city that imposes itself on the characters' psyches.[18] This chorus, to which Woolf repeatedly points, is a mixture of human, natural, and modern city sounds; it is the modern version of Anon's chorus, which, Woolf insists, is "not yet dead in ourselves" ("Anon" 398). There is an underlying conviction in *The Waves* that just by *listening* to the sounds of the real world—the shouts of people on the street, the waves of the sea, the motor of the omnibus, the songs of the birds—characters play their part in a chorus, momentarily affirming a sense of community that seems timeless in Woolf's depiction. Building from Benedict Anderson's study of nationalism and the "imagined community" produced through a simultaneity of experience, par-

---

[18] On the *Virginia Woolf Web*, a computerized count of the frequency of words in *The Waves* shows that the words "roar," "roared," "roaring," and "roars" appear thirty-two times throughout the novel.

ticularly in relation to reading print media, one could theorize such an imagined community based on listening and simultaneous sound experience.[19]

To complicate this notion of the chorus, however, complete choral harmonization is never achieved. While Woolf consistently brings together disparate sounds and demonstrates how her characters function within such sounds, her characters are always already separate, no matter how much they struggle to be a part of the chorus. Indeed, in *To the Lighthouse* the narrator reflects on the ear's tendency to want to harmonize all sounds, but the impossibility of total harmonization. The sounds of the world are composed of

> that intermittent music which the ear half catches but lets fall; a bark, a bleat; irregular, intermittent, yet somehow related; the hum of an insect, the tremor of cut grass, disseevered yet somehow belonging; the jar of a dorbeetle, the squeak of a wheel, loud, low, but mysteriously related; which the ear strains to bring together and is always on the verge of harmonising, but they are never quite heard, never fully harmonised [. . .]. (212)

There is minimal attention to sound in *To the Lighthouse*, though the few instances of reflection on sound, such as the above quotation, are in the "Time Passes" section of the novel, a distinction that clarifies Woolf's self-conscious usage of sound to achieve certain effects and contrasts. In this case, the careful attention to sound heightens the melancholy absence of the Ramsay family and the emptiness of the house. Though Woolf's characters struggle to "belong" and "harmonise" with the sounds of the real world, it is a transitory unification, which in the end only highlights an inability to escape separateness. In *The Waves*, Susan, older and by herself, realizes, "'The bird chorus is over, only one bird now sings'" (242). In the end, there is a sound that cannot be unified completely, and a character that is always separate from the chorus.

Previous to Woolf's diary documentation of war sounds and the writing of *Between the Acts* and "Anon," she portrays a chorus that *sadly* lapses into inevitable separation, but wants ideally to harmonize and unify. As the above descriptions of sound are replaced with "found sound" samples, however, there is a nuance in the relationship between the separated individual and the communal chorus, which hinges on a shift from lamenting separation to insisting on and desiring separation in order to combat completely succumbing to what Woolf called in her diary entry of September 5, 1938, "the herd impulse" (*D5* 166).[20]

---

[19] Greenberg also suggests this in her essay: "Through fiction Woolf is able to imagine a community of shared echoes" (62).

[20] It is of interest to note that Woolf read Freud's *Group Psychology* in December 1939, making a note in her diary, "I read Freud on Groups" (*D5* 252).

Woolf's anxiety over communal feelings of nationalism and her disgust with a patriarchal civilization that produces war (detailed in *Three Guineas*) seems to lead her to an investment in separation and individuality in her later work.[21] Michele Pridmore-Brown persuasively argues that the noise of the gramophone in *Between the Acts*, which initially unites Miss La Trobe's audience with national songs and nursery rhymes, eventually disturbs such absent-minded reception by making her audience aware of the gramophone itself and their manipulation by it. Taking into account the historical context of World War II, Pridmore-Brown claims: "the static or noise inherent in any channel of communication, can serve to fight totalitarianism by encouraging acts of personal interpretation" (411-12). Clearly, Woolf uses the "found sound" samples of gramophone noise to allow for individuality and personal interpretations, though, at the same time, these ticks and chuffs are also shared aural experiences. This paradoxical dimension of "found sound" sampling is partly due to the fact that such samples simultaneously generate collective and personal associations. While "every sound has its cultural tale to tell," real-world sounds are also "imbued with connotations [. . .] and each of us has an individual interpretation of their meaning" (Norman 14, 1). "Found sound" samples do not need to be traced to a singular specific origin in order to signify, and consequently, they provoke common aural associations; it is for this very same reason, however, that listeners develop individual associations with certain sounds, depending on personal experience.

In *Between the Acts*, the "found sound" samples of chuffs and ticks prompt an awareness in the audience of their communal obligation to listen to the pageant. Like the "hoot hoot" and "tick tick," which "hail" Bernard and the characters of *The Waves* back to the mundane world, the songs and sounds of the play pull people from their individual reveries, calling them back to the community, the audience, the chorus of which they are a part (332): "The tick, tick, tick seemed to hold them together, tranced"; "The audience was wandering, dispersing. Only the tick, tick, tick of the gramophone held them together" (82, 154). [22] In fact, it is the ticks and chuffs that reach the audience when the lyrics of the actual chorus of the pageant are "blown away" by the wind (78). At the same

---

[21] Alex Zwerdling finds that while critics often notice that Woolf's novels "move towards a climactic moment of unification," they ignore Woolf's "sense of the pervasiveness of human isolation" (321). Whereas I see Woolf's leanings toward separation in *Between the Acts* as a positive insistence on individuality, however, Zwerdling holds that the novel has only moments of unification, and a predominantly negative tone of isolation.

[22] Bonnie Kime Scott makes a similar point, stating that the gramophone sound "mesmerizes the audience, keeping it in its place" (106).

time, however, because the "found sounds" are generic in nature, characters tend to have individual and personal associations with them. For instance, the ticks of the gramophone make: Bartholomew Oliver mutter about "'Marking time'"; his sister feel the present moment defying time and her old age; William Dodge think of beauty; and Isabella Oliver think of the future and her young age (82).[23] Another "found sound" sample that both keeps the audience together while simultaneously differentiating them is the repeated "Ding, dong. Ding" of the church bell at the end of the pageant. Though this intruding sound triggers collective associations with the "cracked old bell" and "evening service," it still serves to fragment the once unified audience, and forces the dispersal that the gramophone record heralds with the recurring pronouncement, "dispersed are we" (199). Formally separated on the page by ellipses and the "found sound" sample, the fragmented thoughts of the dispersing audience reflect varying interpretations on the meaning of Miss La Trobe's play, as well as a general confusion from the array of different cars that will take the audience members their separate ways (199-201). Like the ticks and chuffs of the gramophone, the sound of the bell, while evoking collective associations, also works to fragment the communication and unity of the audience.

The multitude of personal and communal associations facilitated by the "found sound" samples show that, for Woolf, unification does not preclude separation and individuality. In her essay on "traumatic reverberations" in *Between the Acts*, Judith Greenberg makes a similar claim for the resonant fragments of songs, poetry, conversations, and thoughts of the novel, a mix that "leaves its reader with the desire for unity intertwined with the reality of dispersity, the attempts to communicate alongside the failures of communication" (71). Though Greenberg's reading implies that the resonances of the novel are representative of repressed trauma rooted in disturbance and painful memories, Woolf's "found sound" samples, in contrast, allow her characters to make associations that are not limited to the traumatic. Furthermore, unlike the fragments of prose that Greenberg cites as spurring a "desire for unity" within a negative condition of separation, the "found sounds" of Woolf's last novel hold the audience together while simultaneously insisting on fragmentation and personal interpretations.

---

[23] This is not the first time we see the thoughts of Isabella, Giles, William, Mrs. Manresa and other characters listed, a method that enhances their separation, but also shows the reader their shared predicament of separation. For instance, when they sit after lunch and watch the view, the narrator relates: "Their minds and bodies were too close, yet not close enough. We aren't free, each one of them felt separately, to feel or think separately, nor yet to fall asleep" (65).

Thus, the "found sounds" of *Between the Acts* both acknowledge and combat the communal obligations of patriotism by bringing Woolf's characters together momentarily into a chorus through their shared act of listening, while at the same time, engendering a space in which to make a multiplicity of separate associations and interpretations.[24]

"Found Sound" Samples: The Mechanical, Natural, and Human

Though Woolf utilizes "found sound" to the greatest effect in *Between the Acts*, a gradual development in her technique can be traced beginning with her first experimental novel, *Jacob's Room*. Glimpsing into the life of lonely Mrs. Pascoe, the narrator speculates: "Washing in her little scullery, she may hear the cheap clock on the mantelpiece tick, tick, tick . . . tick, tick, tick. She is alone in the house" (52).[25] The sampled "found sound" of the clock ticking in this scene gives the narrative a heightened sense of realism, as the reader is presented with the word that represents the sound itself, as opposed to a conceptual description of the sound. Although this sound does not unify any characters into a chorus, it does present, in addition to the image of Mrs. Pascoe, a type of aural presence, through the sound of a clock ticking in a silent house. The above example of "found sound" sampling also demonstrates Woolf's complicated notion of sound: it enhances a person's loneliness and separation, as sounds in an empty room only make the emptiness that much more apparent, but it also signifies sameness by referencing a common aural experience. Reading the "found sound" sample of the clock ticking within the novel form, moreover, subtly interrupts the linear narrative of the novel and infuses Mrs. Pascoe's ordinary existence with a poetic quality through the cadence and texture of the repeated sample.

In her study of sound technology and the auditory sensibilities reflected in *Mrs. Dalloway*, Melba Cuddy-Keane rightly remarks that in Woolf's representation of sound, she employs "a combination of disparate sounds—human, natural, and mechanical—broadly diffused from different points in space," as well as a

---

[24] Though they are not "found sound" samples, the tunes played on the gramophone are also often generic, and because of this, they likewise instigate a wide range of associations from the audience, which Bonnie Kime Scott refers to as operating like a "Rorschach test, differentiating character" (107). Usually, the audience is at a loss to name the record being played; the tunes are "[s]omething half known, half not" (*Between the Acts* 182). This gives the melodies even more potential, however, to release in the audience a stream of associations, memories, random lyrics and poems.

[25] One could note that "tick" is a clichéd "found sound" sample, and hence, further demonstrates that *Jacob's Room* marks Woolf's first experiments with "found sound" sampling.

"nonhierarchical mixing of voices and noises" (90).[26] Further evidence of this is found in the mix of Woolf's "found sound" samples, which shows no privileging among the sounds of the modern city, nature and humanity. Woolf's attention to sound, while informed and doubtlessly shaped by advancements in sound technology, is not limited to technological noise. For Woolf, the noise and sounds of technology and industry jostle against the sounds of nature and human voices to reflect a modern subjectivity that is saturated in disparate sounds. In *Jacob's Room* alone, the reader listens to: the cows "[m]unch, munch [. . .]; then again munch, munch, munch" (37); the men making noise, "and then stamp, stamp, stamp—as if they were having at each other—round the room" (102); and trams in Greece that "clanked, chimed, rang, rang, rang" (138).

Within the context of Woolf's developing use of "found sound" sampling, however, it becomes apparent that the above "found sound" samples from *Jacob's Room* are grammatically awkward; they are forced into sentences, and do not stand on their own. In addition, the "found sounds" of *Jacob's Room* are usually solitary experiences for characters, and are not "broadly diffused," uniting characters through shared aural experiences, as Cuddy-Keane suggests the sounds of the airplane and Big Ben do in *Mrs. Dalloway*. One could argue that the technology of the wireless and the gramophone were not common enough for Woolf to think of sound in such a communal and far-reaching way in the first half of 1922, when she published *Jacob's Room*: the BBC transmitted its first broadcast on November 14, 1922 (Woolf's first of three BBC broadcasts was in 1927), and the Woolfs did not obtain an Algraphone until 1925 (*D3* 42). Indeed, Woolf's aesthetic innovations with sound representation develop alongside of auditory technological innovations; hence, her use of "found sounds" and her conception of sound as integral to the modern novel are just beginning in *Jacob's Room*.

An overview of *Mrs. Dalloway* reveals an outburst of onomatopoeia in Woolf's writing. In the first scene of Clarissa opening her windows and descending onto the street to buy flowers the reader hears: "squeak," "burst," "flap," "boomed," "swing, tramp, and trudge," "shuffling and swinging," "jingle," "tapping," "sprung," and "whirling" (1-3). Cuddy-Keane points out that the descriptions of sound throughout *Mrs. Dalloway* reflect a "new aural sensitivity," which Woolf is both reacting to and helping her readers understand (71).

---

[26] Whereas Cuddy-Keane's study is limited to the communal aural experiences of the characters and narrators in Woolf's fiction, her analysis of the effects of new technologies on sound perception in Woolf's time is valuable, as it puts in dialogue Woolf's interest in sound in her novels and short stories and Pierre Schaeffer's ideas on *musique concrète*, as well as John Cage's notion of opening music to the field of sound beyond notation.

New sound technologies surely influenced Woolf's awareness of the new ways in which sound could be recorded and disseminated to the public—engendering an almost wary consciousness of the potential cultural influence of such mediums. To take Cuddy-Keane's analysis a step further, however, the new auditory technology of the first sampler, the phonograph, specifically changed perceptions of sound because it could store and reproduce a sound without the presence of its source.[27] The phonograph, which Edison initially intended to record voices for businesses and family archives, was the first machine that could permanently store the once fleeting sounds of voices and noise; though it also made these sounds seem free-floating, disembodied, and potentially anonymous. The following examples of "found sound" sampling from *Mrs. Dalloway* and *The Years* can be read from within the context of this newfound phonographic experience of hearing sounds as separated from their sources: they are anonymous voices heard from the street, sometimes through windows and walls, and they are often presented as a permanently repeating fixture in the London soundscape.

At street level in *Mrs. Dalloway*, we discover a new kind of sampling that seems randomly recorded as Peter Walsh and Rezia Warren Smith walk down the street. This "found sound" sample is the incoherent song of an old woman, which momentarily connects Peter and Rezia in the narrative through their shared experience of hearing the "found sound" sample of her song. The "frail quivering sound," "*ee um fah um so / foo swee too eem oo*," is recorded and sampled three times in the narrative (87, 89). The narrator's description of the old woman singing on the street as "the voice of no age or sex, the voice of an ancient spring spouting from the earth" with "so rude a mouth, a mere hole in the earth" is rem-

---

[27] The sound reproduction of the phonograph, telephone, and radio has often been described as a split or separation between a sound and its source. R. Murray Schafer refers to this phenomenon as "schizophonia," using the Greek prefix for "split" and the Greek *phone* for "voice"; it "refers to the split between an original sound and its electroacoustical transmission or reproduction" (*Tuning* 90). In his recent comprehensive study, *The Audible Past: Cultural Origins of Sound Reproduction*, Jonathan Sterne finds fault with the built-in negative connotations of Schafer's terminology. While Sterne makes salient points throughout his study, his own definition of sound reproduction is far from satisfying: "modern technologies of sound reproduction use devices called *transducers*, which turn sound into something else and that something else back into sound" (22). The difference here is that Sterne strives for a definition of the technological apparatus itself—how sound is carried from one place to another—while Schafer's definition attempts to imagine how people at the turn of the century may have perceived sound reproduction—the shock of hearing and seeing, for the first time, a sound being reproduced in an "amplified and independent existence" (90).

iniscent of Woolf's description of Anon, the poet, as "sometimes man; sometimes woman," "the common voice singing out of doors," with "no place" and "no name," "often ribald, obscene" (*Mrs. Dalloway* 87, 88; "Anon" 382, 383). Like Anon, who sings "that flowers fade; that death is the end," the old woman sings a song that could apply to anyone about the loss of a lover through death ("Anon" 398). Though written later than *Mrs. Dalloway*, there is an undeniable kinship between Anon, the anonymous poet who connected with the masses and with whom an audience could join in chorus, and the "found sound" sample of the nameless old woman on the street, who momentarily revives Anon for the characters of the modern novel, and textually connects Rezia and Peter. Though Rezia and Peter momentarily participate in the London chorus by listening to the sample, they still fail to make complete sense of the old woman's song and ultimately remain separate, not harmonized, and consumed with their personal tasks.[28] Woolf strives, however, to bring the communal voice of Anon temporarily into her narrative, as the "reader's voice" is slowed with the defamiliarized sample, and the aural dimension of the text is brought to the forefront.

Woolf's portrayal of "found sound" samples from the street multiply and intensify in her penultimate novel, *The Years*, which documents with precision the growing and changing sounds of the city. Such "found sound" samples often signify economic circumstances: those who cannot procure any other job must sell their services on the crowded streets; those who cannot afford private houses must listen to others in adjacent apartments and in the streets below. In 1932, the same year Woolf struck upon the idea for her "Novel-Essay," which was "to take in everything, sex, education, life etc.," she published an essay in *Good Housekeeping*, where she observes: "A thousand such voices are always crying aloud in Oxford Street. All are tense, all are real, all are urged out of their speakers by the pressure of making a living, finding a bed, somehow keeping afloat on the bounding, careless, remorseless tide of the street" (*D4* 129; "Oxford Street Tide" 21). *The Years*, which does indeed take in everything, is particularly attentive to the "real" sounds of the street that Woolf contemporaneously highlights in her essay on Oxford Street. Though the Pargiters are immersed in their sepa-

---

[28] It is interesting to note that J. Hillis Miller, in "*Mrs. Dalloway*: Repetition as the Raising of the Dead," claims that the old woman is singing a translation of the words put to Richard Strauss's "Allerseelen," a song about "the day of a collective resurrection of spirits" (64). Similar to my argument that the "found sound" samples momentarily unify characters, Miller reads the song as heralding the gathering of characters at Clarissa's party, and a resurrection of their memories for one another.

rate thoughts and concerns, they share in the aural experience of men yelling on the streets, and are momentarily united with the chorus of the city. These sampled street sounds embody the paradox of modern living, where the proximity of city life unites people at the same time that it isolates them; characters listen to the real world and feel detached from it while simultaneously they are made a part of it through the act of listening.

In the section of *The Years* devoted to 1910, a year in which Woolf notes elsewhere, "human nature changed" and "human relations [. . .] shifted," Rose Pargiter visits her cousins, Sara and Maggie, sisters who share an inexpensive apartment in a "shabby street on the south side of the river [which] was very noisy" ("Mr. Bennett and Mrs. Brown" 96; *The Years* 162). Public and private sounds are consistently *described* as they penetrate the apartment of the sisters: "A woman shouted to her neighbor; a child cried. [. . .] The swarm of sound, the rush of traffic, the shouts of hawkers, the single cries and the general cries, came into the upper room" (162). The bustle and marketplace of the street, however, are not made vivid until the reader hears two "found sound" samples. First, a disembodied anonymous voice of a man comes through the window, "crying," "'Any old iron? Any old iron?'"; "'Any old iron to sell? Any old iron?'" (171, 172). The second "found sound" sample emphasizes the dialect of the voice, a technique that at once heightens the aural quality of the already defamiliarized sample by misspelling "violets," and also makes the street hawker's cry take on the role of the voice that sings in "the uncouth jargon of their native tongue," the "nameless wandering voice" of Anon ("Anon" 383, 390):

> 'Nice vilets, fresh vilets,' he repeated automatically as the people passed. Most of them went by without looking. But he went on repeating his formula automatically. 'Nice vilets, fresh vilets,' as if he scarcely expected any one to buy. Then two ladies came; and he held out his violets, and he said once more[,] 'Nice vilets, fresh vilets.' [. . .] then began muttering again, 'Nice vilets, sweet vilets.' (173-74)

The stress that the narrator places on the "automatic" nature of this sample makes it seem a predecessor to the mechanical gramophone recording of "found sound" street samples that Miss La Trobe plays for her audience in *Between the Acts*: "Number Ten. London street cries it was called. 'A Pot Pourri'" (157). This record samples the "found sound" of a woman selling lavender on the street, "'Lavender, sweet lavender, who'll buy my sweet lavender,'" which causes two old widows in the audience to remember men in London calling out, "'Any old iron, any old iron to sell?'" and the men selling geraniums and Sweet William "crying: 'All a blowing, all a growing'" (157-58). Woolf's representations of voices from the street, which go from being only metaphorically suggestive of the "automatic" reproduction of the phonograph in *Mrs. Dalloway* and *The Years*, to being mechanically reproduced on the gramophone in *Between the Acts*, seem easily akin to the anonymous "repeat[ing]" voice of Anon ("Anon 397").[29] Woolf's invocation of the phonograph and gramophone, moreover, makes sense when one considers that like the phonograph and later gramophone that connected the masses by reproducing familiar songs and sounds, Anon is portrayed by Woolf as connecting listeners through shared songs and poetry. Woolf, like Miss La Trobe, brings these disembodied voices of the street, which are reminiscent of both the voice of ancient Anon and her/his modern counterpart, the phonograph, into her narrative in order to infuse her fiction with familiar sounds, which will jolt her reader to attention.

Although the above street scene is unrelated to the central narrative and plot of *The Years*, it is crucial to the effect of realism and the documentation of the shifts in English life Woolf reflects in the novel. The "found sound" samples of the street make it difficult for Woolf's characters to live solely within their own thoughts and conventions: they are forced to acknowledge the world outside. As early as 1864, a bill supported by Dickens, Carlyle and Tennyson was proposed to outlaw London street music, a growing annoyance as the noise of a modern urban environment began to inhibit privacy.[30] The luxury of uninterrupted thought became less plausible in a modern city, and *The Years* is full of moments in which characters cannot talk or think because of noisy distractions. In the "Present Day" section of the novel, North Pargiter, just back from a much less hectic Africa, has "his voice [. . .] drowned by the voice" of a "man crying" on the street, "'Old chairs and baskets to mend,'" a "found sound" sample heard twice in the scene (304). He proceeds to drive—a trip consisting of much "hooting"—to visit his cousin Sara, and their conversation is interrupted by sounds such as a trombone and a woman practicing her scales: "The voice of the singer interrupted. 'Ah – h-h, oh-h-h, ah – h-h, oh – h-h'" (311). Woolf herself records such sound interruption in a diary entry full of wartime bleakness from August 28, 1938, as she allows the "ding dong" of a church bell, tolling for the death of a community doctor, to break repeatedly into her thoughts and sentence: "Oh thank God, Ding dong—no, its begun again" (sic *D5* 164). In *The Years*, "found sound" samples interrupt not only the characters within the text, but the lineari-

---

[29] In "Anon," Woolf writes: "He can borrow. He can repeat" (397).

[30] For more on the relation between sound and environment, see R. Murray Schafer's "Music, Non-Music, and the Soundscape" in *Contemporary Musical Thought* Vol. 1 (New York: Routledge, 1992).

ty of the narrative itself is punctured by these samples, which, in turn, induces a heightened aural resonance. When appropriated into the novel form, these commonly heard street cries and sounds become defamiliarized and attention is drawn to their presence, which allows the reader, like Woolf's characters, to register the surrounding world.

Similar to *Mrs. Dalloway* and *The Waves*, *The Years* is full of characters listening (to the war, to their neighbors, to vehicles, to people selling their goods on the streets), and aurally making sense of a city that flows too quickly for the eye to comprehend completely. The modern notion of 'self,' Connor suggests, is one dominated by the auditory rather than visual senses, which opens the 'self' to a plurality of perspectives: "the singular space of the visual is transformed by the experience of sound to a plural space. [. . .] Where auditory experience is dominant, we may say, singular, perspectival gives way to plural, permeated space" (207). This observation about the modern auditory self resonates with Woolf's use of sound in her novels, and the way she uses sound to open a space for a plurality of experience for her characters. The abundance of modern sound is not necessarily a lamentable state for Woolf. She conjures a modern city where people live in close quarters, and the conventions of space and separation among classes is inevitably destroyed by the mere experience of walking down the street. Rishona Zimring points out that in *The Years*, sound descriptions work to disrupt and antagonize characters, while they simultaneously liberate them, allowing for a multiplicity that asks characters to "make something new, something different" (*The Years* 388). Woolf often indicates that urban proximity brings different people together; sounds traverse some of the arbitrary boundaries that convention keeps in place. Lucio P. Ruotolo theorizes that characters within Woolf's fiction that allow for interruption "emerge at times heroically," and, more specifically, the avoidance of interruption by Woolf's female characters leads them dangerously close to patriarchal submission: "To withdraw from an abrasive external world presumes for women in particular an excessive reliance on the protection of men [. . .]" (2). It is the cramped modern city, with its constant interruption of sounds, that allows the Pargiter women to begin to gain the independence and freedom of living in their own apartments—not marrying, but pursuing their goals. The women of the novel cannot be shielded from the sounds of the city and the social diversity that such sounds often signal, and hence, they are not excluded from developing a modern, aurally constructed, sense of self.

Between the Acts: "a new combination of the raw & the lyrical"[31]

The rhetorical effect of "found sound" sampling is exemplified by the persistent gramophone noise repeatedly mixed into the narrative of *Between the Acts*.[32] The "chuff, chuff, chuff" and the "tick, tick, tick" of the gramophone literally act like a choral refrain in the pageant and the novel itself. As previously discussed, these "found sounds" have a twofold effect: they allow the pageant audience to make both personal and communal associations, keeping them momentarily unified in a chorus while allowing individual interpretations; and they punctuate the narrative with a heightened aural quality, as the common words "chuff" and "tick" are made poetic through the defamiliarizing chanting of the machine (chuff: 76-82, repeated seven times, 149-51, three times, 157; tick: 82, twice, 154, twice, 174, 175, 178). It is also of significance, however, that these gramophone sounds are interspersed with the dialogue and songs of the pageant, as well as the thoughts and comments of the audience, which creates a sense of fragmentation, echo and randomness in the narrative.

The fragmented mix of poetry, sounds, pageant lines, character dialogue, newspaper stories, and free indirect discourse that Woolf presents in the narrative of *Between the Acts* points to an overall instability of representation, where readers are regularly left wondering what fragments are taken from outside sources and what is particularly Woolf's invention. Woolf displaces the "real" by

---

[31] This quotation is taken from Woolf's diary entry of January 19, 1940, as she excitedly writes about beginning what she was then calling *Pointz Hall* (*D*5, 259).

[32] There are also instances in this novel that, though not "found sound" sampling, move into the realm of aural experience because of their musical and poetic quality. For example, Woolf mimics a musical tune with her linguistic rhythm and texture: "The tune changed; snapped; broke; jagged. [. . .] What a jangle and a jingle! [. . .] So abrupt. And corrupt. Such an outrage; such an insult; And not plain. Very up to date, all the same. What is her game?" (183). Though not "found sound" sampling, this quotation verifies the extent to which Woolf desired sound to be the dominant force of her last novel. Another remarkably musical passage depicts the flight of birds from a tree: "The whole tree hummed with the whizz they made, as if each bird plucked a wire. A whizz, a buzz rose from the bird-buzzing, bird-vibrant, bird-blackened tree. The tree became a rhapsody, a quivering cacophony, a whizz and vibrant rapture, branches, leaves, birds syllabling discordantly life, life, life, without measure, without stop devouring the tree. Then up! Then off!" (209). Though he does not discuss Woolf's "found sound" samples, Daniel Ferrer notices the "onomatopoeia, shout, gestural language" of the quoted passage, and remarks: "Something is inscribed here which does not pass through the ordinary paths of signification" (121). This is precisely why I import the musical term sampling as a way to approach the sounds of *Between the Acts*, which resist traditional literary explanations.

having a scripted pageant within a novel, which depicts characters who often sound like they are reading scripted lines themselves. For instance: Isa repeats the clichés "in love" and "the father of my children" to herself (14, 48, 207); the refrain of whether it would be wet or dry on the day of the pageant is repeated by different characters (22, 46, 62); and Mrs. Manresa acts her role as the "wild child of nature" and "a thorough good sort," making Giles her "sulky hero" (44, 108, 107). Daniel Ferrer writes of the novel, "the representative function of the narrative signs is continually short-circuited by the invasion of an underlying reality" (120). While the chuffs and ticks seem more "real" in relation to the fabrication of the pageant, the final curtain rising on Isabella and Giles Oliver, and the ultimate knowledge that the novel itself is a representation, further displaces the "real." Woolf consistently seems to point to the fact that though the novel consists only of words, she is in control of those words as the artist; she can shape and change with one simple sentence the fictional world she has created for her characters.

Building from this, one could argue that Woolf destabilizes representation throughout her last novel in order to establish within it her own sense of control. In order to gain this sense of control, Woolf, though bound to the limits of her art, attempts to get as close as possible to bringing the real into her narrative and shaping it. In particular, through her "found sound" sampling, Woolf utilizes the medium of language to manipulate the sounds of the real world for her own aesthetic purposes. Just as the musician can, as Cage terms it, "capture" and "control" the sounds of the real world and shape such sounds into an aesthetic form, Woolf's use of sound in her later writing is possibly an attempt to capture and control the sounds of the darkening and threatening reality of war.

The "found sound" of the church bell, which signals communal associations for Miss La Trobe's audience at precisely the point they are dispersing, resonates with a church bell Woolf herself once recorded in her diary. The previously quoted "ding dong," which interrupts her journal entry from 1938, seems to be associated, for Woolf, not only with the death of a community doctor, but with the war and her observation that Leonard Woolf "is very black" (*D5* 164). In her diary, the bell prompts Woolf to wonder why they settled in a village, affiliating the bell with a sense of small-town closeness that is both comforting and unsettling. By representing the "found sound" of the bell in her fiction, however, Woolf is able to manipulate the sound to her own purposes, as it fragments the thoughts and conversation of her characters. In *Between the Acts*, Woolf controls the associations that the bell can trigger, and has it bring her small-town characters momentarily together while simultaneously affirming their individual interpretations of the play and the separate homes they are about to go to. In a similar manner, one could argue that the "tick tick tick" of the gramophone, mechanically reproduced throughout the pageant, resonates with the ticking bombs of World War II, which had already destroyed two of Woolf's homes. In *Between the Acts*, while the artist, Miss La Trobe, did not create the incidental sounds of the gramophone that "tick" throughout her pageant, similar to the cows bellowing and the rain falling, she depends on the "found sounds" of the real world to jolt her audience to attention, keep them from wandering, and mend fragmentation. The binding aspect of the gramophone ticks calls to mind the threat of war that kept Woolf tied to her community and nation, calling upon her to rally against the Germans and keeping her always attentively listening to the BBC and outside her window. The multiple interpretations that Woolf shows the ticks as engendering in her characters, however, possibly allowed Woolf to enact through her art form a sense of mastery over this dominating sound of war.

On March 24, 1940, Woolf writes about the imminent war, and ends her entry with: "Not a sound this evening to bring in the human tears. I remember the sudden profuse shower one night just before war [which] made me think of all men & women weeping" (*D5* 274). Suggestive of the downpour that relieves the "present time" of Miss La Trobe's pageant and "weep[s] for all people," this diary entry once again shows Woolf waiting and listening for war, wishing for a sound that might represent the human loss (180). But what did Woolf use to relieve her present time? When all is in danger of dispersing irrecoverably into "scraps, orts and fragments," Woolf's use of "found sound" sampling allows her to represent and manipulate the threatening sounds around her into the unifying form of her novel (*D5* 290; *BTA* 189).

Works Cited

Baker, Houston A. Jr. *Black Studies, Rap, and the Academy*. Chicago: U of Chicago P, 1993.

Beer, Gillian. *Virginia Woolf: The Common Ground*. Ann Arbor: U of Michigan P, 1996.

Cage, John. *Silence: Lectures and Writings by John Cage*. Hanover: Wesleyan U P, 1961.

Connor, Steven. "The Modern Auditory I." *Rewriting the Self: Histories from the Renaissance to the Present*. Ed. Roy Porter. New York: Routledge, 1997.

Cuddy-Keane, Melba. "Virginia Woolf, Sound Technologies, and the New Aurality." *Virginia Woolf in the Age of Mechanical Reproduction*. Ed. Pamela L. Caughie. New York: Garland Publishing, 2000.

Ellmann, Richard. *James Joyce.* New and Revised Edition. Oxford: Oxford U P, 1959.

Ernst, David. *Musique Concrète.* Boston: Crescendo Publishing Company, 1972.

Ferrer, Daniel. *Virginia Woolf and the Madness of Language.* Trans. Geoffrey Bennington and Rachel Bowlby. London: Routledge, 1990.

Forster, E. M. *Virginia Woolf.* 1941. London: Folcroft Library Editions, 1971.

Greenberg, Judith. "'When Ears are Deaf and the Heart is Dry': Traumatic Reverberations in *Between the Acts.*" *Woolf Studies Annual* 7 (2001): 49-74.

Holmes, Thomas B. *Electronic and Experimental Music.* New York: Charles Scribner's Sons, 1985.

Kime Scott, Bonnie. "The Subversive Mechanics of Woolf's Gramophone in *Between the Acts.*" *Virginia Woolf in the Age of Mechanical Reproduction.* Ed. Pamela L. Caughie. New York: Garland, 2000.

Laurence, Patricia Ondek. *The Reading of Silence: Virginia Woolf in the English Tradition.* Stanford: Stanford U P, 1991.

Lee, Hermione. *Virginia Woolf.* London: Chatto &Windus, 1996.

Marinetti, Filippo Tommaso. *Futurist Manifesto*, 11 May 1913. *Futurism & Futurisms.* Ed. Pontus Hulten and Palazzo Grassi. Venice, New York: Abbeville Press Publishers, 1986.

Miller, J. Hillis. "*Mrs. Dalloway*: Repetition as the Raising of the Dead." *Critical Essays on Virginia Woolf.* Ed. Morris Beja. Boston: G. K. Hall & Co, 1985.

Morton, Brian. "The World of Popular Music." *Literature and Culture in Modern Britain* Vol. I: 1900-1929. Ed. Clive Bloom. London: Longman, 1993.

Norman, Katherine. "Real World Music." Diss. Princeton U, 1993.

Pridmore-Brown, Michele. "1939-40: Of Virginia Woolf, Gramophones, and Fascism." *PMLA* 113 (1998): 408-421.

Reich, Steve. "It's Gonna Rain." *Steve Reich: Early Works.* Reich Music Publications, 1965.

Rose, Tricia. *Black Noise: Rap Music and Black Culture in Contemporary America.* Hanover: University P of New England, 1994.

Russ, Martin. *Sound Synthesis and Sampling.* Focal Press, 1996.

Ruotolo, Lucio P. *The Interrupted Moment: A View of Virginia Woolf's Novels.* Stanford: Stanford U P, 1986.

Schafer, R. Murray. *The Tuning of the World.* New York: Knopf, 1977.

Shklovsky, Victor. "Art as Technique." *Russian Formalist Criticism, Four Essays.* Trans. and ed. Lee T. Lemon and Marion J. Reis. Lincoln: U of

Nebraska P, 1965.
Sterne, Jonathan. *The Audible Past: Cultural Origins of Sound Reproduction*. Durham: Duke U P, 2003.
Stewart, Garrett. *Reading Voices: Literature and the Phonotext*. Berkeley: U of California P, 1990.
Virginia Woolf Web. "*The Waves*: Words and Frequencies." 14 March 2000. 22 October, 2001
<http://orlando.jp.org/VWWARC/DAT?waveindex.html>
Woolf, Virginia. "'Anon' and 'The Reader': Virginia Woolf's Last Essays." Ed. Brenda R. Silver. *Twentieth Century Literature* 25 (Fall/Winter, 1979): 356-435.
——. *Between the Acts*. 1941. New York: Harcourt, 1969.
——. *The Diary of Virginia Woolf*. Vol. 3. Ed. Anne Oliver Bell. London: Hogarth Press, 1984
——. *The Diary of Virginia Woolf*. Vol. 5. Ed. Anne Olivier Bell. London: Hogarth Press, 1984.
——. *Jacob's Room*. 1923. NY: Harcourt, 1950.
——. "The Leaning Tower." *The Moment and other Essays*. NY: Harcourt, 1974.
——. "Modern Fiction." *The Common Reader: First Series*. Ed. Andrew McNeillie. New York: Harvest/HBJ, 1984.
——. "Mr. Bennett and Mrs. Brown." *The Captain's Death Bed and Other Essays*. New York: Harvest, 1950.
——. *Mrs. Dalloway*. 1925. New York: Harcourt, 1953.
——. "The Narrow Bridge of Art." *Collected Essays*. Vol. 2. New York: Harcourt, 1967.
——. "Oxford Street Tide." *The London Scene: Five Essays by Virginia Woolf*. New York: Frank Hallman, 1975.
——. "Street Haunting." *Collected Essays*. Vol. 4. New York: Harcourt, 1967.
——. "Thoughts on Peace in an Air Raid." *Collected Essays*. Vol. 4. Ed. Andrew McNeillie. New York: Harcourt, 1967.
——. *To the Lighthouse*. 1927. New York: Harcourt, 1955.
——. *The Waves*. 1931. New York: Harcourt, 1959.
——. *The Years*. 1937. London: Grafton, 1977.
Zimring, Rishona. "Suggestions of Other Worlds: The Art of Sound in *The Years*." *Woolf Studies Annual* 8 (2001): 127-156.
Zwerdling, Alex. *Virginia Woolf and the Real World*. Berkeley: U of California P, 1986.

Guide to Library Special Collections
This guide updates the information in volume 10.

Name of Collection: The Beinecke Rare Book and Manuscript Library

Contact: Vincent Giroud, Curator of Modern Books and Manuscripts
Patricia Willis, Curator of American Literature

Address: Yale University Library
P.O. Box 208240
New Haven, CT 06520-8240

URL: www.library.yale.edu/beinecke/brblhome.html

Hours: Mon.-Thurs. 8:30AM-8PM
Fri. 8:30AM-5PM

Access Requirements: Register at the circulation desk on each visit.

Holdings Relevant To Woolf: General Collection includes autograph manuscript of "Notes on Oliver Goldsmith." Comments on Edward Gibbon, William Beckford Collection. Letters from Virginia Woolf in the Bryher Papers, the Louise Morgan and Otto Theis Papers, and the Rebecca West Papers. Related material: 41 letters from Vita Sackville-West to Violet Trefusis; files relating to Robert Manson Myers's *From Beowulf to Virginia Woolf* in the Edmond Pauker Papers.

Yale Collection of American Literature includes typewritten manuscripts of "The Art of Walter Sickert," "Augustine Birrell," "Aurora Leigh," "How Should One Read a Book?" "Letter to a Young Poet," "The Novels of Turgenev," "Street Haunting." Dial/Scofield Thayer Papers: manuscripts of "The Lives of the Obscure," "Miss Ormerod," and "Mrs. Dalloway in Bond Street." Letters from Virginia Woolf in the William Rose Benet Papers, the Benet Family Correspondence, the Henry Seidel Canby Papers, the Seward Collins Papers, the Dial/Scofield Thayer Papers, and the *Yale Review* archive. Material relating to translat-ions of Woolf in the Thornton Wilder papers. Related material: Clive Bell, "Virginia Woolf" (Dial/Scofield Thayer Papers); 43 letters from Leonard Woolf to Helen McAfee (*Yale Review*); 11 letters from Leonard Woolf to Gertrude Stein.

Name of Collection: The Henry W. and Albert A. Berg Collection of English and American Literature

Contact: Isaac Gewirtz, Curator

Address: New York Public Library, Room 320
Fifth Avenue & 42nd Street
New York, NY 10018

Telephone: 212-930-0802
Fax: 212-930-0079
E-mail: igewirtz@nypl.org

Hours: Tues./Wed. 11AM -6:00PM
Thurs.-Sat. 10AM-6:00PM
Closed Sun., Mon. and legal holidays

Access Requirements: Apply for card of admission at Office of Special Collections, Room 316. Traceable identification required. Undergraduates working on honors theses need letter from faculty advisor.

Restrictions: Virginia Woolf's MSS are now made available on microfilm. N.B. *All the Berg's Woolf MSS are on microfilm published by Research Publications and available at many research libraries.*

Holdings Relevant To Woolf: Manuscripts of *Between the Acts, Flush, Jacob's Room, Mrs. Dalloway* (notes and fragments), *Night and Day, To the Lighthouse, The Voyage Out, The Waves, The Years*; 12 notebooks of arti-

GUIDE TO LIBRARY SPECIAL COLLECTIONS 163

cles, essays, fiction and reviews, 1924-1940; 36 volumes of diaries; 26 volumes of reading notes; correspondence with Vanessa Bell, Ethel Smyth, Vita Sackville-West and others. Su Hua Ling Chen's Bloomsbury correspondence.

Name of Collection: The British Library Manuscript Collections

Contact: Manuscripts Enquiries

Address: 96 Euston Road
London NW1 2DB
England

Telephone: 0207-412-7513
Fax: 0207-412-7745
E-mail: mss@bl.uk

Hours: Mon 10:00-5:00PM
Tue-Sat: 9:30-5:00PM

Access Requirements: British Library Reader Pass (signed I.D. required and usually proof of post-graduate academic status, or other demonstrable need to use the collections—see www.bl.uk). In addition, access to most literary autograph material only available with letter of recommendation.

Restrictions: Paper Copies, Microfilms, and Photography of selected items available upon receipt of written authorization for photo duplication from the copyright holder.

Holdings Relevant To Woolf: Diaries 1930-1931 (microfilm); Mrs. Dalloway and other writings (1923-1925) three volumes; letter from Leonard Woolf to H. G. Wells (1941); two letters from Virginia Woolf and three letters from Leonard Woolf to John Lehmann (1941); letter written on behalf of Leonard Woolf to S. S. Koteliansky (1946); notebook in Italian kept by Virginia Woolf; notebook of Virginia Stephen (1906-1909); A sketch of the past revised ts (1940); letters from Virginia Woolf in the correspondence files of Lytton and James Strachey; letter from Virginia Woolf to Mildred Massingberd; letter from Virginia Woolf to Harriet Shaw Weaver (1918); letters from Virginia Woolf to S. S. Koteliansky (1923-27); letter from Virginia Woolf to Frances Cornford (1929); letter from Virginia Woolf to Ernest Rhys (1930); correspondence of Virginia Woolf in the Society of Authors archive (1934-37); letter and postcard from Virginia Woolf to Bernard Shaw (1940); three letters (suicide notes) from Virginia Woolf (1941); two letters from Virginia Woolf and three from Leonard Woolf to John Lehmann (1941).

"Hyde Park Gate News" 1891-92, 1895 (add. MSS 70725, 70726). Letters of Virginia and Leonard Woolf to Lady Aberconway, 1927-1941. Letter from Virginia Woolf to Frances Cornford. Collection of RPs ("reserved photo copies"–copies of manuscrips exported, some subject to restrictions).

Name of Collection: Harry Ransom Humanities Research Center

Contact: Research Librarian

Address: The University of Texas at Austin
P.O. Box 7219
Austin, TX 78713-7219

Telephone: 512-471-9119
Fax: 512-471-2899
E-mail: reference@hrc.utexas.edu

Hours: Mon.-Fri. 9AM-5PM

GUIDE TO LIBRARY SPECIAL COLLECTIONS 165

       Sat. 9AM-NOON
       Closed holidays; intersession Saturdays; one week each in late May and late August.

Access Requirements: Completed manuscript reader's application; current photo identification.

Restrictions: Photocopies of selected items available upon receipt of written authorization for photoduplication from the copyright holder.

Holdings Relevant To Woolf: The manuscript collection includes the typed manuscript with autograph revisions of *Kew Gardens,* and the typed manuscript and autograph revisions of "Thoughts on Peace in an Air Raid." The Center holds 571 of Woolf's letters, including correspondence to Elizabeth Bowen, Lady Ottoline Morrell, Mary Hutchinson, William Plomer, Hugh Walpole and others. Further mss. relating to Virginia Woolf include letters to her from T. S. Eliot and reviews of her work. A substantial collection of the first British and American editions of Woolf's published works, as well as 130 volumes from Leonard and Virginia Woolf's library and a collection of books published by the Hogarth Press, is also housed. An art collection holds a landscape painting of Virginia's garden and a series of Cockney cartoons in a sketch book, signed "V.W." The center also has extensive holdings of materials related to Leonard Woolf, Ottoline Morrell, Mary Hutchinson, Lytton Strachey, Dora Carrington, E. M. Forster, Clive Bell, Roger Fry, Vanessa Bell, Bertrand Russell, Elizabeth Bowen, William Plomer, Stephen Spender and Hugh Walpole.

Name of Collection: King's College Archive Centre

Contact: Rosalind Moad, Archivist

Address: King's College
Cambridge CB2 1ST

Telephone: 01223-331444
Fax: 01223-331891
E-mail: archivist@kings.cam.ac.uk

Hours: Mon.-Thurs. 9:30AM-12:30PM and 1:30PM-5:15PM. *Closed during public holidays and the College's annual periods of closure.*

Access Requirements: Proof of ID, letter of introduction, appointment in advance.

Holdings Relevant To Woolf: Woolf MSS and letters: Minute book, written up by Clive Bell, of the meetings of a play-reading society, with cast lists and comments on performances by CB. Dec. 1907-Jan. 1909, Oct. 1914-Feb. 1915. Players included variously Clive & Vanessa Bell, Roger & Margery Fry, Duncan Grant, Walter Lamb, Molly MacCarthy, Adrian & Virginia Stephen, Saxon Sydney-Turner. *Freshwater, A Comedy*—photocopy of editorial typescript prepared from the MSS at Sussex University and Monk's House; photcopy of covering letter from the publisher to "Robert Silvers," 1.29.1976. Papers relating to the Virginia Woolf Centenary Conference held at Fitzwilliam College, Cambridge, 9.20-22.1982. TS with corrections of "Nurse Lugton's Curtain." Typed transcript of R. Fry's memoir of his schooldays. Correspon-dence with Clive Bell, Julian Bell, Vanessa Bell, Richard Braithwaite, Rupert Brooke, Mrs. Brooke, Katharine Cox, Julian Fry, Roger Fry, John Davy

GUIDE TO LIBRARY SPECIAL COLLECTIONS 167

Hayward, J. M. Keynes, Lydia Keynes, Rosamond Lehmann, Charles Mauron, Raymond Mortimer, G. H. W. Rylands, J. T. Sheppard, W. J. H. Sprott, Thoby Stephen, Madge Vaughan. Woolf-related archival collections held: Charleston Papers; Rupert Brooke Papers; E. M. Forster Papers; Roger Fry Papers; J. M. Keynes Papers; J. T. Sheppard Papers; W. J. H. Sprott Papers. Various works of art by Vanessa Bell, Duncan Grant, and Roger Fry, held in various locations around King's College. Access via Domus Bursar's secretary.

Roger Fry Papers: sketchbooks, 1880s-1920s. The papers of George Humphrey Wolferstan ('Dadie') Rylands (1902-99).

Name of Collection: The Lilly Library

Contact: Breon Mitchell, Director
Saundra Taylor, Curator of Manuscripts

Address: The Lilly Library, Indiana University
1200 East Seventh Street
Bloomington, IN 47405-5500

Telephone: 812-855-3143
Fax: 812-855-3143
E-mail: liblilly@indiana.edu, mitchell@indiana.edu
taylors@indiana.edu

Hours: M-F 9-6; Sat. 9-1;
Closed Sundays and Major Holidays

Access Requirements: Valid photo-identification; brief registration procedure.

Restrictions: Closed stacks; material use confined to reading room; wheelchair accessible reading room and exhibitions (but no wheelchair-accessible restroom)

Holdings Relevant To Woolf: Corrected page proofs for the British edition of *Mrs Dalloway*; letters to Woolf from Desmond and Mary (Molly) MacCarthy; 77 letters (published in *Letters*) from Woolf to correspondents including Donald Clifford Brace, Robert Gathorne-Hardy, Barbara (Strachey) Halpern, Richard Arthur Warren Hughes, Desmond MacCarthy and Molly MacCarthy; "Preliminary Scheme for the formation of a Partnership between Mr Leonard Sidney Woolf and Mr John Lehmann to take over The Hogarth Press" (includes contract signed by Lehmann, LW, and VW, and receipt for Lehmann's payment to VW to purchase VW's share in the Hogarth Press); photographs of VW, LW, Lytton Strachey, Strachey family, Roger Fry, and Vanessa Bell (Hannah Whitall Smith mss.); (Richard) Kennedy mss. (four hand-colored lithographs of VW: artist's proofs for RK's portfolio, VIRGINIA WOOLF: "AS I KNEW HER"; Sackville-West, V. mss. (10,529 items: includes the correspondence of Vita Sackville-West, and Harold Nicolson); MacCarthy mss. (ca. 10,000 items: papers of Desmond and Molly MacCarthy); correspondence between LW and Mary Gaither regarding publication of *A Checklist of the Hogarth Press* (1976, repr. 1986); Todd Avery, *Close and Affectionate Friends: Desmond and Molly MacCarthy and the Bloomsbury Group* (The Lilly Library / Indiana University Libraries, 1999).

Name of Collection: Archives and Manuscripts, University of Maryland, College Park, Libraries

Contact: Beth Alvarez, Curator of Literary Manuscripts

GUIDE TO LIBRARY SPECIAL COLLECTIONS 169

Address: University of Maryland Libraries
College Park, MD 20742

Telephone: 310-405-9298
Fax: 301-314-2709
E-mail: alvarez@umd.edu

Hours: Mon.-Fri. 10AM-5PM, Sat. Noon-5PM.

Access Requirements: Photo ID.

Holdings Relevant To Woolf: Papers of Hope Mirrlees contain five autograph letters and postcards (1919-28) from Virginia Woolf to Mirrlees. Also in the collection are 113 letters from T. S. Eliot to Mirrlees, and three letters from Lady Ottoline Morrell to Mirrlees.

Name of Collection: Monks House Papers/Leonard Woolf Papers/Charleston Papers/Nicolson Papers

Contact: Dorothy Sheridan, Head of Special Collections

Address: University of Sussex Library
Brighton
Sussex BN1 9QL
England

Telephone: 01273-678157
Fax: 01273-678441
E-mail: Library.Specialcoll@sussex.ac.uk

Hours: By appointment

Access Requirements: Letter, to be received *before* visiting. Photocopying strictly controlled.

Holdings Relevant To Woolf: The University of Sussex holds two large archives relating to Leonard and Virginia Woolf: The Monks House Papers, primarily correspondence and MSS of Virginia Woolf, including the three scrapbooks relating to *Three Guineas*; and The Leonard Woolf Papers, primarily correspondence and other papers of Leonard Woolf. (Monks House Papers are available on microfilm in many research libraries.) The Charleston Papers consist in the main of letters written to or by Clive and Vanessa Bell and Duncan Grant which had accumulated in their home; the library houses Quentin Bell's photocopied set. Also included are c. 900 letters from Maria Jackson to Julia and Leslie Stephen (Charleston Papers Ad. 1); letters from Roger Fry, Maynard Keynes, Lytton Stachey, Virginia Woolf, Vita Sackville-West, E. M. Forster, T. S. Eliot, Frances Partridge and others. The Nicolson Papers complement these three Sussex archives relating to the Bloomsbury Group, and consist of Nigel Nicolson's correspondence relating to his editorial work as principal editor of the six-volume *Letters of Virginia Woolf*, published between 1975 and 1980.

The Bell Papers. A. O. Bell's correspondence relating to her editorial work on Virginia Woolf's Diaries. A parallel collection to Nicolson Papers.

Colection level description may be accessed at www.archiveshub.ac.uk

Name of Collection: Archives & Manuscripts

Contact: Michael Bott, The Archivist

Address: The University of Reading, The Library,
Whiteknights
P.O. Box 223
Reading RG6 6AE
England

GUIDE TO LIBRARY SPECIAL COLLECTIONS 171

Telephone: 0118-931-8776
Fax: 0118-931-6636
E-mail: g.m.c.bott@reading.ac.uk

Access Requirements: Appointment needed to consult material. Permission required to consult or copy material in the Hogarth Press and Chatto & Windus collections from Random House, 20 Vauxhall Bridge Road, London SW1V 2SA, UK.

Holdings Relevant
To Woolf: Hogarth Press (MS2750): editorial and production correspondence relating to publications of the Press including Woolf's own titles. Production ledgers 1920s-1950s. Correspondence between Leonard Woolf and Stanley Unwin about progress with his collected edition of the works of Freud.
Chatto & Windus (MS2444): small number of letters 1915-25; 1929-31.
George Bell & Sons (MS1640): 5 letters from Leonard Woolf 1930-66.
Routledge (MS1489): Reader's report by Leonard Woolf on George Padmore's "Britannia rules the blacks" (1935); "How Britain rules Africa."
Megroz (MS1979/68): 2 letters from LW, 1926.
Allen & Unwin (MS3282): Correspondence with LW 1923-24; 1939-40; 1943; 1946; 1950-51, including letters concerning a reprint of *Empire and Commerce in Africa*, and concerning ill-founded rumors about the Hogarth press.

Name of Collection: Frances Hooper Collection of Virginia Woolf Books and Manuscripts/Elizabeth Power Richardson Bloomsbury Iconography Collection.

Contact: Karen V. Kukil, Associate Curator of Rare Books

Address: Mortimer Rare Book Room
William Allan Neilson Library
Smith College
Northampton, MA 01063

Telephone: 413-585-2906
Fax: 413-585-4486
E-mail: e-mail: kkukil@email.smith.edu
URL: www.smith.edu/libraries/libs/rarebooks

Hours: Mon.-Fri. 9AM-5PM

Access Requirements: Appointment to be made with the Curator.

Holdings Relevant To Woolf: The Hooper Collection emphasizes Woolf as an essayist but also includes many Hogarth Press first editions, limited editions of Woolf's works, and translations. The collection includes page proofs of *Orlando*, *To the Lighthouse*, and *The Common Reader*, corrected by Woolf for the first American editions, a proof copy of *The Waves* that Woolf inscribed to Hugh Walpole, and the proof copies of *The Years* and of *Flush*. The Collection also has one of the deluxe editions of *Orlando* that was printed on green paper. Other items include twenty-two pages of reading notes from 1926, three pages of notes on D. H. Lawrence's *Sons and Lovers*, thirty-three pages of notes for *Roger Fry*, a six-page ms. "As to criticism," a five-page ms. of "The Searchlight," and a fourteen-page ms. of "The Patron and The Crocus." The Hooper Collection also owns 140 letters between Woolf and Lytton Strachey as well as other correspondence, including a 13 February [1921] letter to Katherine Mansfield and ten letters to Mela and Robert Spira.

The Richardson Collection is a working collection of books and materials used by Richardson in preparing her *Bloomsbury Iconography*. It includes Leslie Stephen's photograph album, ninety-eight original exhibition catalogs dating back to 1929, clippings and photcopies of such items as reviews of early Woolf works, and Bloomsbury material from British *Vogue* of the 1920s. The Collection also has three preliminary pencil drawings by Vanessa Bell for *Flush*.

The Mortimer Rare Book Room also owns Woolf's 1916 Italian ms. notebook and her corrected typescripts of "Reviewing" and "The Searchlight." In addition, there is a 1923 photograph of Woolf at Garsington. Original cover designs for Hogarth Press publications include *The Common Reader*, *On Being Ill*, and *Duncan Grant*. The Mortimer Rare Book Room also has a Sylvia Plath Collection that includes eight of Woolf's books from Plath's library, several of which are underlined and annotated, as well as Plath's notes from her undergraduate English 211 class at Smith (1951-2) in which she studied *To the Lighthouse*.

Recent Acquisitions: Virginia Woolf's 26 February 1939 letter to Vita Sackville-West, a 1931 bronze bust of Virginia Woolf by Stephen Tomlin, and a 1923 Hogarth Press edition of T.S. Eliot's *The Waste Land*.

Name of Collection: Woolf/Hogarth Press/Bloomsbury

Contact: Robert C. Brandeis

Address: Victoria University Library
71 Queens Park Crescent E.
Toronto M5S 1K7
Ontario
Canada

Hours: Mon.-Fri. 9AM-5PM
URL: http://library.vicu.utoronto.ca/special/bloomsbury.htm
E-mail: vic.library@utoronto.ca

Access Requirements: Prior notification; identification.

Restrictions: Limited photocopying.

Holdings Relevant To Woolf: This collection, the most comprehensive of its kind in Canada, contains all the work of Virginia and Leonard Woolf in various editions, issues, variants and translations; all the books hand printed by Leonard and Virginia Woolf at the Hogarth Press, including many variant issues and bindings, association copies and page proofs; a nearly comprehensive collection of Hogarth Press machine printed books to 1946 (the year Leonard Woolf and the Press joined Chatto & Windus) including presentation copies, signed limited editions, page proofs, variants as well as substantial amounts of ephemera. The collection is also very strong in Bloomsbury art, especially the decorative arts, and contains important examples of Omega Workshops publications and exhibition catalogues. Vanessa Bell correspondence/MSS; Leonard Woolf correspondence; Ritchie family materials and correspondence re: Anne Thackeray Ritchie/Stephen family. Vanessa Bell dustwrapper designs for Woolf novels; Quentin Bell correspondence; S. P. Rosenbaum mss. 97 additional items: Ephemera Collection.

GUIDE TO LIBRARY SPECIAL COLLECTIONS 175

Bronze bust of Lytton Strachey by Stephen Tomlin (1901-37). A companion piece to Tomlin's bronze of Virginia Woolf. More than 150 additional items including Hogarth Press variant bindings and proof copies; translations of Virginia Woolf and Leonard Woolf; ephemera; including Hogarth Press: Complete Catalogue of Publications to 1939 with annotations by Leonard Woolf; materials relating to Bloomsbury Art and Artists including the catalogue of the second post impressionist exhibition, 1912, and catalogues relating to Vanessa Bell and Duncan Grant exhibitions.

Recent Acquisitions: 228 items, including Hogarth Press proof copies; Hogarth Press publication catalogues; bronze medal of Virginia Woolf by Marta Firlet; oil on canvas portrait of Amaryllis Garnett by Vanessa Bell (c.1958); Duncan Grant and Vanessa Bell designed Clarice Cliff dinner plates.

Name of Collection: Library of Leonard and Virginia Woolf (Washington S U)

Contact: Laila Miletic-Vejzovic, Head Manuscripts, Archives and Special Collections
E-mail: vejzovic@wsu.edu

Address: Washington State University Libraries
Pullman, WA 99164-5610
URL: www.wsulibs.wsu.edu/holland/masc/masc.htm

Hours: Mon.-Fri. 8:30AM-5PM

Access Requirements: Letter stating nature of research preferred; student or other identification.

Restrictions: Materials must be used in the MASC area under supervision. Photocopying or photographing is permitted only when it will not harm the materials and is permitted by copyright.

Holdings Relevant
To Woolf: WSU has the Woolfs' basic working library including many works which belonged to Virginia's father, Sir Leslie Stephen, and other family members. Over 800 titles came from their Sussex home, Monks House, including some works bought at auction soon after Leonard Woolf died in 1969. Later additions include: 1,875 titles from his house in Victoria Square, London; 400 titles from his nephew Cecil Woolf; and over 60 titles from Quentin and Anne Olivier Bell. WSU has been actively collecting: all works in all editions by Virginia; all titles by Leonard; works published by the Woolfs at the Hogarth Press through 1946; books by their friends and associates, especcially those by Bloomsbury authors and about Bloomsbury artists; relevant correspondence and original works of art. Original artwork by Vanessa Bell; scattered letters by Vanessa Bell, E. M. Forster, Roger Fry, Leslie Stephen, Lytton Strachey, and Leonard Woolf. Original artwork by Richard Kennedy for illustrations in his book *A Boy at the Hogarth Press*; scattered letters by Roger Fry, Leslie Stephen, Ethel Smyth, and Leonard Woolf. Virginia Woolf's initialed copy of *Cornishiana*; Leonard Woolf's annotated copy of *An Anatomy of Poetry* by A. William-Ellis; Leslie Stephen's copy of *Lapsus Calami and Other Verses*, inscribed by James Kenneth Stephen. Several letters from Virginia Woolf, including two written in 1939 to Ronald Heffer, and a letter to Edward McKnight Kauffer. New in the Hogarth Press Collection are a copy of E. M. Forster's *Anonymity, an Enquiry*, bound in cream paper boards, and what Woolmer calls the third label state of Forster's *The Story of the Siren*.

GUIDE TO LIBRARY SPECIAL COLLECTIONS 177

Name of Collection: Yale Center for British Art

Contact: Elisabeth Fairman, Associate Curator forRare Books

Address: 1080 Chapel Street
P.O. Box 208280
New Haven, CT 06520-8280

E-mail: elisabeth.fairman@yale.edu

Hours: Tues.-Fri. 10AM-4:30PM

Access Requirements: Permission needed in order to reproduce.

Holdings Relevant
To Woolf: Rare Books Department: 94 letters from Vanessa Bell and Duncan Grant to Sir Kenneth Clark. Prints & Drawings Department: 2 designs by Vanessa Bell and 2 studies by Duncan Grant. Paintings Department: 1 painting by Vanessa Bell, 2 by Duncan Grant (including a portrait of Vanessa Bell).

Reviews

The Katherine Mansfield Notebooks: Complete Edition. Ed. Margaret Scott (Minneapolis: U of Minnesota P, 2002) Volume One xxv + 310 pp; Volume Two, xviii + 355 pages (Combined in one edition)

When the *The Journal of Katherine Mansfield, 1914-1922* was published in 1927, four years after Mansfield's tragically early death from tuberculosis, people who had known her quite well were perplexed: the sexually transgressive, sardonic, sometime comedienne and performance artist emerged in her private notebooks as a sexless saint, part mystic, part martyr. Lytton Strachey, for one, found the *Journal* "quite shocking and incomprehensible": "I see Murry lets out that it was written for publication—which no doubt explains a good deal. But why that foul-mouthed, virulent, brazen-faced broomstick of a creature should have got herself up as a pad of rose-scented cotton wool is beyond me," he wrote in a letter to a friend (Holroyd 928). Virginia Woolf, who reviewed the *Journal* for the New York *Herald Tribune* on 18 September 1927, was more generous. Ambivalent about Mansfield's sexual promiscuity and alliances with what Woolf considered a literary underworld—"We could both wish that ones first impression of K. M. was not that she stinks like a—well civet cat that had taken to street walking. In truth, I'm a little shocked by her commonness at first sight; lines so hard and cheap," she infamously remarked upon first meeting her (*D1* 58)—Woolf's review nonetheless praises Mansfield for her attitude toward writing and for her desperate search for what Woolf terms "something unexpressed ... something solid and entire" that would deepen and enrich her fiction (*Women and Writing* 186):

> No one felt more seriously the importance of writing than she did. In all the pages of her journal, instinctive, rapid as they are, her attitude towards her work is admirable, sane, caustic, and austere. There is no literary gossip; no vanity; no jealousy. Although during her last years she must have been aware of her success she makes no allusion to it. Her own comments upon her work are always penetrating and disparaging. Her stories wanted richness and depth; she was only "skimming the top—no more." (186)

Still, Woolf's review suggests a disparity between her own impressions of Mansfield and that conveyed by the journal; entitled "A Terribly Sensitive Mind," the review invokes this phrase so often that it finally becomes an ironic undercutting of Mansfield's supposed use of the journal as a "mystic companion" (184).

As it turns out, Mansfield's friends and acquaintances had good reason to wonder about the self-presentation created in the *Journal*. In 1957, when the Alexander Turnbull Library in Wellington, New Zealand, acquired the bulk of Mansfield's unpublished writings, the scholar Ian A. Gordon discovered that the *Journal* was a "brilliant... editorial patchwork" created by Mansfield's husband John Middleton Murry from an enormous and amorphous and almost illegible tangle of material, including "four ordinary and rather empty diaries for the years 1914, 1915, 1920 and 1922; about thirty notebooks containing fragments of stories, scenes, snatches of conversation, ideas, notes from reading, quotations, calculations of household finances, unposted letters; and finally, about one hundred loose sheets of equally heterogeneous material" (Stead, "Introduction" 13). Still to come was the revelation that Murry had been in the habit of selling off portions of the material as his financial needs dictated; the Turnbull Library collection includes a letter from Murry in which he offered to sell one of the notebooks for the price of a new tractor for his farm (Scott, xiii). Most of these manuscript portions ended up in the private hands of the American collector Mrs. Edison Dick, who sometime in the 1990s deposited the manuscripts in the Newberry Library in Chicago. Assuming that most of the manuscripts have now been located, Mansfield's unpublished writings to date consist of 53 miscellaneous notebooks and "several hundred loose pages of scribble" (Scott xiii). Margaret Scott, the co-editor of the five-volume edition of Mansfield's letters published by Clarendon Press, has worked on transcribing and organizing this material since 1989; her herculean labor has resulted in an indispensable text for Mansfield scholars as well as modernist scholars more generally, *The Katherine Mansfield Notebooks: Complete Edition*. As Scott herself somewhat self-deprecatingly states, "This material—the whole raft of it—is so rich in reflections of, connections with, roots of, hints at, variations of her best work that to explicate it all would take more lifetimes than I have at my disposal. I have therefore confined myself to a presentation of the text of these manuscripts, together with such descriptive and explanatory notes as will help to convey their essential nature. This is the raw material for an infinite number of investigations" (xv).

The immediate effect of this path-breaking book will be to correct the erroneous impression of Mansfield developed by Murry after her death that to some extent still tarnishes her literary reputation. In fact, Mansfield herself had not wanted most of this material published. In her will of 14 August 1922 she bequeathed her unpublished manuscripts to her husband, but added, "I should like him to publish as little as possible and tear up and burn as much as possible he will understand that I desire to leave as few traces of my camping ground as possible" (cited by Stead, 10). A letter to Murry to be opened in event of her death reiterates this desire: "All my manuscripts I leave entirely to you to do what you like with. Go through them one day, dear love, and destroy all you do not use. Please destroy all letters you do not wish to keep and all papers. You know my love of tidiness. Have a clean sweep... and leave all fair—will you?" (cited by Stead, 10). While scholars must remain grateful that Murry disregarded these instructions, his self-serving use of the material and his narcissistic shaping of Mansfield's legacy distorted her biographical complexity and literary achievements for decades. Immediately following her death, Murry published *Poems by Katherine Mansfield* (1923), followed by the *Journal* (1927), a two-volume selection of her letters (1928), a collection of her reviews entitled *Novels and Novelists* (1930), *The Scrapbook of Katherine Mansfield* (1939), *The Letters of Katherine Mansfield to John Middleton Murry* (1951); and *Katherine Mansfield's Journal: Definitive Edition* (1954), a volume which combined the earlier journal with entries from the *Scrapbook* as well as previously unpublished material. In addition to these texts, Murry brought out two posthumous collections of Mansfield's stories, *The Dove's Nest and Other Stories* (1923) and *Something Childish and Other Stories* (1924). Murry's decision to publish Mansfield's incidental verse and fiction that was either unfinished at her death or rejected by Mansfield during her life was unfortunate: Murry did not make clear that Mansfield had not intended publication of this material, and since much of it is highly sentimental it did little to consolidate her literary achievements. Mansfield's reputation fared somewhat better with the publication of the journals and letters, although here too Murry's editorial inconsistency wreaked havoc. The 1927 *Journal* was immensely successful, so successful that Murry brought out the *Scrapbook* twelve years later, which then gave the erroneous impression that Mansfield had kept two types of notebooks, one a journal, the other a compendium of ideas about books and stories. The 1954 "definitive edition" of the *Journal* simply confused matters even more. Scholars working with these texts faced tremendous difficulty determining their scholarly integrity and usefulness.

Perhaps more damaging than Murry's irregularities as an editor was his dissemination of an image of Mansfield that is considerably more angelic and sentimental than the biographical record supports. Brigid Brophy, commenting on Murry's handling of Mansfield's image, summed it up thus:

> Once upon a time a sensitive soul was born in New Zealand, took the name Katherine Mansfield, and came to Europe, where she wrote evocative fragments, loved delicately, and died young—technically of pulmonary tuberculosis but really because life was too gross for her. Fortunately, this banal person never existed. Katherine Mansfield was in the habit of running up spare personalities for herself; one evening she would wear the decadent sophisticate, the next the unfathomable Russian. The fragile stray from elfland was the least pleasing of her creations but the longest-lasting—because it had the backing of her second husband, John Middleton Murry; and not only did Murry represent

her after her death, but throughout their life together she was trying—to the point of falsifying her true personality—to capture his approval or even his attention. (255)

As C. K. Stead notes, "Murry's promotion of his wife's literary remains brought him royalties. . . and increased her fame. . . He transcribed, edited and wrote commentaries tirelessly but in a way which encouraged a sentimental, and sometimes falsely mystical, interest in her talent. He could not keep himself out of the picture either, seeking the development of her art always in relation to the development of her feeling for him. . . He antagonized many people previously well-disposed towards her writing and perhaps ensured something of a reaction against it at the same time that he was making it more widely known" (10-11). Virginia Woolf's sense that Murry interfered with her friendship with Mansfield seems germane here: "there was Murry squirming and oozing a sort of thick motor oil in the background," she observed in a letter to Vita Sackville-West (*L4* 366). Murry similarly inserted himself into his editing of Mansfield's work, perhaps not surprising for a man who inscribed on Mansfield's grave "Katherine Mansfield: Wife of John Middleton Murry." Yet as Stead observes, "There was certainly bad taste in his manner of presenting his wife's work but it could not have been otherwise, he being the man he was, and there was no one else to do the job" (11). Margaret Scott even more generously asks us to imagine the courage and tenacity Murry brought to the task of deciphering Mansfield's writing: "He struggled on. . . and whatever he did manage to read he published, without defensive explanations. . . This courage and honesty. . . served only to harden the public perception of KM as the suffering and dying genius, and Murry as the cold, careless, inadequate husband. This was cruelly unfair to him" (xvii). Scott points to the difficulties Murry faced—a life in disarray, financial troubles, lack of familiarity with New Zealand—and concludes, "In the light of these difficulties his achievement is astonishing. Only another transcriber, coming after him, can perceive the quiet dogged hard labour he put into these volumes. He commands a respect and an admiration that no amount of disapproval of his editorial methods can diminish" (xvii).

Still, it is only now that Mansfield scholars have access to carefully edited editions of Mansfield's journals and letters (the fifth volume of the Clarendon Press edition of the letters is still forthcoming as of this writing). For Woolf scholars, a comparison is instructive. The judicious management of Woolf's estate by her family members ensured that her diaries and letters appeared in standardized, scholarly editions as early as was feasible. In his introduction to the first volume of her letters, Woolf's nephew, the late Quentin Bell, noted that the family had long recognized the diary as possessing "major historical and biographical importance" and he elaborated thus on its literary merits: "in calling it a masterpiece I mean to indicate that it is a literary achievement equal to though very different from *The Waves* or *To the Lighthouse*, having the same accurate beauty of writing but also an immediacy such as one finds only in diaries; it is in fact one of the great diaries of the world" (*D*1 xiii). Similarly, Nigel Nicolson and Joanne Trautmann, the editors of Woolf's letters, write of the decision to publish her letters unabridged: "Virginia Woolf will be read and written about for centuries to come. Her letters preserve her personality, the very tone of her voice, even more faithfully than her books. They explain many incidents in her life, and the genesis of her ideas and style" (*L*1 ix). For those of us who have worked on comparative studies of Mansfield and Woolf, the disparity between the two bodies of material has been very difficult to finesse. A slow trickle of texts—C. K. Stead's highly selective *Katherine Mansfield: Letters and Journals* (Penguin 1977), Ian A. Gordon's *The Urewara Notebooks* (1978), and most recently, Persephone Press's edition of Mansfield's writing during the last year of her life, *The Montana Stories* (2002)—have served as tantalizing glimpses of material Murry chose to gloss over or eliminate altogether.

Scott's two-volume edition finally gives us a Mansfield her friends would find more recognizable. To begin with, readers will now be able to examine Mansfield's earliest attempts to write about her friends, her family, and her love for and appreciation of New Zealand, what she later called her "undiscovered country." Roughly two-thirds of the first volume consists of Mansfield's adolescent writing, up to the time she left New Zealand for good in 1908. As Scott remarks, "Murry used only a fraction—less than a sixth—of this material in the *Journal* and *Scrapbook*, presumably because he thought it immature, which it is, and uninteresting, which it is not. It is a goldmine of biographical and psychological information, and clearly shows the emergence of themes and situations that were to preoccupy her for the rest of her life. It also, inevitably, changes to some extent our perception of her life at that time" (xviii). Readers will be interested to see how early Mansfield carved out for herself a vocation as an artist, how she claimed sexual experimentation—with both men and women—as part of this vocation, and how her boldness and courage allowed her to challenge and finally to reject her bourgeois family's expectation that she become a middle-class lady, wife, and mother. At the same time, Mansfield's adolescent fascination with death now seems prescient: her boldness easily shaded into recklessness and impulsivity, traits that lead to the mistakes in judgment (particularly about sex) that would eventually result in her estrangement from her family and that would contribute to the deterioration of her health and her death from tuberculosis at age thirty-four. As Claire Tomalin has remarked in her biography of Mansfield,

It could even be said that her story hinges on a single physical fact. By becoming pregnant during the first month of her passionately sought freedom in London, she set in motion a sequence of events which ran to her death fourteen years later, events which darkened her relations with her family most unfortunately; which profoundly affected both her marriages; which involved her reputation as a writer; and which destroyed the foundations of her bodily health. It is a bleak, inescapable, cautionary tale, reading more like one of George Eliot's plots of nemesis than any of the modernist works of Katherine herself or her contemporaries, and involving her in exactly those desperate, secret stratagems into which the heroines of Victorian fiction—Mrs. Transom, Lady Deadlock, Lydia Glasher, Gwendolyn Harleth—were so often forced. (7)

It is poignant in this context to read entries in which Mansfield longs for the succor of her grandmother and a return to the safety of the childhood and family which she believed she had lost for good. Scott observes that "[t]he struggle between the cautious and reckless side, strongly hinted at in these notebooks, was severe and, in a sense, fatal": "From the moment she knew she had won the battle with her father and was to be allowed to go, she also knew that there could be no turning back to her family—ever. Even when, not much later, she found herself up to her neck in disaster, and during all her subsequent anguished longings for a home, she felt that she had forfeited her right to go home" (xx).

The second volume of the *Notebooks* visits terrain more familiar to the readers of Murry's earlier editions of the *Journal* and the *Scrapbook*. Here again, however, much is new and of interest. That Mansfield's mission to write changed drastically after the death of her younger brother while he was in military training in 1915 is a critical commonplace, but one that seemed peculiarly uncontextualized and even unconvincing in Murry's editions. But as Scott explains, the newly published evidence of the *Notebooks* demonstrates that "Leslie was always important to KM . . . one had been left with a suspicion that in KM's extreme reaction to his death she may have been over-dramatising him and herself and the significance of his death for her. It can now be seen that this was not so. All the pain and grief she described were truly felt" (xxi). The loss of other friends, such as Rupert Brooke, added to Mansfield's anguish and deepened her resolve to write fiction of greater depth and richness than she had yet achieved. And, from 1918 on, Mansfield's notebooks increasingly detail her suffering from advanced gonorrhea and tuberculosis and her intensified search for health, even as she desperately wrote against time. She produced almost all of her best fiction during the last two years of her life, and the late notebooks in particular become a source of relief for the restless mind physically housed in a body that could do no more than sit at a table and put pen to paper. As Scott remarks, the late notebooks, "because of their urgency, constitute an even richer and more complex omnium gatherum than the earlier ones" (xxiii). To read through the jumble of unposted letters, poems, story ideas, and lines for reviews in the order in which they were originally written is truly to appreciate the unfulfilled talent and tragedy of Mansfield's truncated career.

Woolf scholars may be disappointed that Mansfield does not say more about her friendship with Woolf (the single reference to Woolf simply notes a social engagement for 1 July 1920). Yet the *Notebooks* flesh out the Mansfield whom Woolf described as vital and necessary to her development as a writer. In a letter of 8 August 1931 to Vita Sackville-West, Woolf recalls how Mansfield "had a quality I adored and needed; I think her sharpness and reality—her having knocked about with prostitutes and so on, whereas I had always been respectable—was the thing I wanted then. I dream of her often—now thats an odd reflection—how one's relation with a person seems to be continued after death in dreams, and with some odd reality too" (*L4* 366). She continued to haunt Woolf throughout her life, a "faint ghost, with the steady eyes, the mocking lips, &, at the end, the wreath set on her hair" (*D3* 50). Hermione Lee has called Mansfield's haunting presence in Woolf's life evidence of "unfinished business," the sense of regret we feel about people "with whom we have not completed our conversation" (Lee 394). Readers of these notebooks may find themselves similarly haunted, for Mansfield's conversation with the world was far from over when she died in 1923.

—Patricia Moran, *University of California, Davis*

Works Cited

Brophy, Brigid. "Katherine Mansfield." *London Magazine* (December 1962). Rpt. in *Don't Never Forget: Collected Views and Reviews*. London: Jonathan Cape, 1966. 255-263.

Gordon, Ian A. "The Editing of Katherine Mansfield's *Journal* and *Scrapbook*." *Landfall* 13. 1 (March 1959): 62-69.

———. ed. *The Urewara Notebooks*. By Katherine Mansfield. Wellington: Oxford UP, 1978.

Holroyd, Michael. *Lytton Strachey: A Biography*. New York: Holt, Rinehart, and Winston, 1967.

Lee, Hermione. *Virginia Woolf*. New York: Knopf, 1997.

Mansfield, Katherine. *The Collected Letters of Katherine Mansfield*. Ed. Vincent O'Sullivan. New York and Oxford: Clarendon Press. Vol. 1, 1984; Vol. 2, 1987; Vol. 3, 1993; Vol. 4, 1996; Vol. 5 (forthcoming).

———. *The Montana Stories*. London: Persephone Press, 2002.

Stead, C. K., ed. "Introduction." *Katherine Mansfield: Letters and Journals, A Selection.* Harmondsworth and New York: Penguin, 1977.
Tomalin, Claire. *Katherine Mansfield: A Secret Life.* New York: Knopf, 1988.
Woolf, Virginia. *Women and Writing.* Ed. Michèle Barrett. San Diego: Harcourt, 1980.

A Shrinking Island: Modernism and National Culture in England. Jed Esty (Princeton: Princeton UP, 2004) 226 pp.
Sapphic Primitivism: Productions of Race, Class, and Sexuality in Key Works of Modern Fiction. Robin Hackett. (New Brunswick, New Jersey: Rutgers UP, 2004) 150 pp.
Colonial Odysseys: Empire and Epic in the Modernist Novel. David Adams. (Ithaca: Cornell UP) 225 pp.

In *Three Guineas*, Virginia Woolf warns of "ruin," should "we in the intensity of our private emotions forget the public world. Both houses will be ruined, the public and the private. . .for they are inseparably connected" (*TG* 142-3). Indeed, Woolf was consistently interested in the social and political contexts in which she lived and wrote, from her overt commentary on the connected nature of public and private existence to her use of subtle imagery that invokes global realities in the midst of her characters' most private ruminations. Recent Woolf criticism reflects the author's global and local sensibilities, as Maren Linett asserts in her characterization of a recent critical trend toward "thick contextualization" (Linett 225). Woolf's critical engagement with British imperialism, which she represents at its height and in the decline that occurred during her lifetime, provides critics with a particularly rich and compelling context. In the ten years since the publication of Kathy Phillips' *Virginia Woolf Against Empire*—admired by critics for its important foray into postcolonial methodology and taken to task for its reductive reading of Woolf's complex stance on imperialism (Kennedy and Rosenman)—scholars of modernism have drawn out more nuanced analyses of Woolf's and other modernists' responses to empire. Three such books are Jed Esty's *The Shrinking Island*, Robin Hackett's *Sapphic Primitivism*, and David Adams' *Colonial Odysseys*, all of which include chapters on Woolf. These works address Woolf's take on empire through their respective themes of empire and national identity (Esty), the impact of imperialism on modernist constructions of race and gender (Hackett), and imperial conscriptions of the modernist journey (Adams).

Taken together—and in varying degrees on their own—these works reveal not only Woolf's stance on British imperialism, but the more pressing issue of the inconsistency of Woolf's and other modernists' conflicted corroborations as well as critiques of imperialism. Between her overtly anti-imperial statements in *Three Guineas* and her use of colonial tropes of representation in her novels; between her eschewal of what she saw as an exclusive, exploitative model of the imperial British state and her ardent desire to *belong* (through her active revisions to English history in *Between the Acts* and *Orlando*, for example), Woolf struggled with the politics of her citizenship in an imperial nation. In part because the books by Esty, Hackett, and Adams discuss Woolf in the context of larger arguments about modernism, they seek not to advance a judgment on Woolf's political positions, but to work out specific questions as they arise in individual works. In so doing, they present close readings of several of Woolf's novels (only Adams spends half a chapter on her non-literary writings) through which they reveal a basic tension between Woolf's anti-imperialism and her project of defining and claiming English identity during an imperial moment in her nation's history.

Esty addresses this tension through his focus on Woolf's participation in what he sees as a move among British modernists to establish national culture in the face of the Empire's decline. In a riff on Hugh Kenner's *The Sinking Island*, Esty argues in *A Shrinking Island* that the decline of the Empire did not herald a concurrent "aesthetic decline but [rather] cultural revival" (8). Esty founds his analysis on the concept of the "anthropological turn," which he defines as "the discursive process by which English intellectuals translated the end of empire into a resurgent concept of national culture" (2). As English universalism dwindled in the face of an increasingly unstable and dismantled empire, Esty observes an "emergent significance of English particularism" among such writers as T. S. Eliot, E. M. Forster, and Woolf. Given that these writers' careers span from the time when English universalism was available to English writers to the decline of such universalism, Esty necessarily focuses on the authors' later works. He reads an aesthetic as well as sociological coherency in the "insular integrity" of late modernist works, which "seemed to mitigate some of modernism's characteristic social agonies while rendering obsolete some of modernism's defining aesthetic techniques" (2). Thus he establishes the literary territory of his project in thematic, historical, and aesthetic terms that allow him to concentrate on an effective cross-section of late modernist texts (if not to substantiate the point that in these late works the "*latent* nativism of Forster, Woolf, and Eliot came to the surface" [86, emphasis mine]). Within the clearly established parameters of Esty's study, his point about the anthropological turn of late British modernist texts is well-taken.

Esty's argument works particularly well for the texts he selects for analysis under the chapter heading in which Woolf appears: "Insular Rites: Virginia Woolf and the Late Modernist Pageant-Play." By contextualizing the pageant play as such, Esty offers a comprehensive look at the revived genre that appears in *Between the Acts*. Esty chronicles numerous pageant play productions, and he sets up his reading of the pageant play in Woolf's novel by first addressing J. C. Powys's *A Glastonbury Romance*, Eliot's *The Rock*, and Forster's *Abinger Pageant* and *England's Pleasant Land*. It is Woolf's use of the pageant, Esty argues, that makes *Between the Acts* the revisionary history of England that she was unable to fully accomplish in *The Years*: "The pageant-in-novel design allowed Woolf to introduce a folkloric choral element... without relinquishing the familiar techniques of her distinctive narrative style" (87). The pageant serves to convey a more connected, communal artistic medium for writers whose work was generally perceived to be elitest and alienated. While Esty shows how his framing device of the anthropological turn of late British modernism does apply to Woolf, and while the pageant does introduce an unusual note of communal values in the novel, the fact that Woolf does not write a pageant as such but splices it into her modernist text, also sets her apart from those writers who use the pageant to express a nostalgic or nationalistic portrait of England. This is a key point, given Woolf's deep mistrust of nationalistic and patriotic ideology and her dread of the fascism she already saw on the Continent. Esty notes that "several times in the novel, Woolf reverses course between collective and recuperative ideas of Englishness and her fundamental wariness (as both artist and woman) about any kind of national or collective participation" (87).

In his reading of *Between the Acts*, Esty compares the implicit discourse on nation and empire that plays out in the characters' lives to the pageant play that brings them together. Woolf's basic aesthetic of gathering versus dispersal, universalism versus atomism, pervades even through her use of the communal, universalizing drama at the center of the novel. Thematically, this aesthetic sensibility signifies the rift between community on the one hand, and corrosive and ultimately destructive appropriations of community on the other. Thus the question of national community is central, for Woolf's delicate balance between trying to redefine English culture while evading nostalgia and nationalism results in such an ironic rendering of English history that we are left wondering where and how to read a recuperative portrait of Englishness. The fact that Woolf writes a pageant within her novel signals to us the project of narrating English culture. The parodic nature of this pageant, along with the novel's conclusive "dispersed are we"—chanted of course in unison—qualifies that project. The extent to which *national* culture bears on Woolf's aesthetic of gathering and dispersal in *Between the Acts* is at times tenuous because her novel offers more allegorical reflections on how communal history is constructed and reflected in art. The allegorical level of the novel is arguably as salient as Woolf's construction of a redemptive English narrative. Can we read a constructivist agenda in Woolf's critical, wary encounters with nationalism—given the links she makes between nationalism, patriotism, patriarchy, and fascism in her late writings? Esty confirms his argument that "Woolf's cultural turn proceeds under the sign of the nation because it seemed both possible and necessary to resignify England as a meaningful (but geopolitically minor) social collective" (105) by pointing to the structural and generic English codes in the novel, and finally by reminding us that Woolf's concurrent, unfinished work was that of writing a history of English literature. Yet, a strength of Esty's analysis is his ongoing acknowledgement of Woolf's ambivalence toward national identity and the extent to which this conflict destabilizes even the narrative of "national retrenchment" (107) that can be read in her last novel.

Whereas most readings of the imperial context of modernism seek out colonial allusions and imagery, Esty's examination of the anthropological turn of late modernism leads him to seek out contained narratives of Englishness that do not rely on colonial othering, but on writers' attempts to define culture within the national and geographic boundaries of a finite, contracting space that became apparent as the British empire came apart. In a more pronounced postcolonial approach, Robin Hackett points to empire as an underlying playing field for the white modernist imagination. In *Sapphic Primitivism*, she employs the methodology Toni Morrison develops in *Playing in the Dark: Whiteness and the Literary Imagination*, by showing how white literature is signified by fundamental notions of racial difference. In this view, even shrinking islands in search of collective, internal histories are located in the contact zones of empire, and the most insular of rites play out against excluded others.

The term "Sapphic Primitivism" is one that Hackett sketches out briefly as the reliance of modernist portrayals of homoerotic desire (which Hackett sometimes uses interchangeably with "female sexual autonomy") on the primitivist categorization of racial others. As Hackett puts it, Sapphic primitivism is "a mode of writing in which figurations of blackness and working-class culture appear as constitutive elements of white-authored fictional representations of female sexual autonomy including homoerotics" (3). Hackett further establishes her terms in the opening chapter on "The Homosexual Primitivism of Modernism," in which she presents nineteenth and early twentieth-century anthropological and psychological research that, in trying to understand other cultures' sexual behavior, tended to equate racial difference with sexual perversion, thus producing a climate wherein the converse was true: that is, modern writers could connote non-normative sexuality through allusion to racial difference.

Unlike Esty's focalized English study, Hackett's is somewhat comparative in nature (although she assumes a certain coherency by using the term "Euro-American") in that she presents readings of Woolf and Sylvia Townsend Warner, along with the South African Olive Schreiner and American Willa Cather. Her chapter on Woolf, "Empire, Social Rot, and Sexual Fantasy in *The Waves*," builds on analyses that have established the novel's engagement with colonial critique, and Rhoda's homoerotic desire. Hackett links these two lines of analysis through an attentive reading of the colonial imagery Woolf uses to signify Rhoda's sexual experiences and desires: tigers, Arab warriors, rotting tropical forest floors, and decaying Indian landscapes indicate a colonial locus in Woolf's figurations of Sapphism. In arguing that Woolf uses "blackness and colonial place" as "what Roland Barthes would call a third meaning—an 'obtuse' meaning that exists like a fold or crease beyond the obvious meanings of communication and signification" (60), Hackett acknowledges the difficulties in defining this "obtuse" field of signification. Her collapse of such diverse images and places as India, Africa and Turkey; maggots, decay, and blackness into the descriptor "colonial" serves her reading well, but provokes further questions. Similarly, Hackett includes the point that Mediterranean regions of Europe, referred to by Victorians as the "Sotadic Zone," were characterized in a manner similar to that of colonial regions. Like the colonies, the Sotadic Zone was seen as a space of sexual degeneracy and laxity; however, references to "sotadic/colonial" (80) imagery elide important political distinctions that might be brought to bear on Hackett's generally compelling reading of Woolf's imagery.

The notion that, in the wake of the Radclyffe Hall trial, writers felt that they had to silence and suppress representations of homoerotic desire is apt; the idea that colonial discourse was a more acceptable system of signification is intriguing, and the argument that *anti-imperial* discourse could simultaneously serve to convey hidden sexual transgression is complicated. For instance, as Hackett notes, Woolf's anti-imperial critique simultaneously mirrors colonial discourse at times. The upshot of Hackett's chapter really seems to be that an underlying discourse on *degeneration*—degeneration of nature, of the body, of culture, of empire—serves to signify lesbianism in *The Waves*. For example, Hackett concludes that "a description of Rhoda in Bernard's summary similarly aligns her with corruption as well as with colonial places... there is also a parallel between Bernard's image of sexual love and Rhoda's image of rot and blackness" (82). To the extent that degeneration was equated with racial and sexual otherness, colonialism functions as a stand-in. Hackett's rich and provocative, if not entirely disentangled, discussion does successfully achieve her stated goal: "to disrupt the coherence of whiteness as well as heterosexuality" (150).

Hackett alludes to Greek legacy in passing in her discussions of the Sotadic factor in modernist fiction and of course in her use of the figure of Sappho. In another project that considers Greek legacy much more explicitly, David Adams builds on such work as Karen Lawrence's excellent *Penelope Voyages* to examine modernists' reception of the epic tradition in *Colonial Odysseys: Empire and Epic in the Modernist Novel*. Because Adams' emphasis is mostly on odysseys and epics in his examination of Woolf, Forster, James Joyce, Joseph Conrad, and Evelyn Waugh, empire serves less as an integral topic than as a historical backdrop for his analysis of the modernist odyssey. Empire functions as a global totality that orchestrates and controls modernist voyages, and serves to fill in geographical and ontological maps. The modern attempt to transpose the epic tradition of exploring and establishing the self through odyssey is inflected by an imperial context which creates a subtext of "anxiety about imperial disintegration, transforming the odyssey into an increasingly morbid reflection on national identity and the meaning of 'home'" (3). If the classical odyssey serves as a means of controlling and defining one's destiny, the colonial odyssey exposes philosophical questions about home and death that persist against the backdrop of the geopolitical totality of empire. In the face of the modernist fragmentation of absolutes, Adams proposes that modernist writers enact a "reoccupation" of this empty metaphysical space: "The attempt to answer theological questions with secular ideas, to fill the god-shaped hole with human constructs, is what Hans Blumenberg calls 'reoccupation'" (4). It is this idea of reoccupation that Adams pursues in his analysis of modernist works.

Adams begins appropriately with Homer, Virgil, and Dante in order to establish the epic tradition upon which modernists build. The chapter on Woolf, "Shadows of a 'Silver Globe': Woolf's Reconfiguration of the Darkness," is divided into an analysis of Woolf's engagement with classical antiquity and with modern Greece in her letters, diaries, travels, and others' accounts, and a reading of two novels. Given his argument that modernist voyages emphasize the voyage *out*, and that they characteristically confront eroding truths, Adams' most convincing section is on *The Voyage Out*. Although he includes an analysis of *Ulysses* earlier in the book, and although he notes the important parallel odyssey theme in *Mrs. Dalloway*, he opts for *To the Lighthouse* to conclude his argument, reading in it a contraction of the themes of Woolf's first novel. Between the two novels, he charts a move away from the modernist desire to "reoccupy" the empty space of death in Woolf: Rachel Vinrace voyages out into the perilous emptiness of secular death whereas Lily Briscoe develops a willingness to live with the trace of the unredeemable emptiness of death in her art. Woolf, he concludes, "displays a tension... between the pressure to reoccupy the epistemological position and the need to excise it from the body of human knowledge" (201). Adams meditates on questions of totality, epistemological and ontological reoccupation—in short what Rachel refers to as "the meaning of it all"—as such broad philosophical ideas become manifest in modernist revisions of the epic tradition, subtly inflected by the context of empire.

The "thick" context of empire is explored in these readings of Woolf and other modernists as it bears on aesthetic, cultural, political, and philosophical questions. No longer is the question that of judging these writers' politics, but rather of understanding how the larger politics of location, race, and nation are negotiated in modernist texts. Woolf's anti-imperialism emerges as a major source of tension in her work, whether with regard to her ambivalent position on nationalism or her aesthetic participation in colonial othering. These three books address her complex responses to empire through a variety of critical lenses that combine postcolonial theory with cultural studies, structuralist, feminist, and historicist angles, thus indicating a rich and expanding area of Woolf criticism and showing that—as is always the case with Woolf— "[f]ifty pairs of eyes were not enough to get round that one woman" (*TTL* 198).

—Erica L. Johnson, *Chatham College*

Works Cited

Kennedy, Jennifer T. Review of *Virginia Woolf Against Empire* by Kathy Phillips. *Modernism/modernity* 3.2 (1996): 123-4.

Linnet, Maren. "From Supernova to Manuscript Page: Circling Woolf." *Modern Fiction Studies* 50.1 (Spring 2004): 224-240.

Rosenman, Ellen Bayuk. Review of *Virginia Woolf Against Empire* by Kathy Phillips. *Modern Fiction Studies* 42.1 (1996): 176-7.

Woolf, Virginia. *Three Guineas.* New York: Harcourt Brace, 1938.

——. *To the Lighthouse.* San Diego: Harcourt Brace, 1989.

Psychoanalysis, Psychiatry, and Modernist Literature. Kylie Valentine (Hampshire and New York: Palgrave Macmillan) viii + 224 pp.
Cultures of the Death Drive: Melanie Klein and Modernist Melancholia. Esther Sanchez-Pardo. (Durham: Duke UP, 2003) xii + 490 pp.

The depiction of Virginia Woolf as a neurotic recluse in Stephen Daldry's film version of Michael Cunningham's *The Hours* will continue to provide occasions to defend the other Woolf: the public intellectual, the busy publisher, the humorous conversationalist, etc. Many Woolf scholars have stalwartly resisted fetishizing mental illness, in general, and Woolf's mental illness, in particular, as a source of creativity. And anyone who teaches Woolf in the United States is accustomed to fielding questions from students indicating that in the culture at large, the received wisdom on Woolf begins with the assumption that she was depressed, mad, schizophrenic, or some combination thereof. An abiding fear is that Woolf's texts will simply be mined for evidence of her mental condition, not appreciated as works of art. Yet one hankers at the very least to acknowledge mental illness, and to understand some of its causes and effects. Where to begin dismantling the clichés about Woolf's troubled state of mind? How to find the subtle vocabulary that defetishizes, without dismissing, Woolf's mental illness? Works such as Roger Poole's *The Unknown Virginia Woolf*, Thomas Caramagno's *The Flight of the Mind: Virginia Woolf's Art and Manic-Depressive Illness*, Hermione Lee's biography of Woolf, Louise DeSalvo's *Virginia Woolf: The Impact of Childhood Sexual Abuse On Her Life and Work*, and Elizabeth Abel's *Virginia Woolf and the Fictions of Psychoanalysis*, to mention just a few, already provide thoroughgoing investigations of the psychodynamics of Woolf's life and work. Yet two new studies of psychoanalysis and modernism, both representative of interdisciplinary work in the field of cultural studies, add a potentially rich source of answers to questions about how to understand mental distress in a larger context, while at the same time raising others: what are the advantages and limits of interdisciplinary work for interpreting literary texts? Does the historicization of psychoanalysis dislodge or bolster its role as a master narrative? Do Woolf's mental troubles—or those of her contemporaries—arise from personal losses and traumas, or from cultural ones? Which stories about "the modernist era" do we find to be most useful—or, to pose the question in a less postmodern vein, which account is the accurate one, and what methodology will produce it?

Kylie Valentine's study seeks to explain how psychoanalysis, psychiatry, and modernism produced different models of madness, always with an eye toward treating the *experience* of madness as unique and complex. The emphasis on experience is important. Valentine's introduction contains a miniature critique of cultural studies, in general, and Foucault's contributions to it, in particular:

"Experience deserves to be trusted as a category with connections to discourse, but not as reducible to it" (19). I take Valentine to mean "discourse" in the sense of Foucault's "discursive practice," with its institutional base. Valentine seeks to uncover non-institutional, individual experiences and languages. Still, much of Valentine's work depends on establishing madness as a cultural and clinical construction. The first three chapters, on "Modernism," "Psychiatry," and "Madness," provide illuminating discussions of each, while carefully synthesizing all three. The second half of the book delves into the work of individual writers, all women, who were, in their lives and their work, linked to madness: Woolf, Emily Holmes Coleman, and Antonia White. Valentine's book offers two major tools of analysis to Woolf scholars: the new ways in which she historicizes madness, and the comparison of Woolf to other, less well known, modernist women writers. Although Valentine does not pursue this line of thought, another fruitful comparison would be between Bloomsbury's intimate circle, and that of Hayford Hall, the Dorset estate where Peggy Guggenheim played hostess not only to Coleman and White, but to Djuna Barnes and others.

The introduction formulates ideas that resonate throughout the book: the need for understanding how the institutions of psychiatry and psychoanalysis developed in tandem, often in competition with each other; the need for revising certain feminist readings of madness (while at the same time offering a revision that will, it turns out, be feminist in its own right); the attraction of a version of modernism that foregrounds social change: "Feminist and working-class mobilisation and transformation in the field of class relations rendered social revolution an imaginative possibility; a revolution that was both desired and feared" (24). Feminist investigations into the history of madness "tend to neglect the professional and institutional history of psychiatry" (11); thus, Valentine intends to correct previous omissions. Valentine's critique of feminism cuts deeper, however. In particular, she points out that arguments such as Elaine Showalter's that view women's madness as a form of political oppression do "violence to the varieties of experiential mental distress and the consequences of being diagnosed with schizophrenia" (18). Throughout the book, then, Valentine is always careful not to simplify "the complexity and individuality of mental distress" (18) even as she provides histories of both institutions and discourses. In fact, by devoting the last several chapters to literary texts, Valentine valorizes literature itself as something closer to "experience" than to "discourse."

The chapters on modernism, psychiatry, and madness provide both lucid surveys and detailed textual explications that persuade the reader of the rewards of carefully executed interdisciplinary work, and of the difficulty of disentangling madness from discourse analysis. In explaining the connections between literature and psychoanalysis, the chapter on "Modernism" discusses H.D.'s analysis with Freud, Ernest Jones' reading of Shakespeare compared with T. S. Eliot's, and the circulation of the term "ego" in the modernist milieu in relation to James Strachey's translation of "ich" as "ego" (53). The chapter also contains a compelling comparison of Freud's construction of the female reader's "fevered, absent reading" (46) with Eliot's masculinization of modernism in "Tradition and the Individual Talent" (47-8). After setting up this gendered opposition, however, Valentine emphasizes the shared concerns of literature and psychoanalysis: "For all the modernist emphasis on the technical and impersonal, modernist literature was concerned with sensation, emotions, and desire. And for all its technical analysis of literature, psychoanalysis was concerned with the same things" (51).

In the chapters on "Psychiatry" and "Madness" Valentine offers a nuanced, scrupulously detailed account of the tension between mentalist and physicalist approaches to madness in the interwar struggles for authority of psychoanalysis and psychiatry. The relevance to literary interpretation: to provide access to "the visibility of madness to the non-medical public, and to modernist writers and artists in particular" (64). Valentine discusses psychoanalysis and psychiatry in terms of struggles for authority, including a detailed section on the role of women's work in British psychoanalysis (that work, Valentine persuasively argues, was central, not marginal). Valentine also analyses the impact of World War I on both institutions, especially the "therapeutic optimism associated with the war neuroses [which] produced a kind of speculative optimism about treating the psychoses" (80); later, pessimism overtook the initial optimism, and anti-analysts targeted that pessimism in their attacks on psychoanalysis. As Valentine states in the introduction, the beginning of World War II marked both the end of the modernist era and physicalist psychiatry's defeat of psychoanalysis (a defeat, one guesses, that Valentine mourns, and one that may explain, in part, why psychoanalysis, along with modernism, has found some refuge in the academy).

Valentine moves on from the analysis of institutions to explore ways in which madness may be understood in its "historical and geographical specificity" (96). To do this, Valentine turns away from broad institutional histories to "narratives: by patients, clinicians, theoreticians, novelists, critics," raising the questions "what texts to believe, and what reading practices to engage" (99). Valentine privileges the work of novelists, who also happen to be patients and critics. The chapter on "Madness" lays out the reasons, then, for the book's second half: its literary interpretations. "[M]odernist writers such as H.D., Virginia Woolf, Emily Holmes Coleman and Antonia White analyse the political inflections of madness, the institutional forms of psychiatry, the discourses of psychoanalysis, and experiential distress . . . modernist literature introduces a new recognition of the sexed production of madness and feminist analysis of this production" (101). Wishing, again, to argue that "experience" is irreducible to "discourse," Valentine ends up valorizing literary expression as able to provide "particularity" (93) and access to "experiential madness" while also asking the reader to bear in mind "culturally recognisable madness" and "madness as clinical construction" (108). Not just any literary expression, however: modernism especially is understood by Valentine to possess "confidence and optimism . . . an environment where literature seemed not only important, but the most important force in social change" (61). As Valentine moves towards modernist literature, she foregrounds its role as an instrument of change, and in particular the feminist value of women's writing that provides "a new framework of interpreting madness politically" (110).

Valentine emphasizes Woolf's, White's, and Coleman's triple roles as creative writers, patients, and critics. Each in her own way is a feminist critic of the discourses constructing madness; each knows madness from experience, but writing confers a privileged outsider status in relation to the institutions that seek to categorize the madwoman. Each, then, is not a victim, but actively involved in self-creation. Thus: "[Woolf] was aware of, and deployed, the clinical and legal differentiations between mental illness, feeble-mindedness and idiocy" (139); "Woolf's work contributed to the imaginative possibilities of modernism: connecting a transformation of the self to a transformation of the social" (137); "Woolf was a conscious and deliberate translator of the cultural and clinical representations of madness circulating through the modernist field" (142); and "[m]adness does not dominate Woolf's writing" (148). Much of Valentine's representation of Woolf as a critic, rather than as a victim, of madness relies on a lengthy reading of *Mrs. Dalloway* that makes the uncontroversial claim that Septimus Smith is not an autobiographical figure. One wishes for more: it would be useful to read Valentine's commentaries, in light of her careful institutional histories, on other "mad" figures in Woolf's fiction (e.g. Rhoda, Rachel Vinrace, or Sara Pargiter), or on the voice of "On Being Ill." However, scholars and teachers of Woolf will find that White's *Beyond the Glass* and Coleman's *The Shutter of Snow* provide intriguing contextualization for Woolf's work within the larger framework of a "range of modernist interventions into madness and psychiatry [that] is broader than has been acknowledged" (196). Valentine presents White's and Coleman's writing as deliberate and self-conscious confrontations with madness, framing their work, in distinction from Woolf's, as "minor" literature in Deleuze and Guattari's sense: the "use of a dominant language by a minority" (175). Of White, for example, Valentine writes that she "is able to stage a meaningful, politicized madness that is both response to and product of a femininity that is staged in the same way" (186); of Coleman: "The privileging of Marthe's perspective in the text is a redress to [a] power imbalance; as is her consistent awareness of the positions of others while they have no awareness of hers" (190). Increasingly, Valentine uses verbs such as "intervene" and "undermine" to characterize Coleman's and White's texts as self-aware commentary on the social and cultural position of the sufferer of madness.

Whereas the literary "interventions" of Valentine's study arise from a version of modernism defined as an optimistic "moment of creative and cultural possibility" (147), Sanchez-Pardo zeroes in on a more troubled modernism in which literature is viewed less as an intervention, and more as evidence of struggles with a culturally pervasive psychic disorder: melancholia. Although "melancholia" is defined as "an obsolescent term for what is now called depression" in Charles Rycroft's *A Critical Dictionary of Psychoanalysis*, it has not lost its currency in literary studies, nor is it likely to, although it will probably always have to bow to the authority of "trauma." Freud's 1917 essay "Mourning and Melancholia," with its distinction between normal and abnormal reponses to loss, provides the basic taxonomy of psychic states deployed by such interpreters of literary elegy as Peter Sacks (*The English Elegy: Studies in the Genre from Spenser to Yeats*) and Jahan Ramazani (*Poetry of Mourning: The Modern Elegy from Hardy to Heaney*). Melanie Klein's studies of infants and children, and her theory that normal and abnormal responses to loss (of the mother) must be understood as intrinsic to all development, have also proven to be of great interest to readers of literary, and especially—though not exclusively—modernist texts. Elizabeth Abel's 1989 *Virginia Woolf and the Fictions of Psychoanalysis* is the groundbreaking work and remains the outstanding resource on Klein and her relevance to reading Woolf; Lyndsey Stonebridge's 1998 *The Destructive Element: British Psychoanalysis and Modernism* is more general, but also contains an extensive look at *Between the Acts* through the lens of Kleinian psychoanalysis.

Sanchez-Pardo's study again reads Woolf with Klein, in a lengthy chapter that compares maternal absence in *To the Lighthouse* with maternal absence in the "lit houses" to be found in the paintings of Rene Magritte (who, like Woolf, lost his mother at the age of thirteen). In the end, Sanchez-Pardo reads *To the Lighthouse* as an irredeemably melancholy text, and Lily, in particular, as a case study in melancholia. There is no Kleinian reparation, no triumph over loss, no "normal" work of mourning, finally, in Sanchez-Pardo's interpretation of *To the Lighthouse*. "Woolf herself questions the reparative quality of art by presenting instead a *Künstlerroman* about the failures of the artist and the fault lines of the artistic career and the artistic paradigm in modernism" (271). Lily's "vision" at the end of the novel may be mere "delusion" (271), and the "quasi-mystical modernist epiphanic moment" may indeed be "the psychotic delirium of hallucination" (272). The end of the novel leaves Sanchez-Pardo with the unanswered, and for her unanswerable, question: "where is the labor of melancholia to be closed and how can we begin the work of mourning?" (272). The question is unanswerable because Sanchez-Pardo wants to ask, in the end, whether all reading and writing are "entombments" or "memorials to all the cultural and emotional losses of our pasts" (272). If, as she speculates, all reading and writing express a "deeper melancholia," then, she implies, reading and writing are not reparative, do not help mourners overcome loss, but instead allow the reader or writer to languish in a state, among other things, of self-destruction. That writers or artists are prone to self-destruction has a familiar ring to it, whether we find it in "the very temple of Delight" where Keats' Melancholy has her "sovran shrine" or in the posthumous fascination with rock musician and suicide Elliott Smith. The list goes on.

Sanchez-Pardo does not consistently argue that all reading and writing are melancholic. Rather, she intends to single out the melancholia of modernism in particular. This raises important questions. Can the artistic innovations of modernism be likened to, or explained by, certain psychic states? Is modernism peculiarly melancholic, and if so, because of what historical circumstances? Regarding the former question, Sanchez-Pardo asserts that "modernist art and literature, with their emphasis on spatialization and the relevance of forms, reveal a troubled aesthetic state pervaded with melancholia" (215). Like others, Sanchez-Pardo has been struck and perhaps troubled by the interior landscape suggested by the Kleinian psychoanalysis of infants and children, a landscape littered with shattered lost objects, or, as she puts it, "a derelict space in ruins" (215). Since "fragmentation" is one of the most common terms to be found in descriptions of modernist art, it is tempting to find a meaningful analogy between Klein's broken worlds and modernism's. The next step is to find a common cause for both, which Sanchez-Pardo indeed asserts: "After the golden age of melancholy in the Renaissance, modernism appears with a revival of the melancholic affliction in a specific historical conjuncture after World War I" (215). Sanchez-Pardo periodizes modernism as a movement that takes place "between the two world wars" (217) and she defines the "cultures of the death drive" as "a variety of forces that produce melancholia . . . . after the wars" (194) (there is some confusion, therefore, about whether modernism ends with, or continues after, World War II). The impact of World War I on modernist writing is not to be underestimated, and Sanchez-Pardo is not alone in finding the "pervasion" of postwar melancholia. Ramazani, for example, argues that in the twentieth century, poetic elegies are violent and recalcitrant, and emphasize masochism, irresolution, irredemption, aggression, and self criticism. Their psychic basis is in melancholia, and they create a cultural space for grief in opposition to a dominant discourse that anaesthetizes death and idealizes consolation. In *The Ability to Mourn: Disillusionment and the Social Origins of Psychoanalysis*, Peter Homans also makes a strong case for singling out the 1920s as a period in which the concerns of British object relations can be understood to arise from the conditions of a grief-stricken society unable to complete the work of mourning. The question remains, however, whether modernist melancholia begins with World War I. After all, Sanchez-Pardo defines melancholia as "a malaise affecting the 'privileged' victims of a new urban, industrialized, and capitalist world order" (194) which did not begin in 1914; she also claims that these victims are "women, lesbians, gay men, blacks, Jews, ethnic minorities, and in general those who suffered the consequences of deterritorialization and diaspora" (194), again, not a victimization originating with World War I. The historical vagueness of Sanchez-Pardo's book is belied by the brevity of what might have been the most important chapter, and should, perhaps, have been the introductory one, "Modernist Cultures of the Death Drive."

The driving passion of Sanchez-Pardo's study is for the explanations offered by Kleinian object-relations, to which seven out of twelve chapters are devoted. The remaining five chapters concern, aside from the one chapter discussed above, Kleinian analyses of textual and visual materials: by Woolf (with Magritte), Lytton Strachey, Djuna Barnes, and Countee Cullen. By contrast with Valentine's chosen literary works, Sanchez-Pardo's tend not to offer interventions or commentary; instead, they are examples of deadlocked melancholia. The exception is Barnes, whose oeuvre, Sanchez-Pardo argues, destabilizes gender and sexuality, deciphers cultural inscriptions, and "unveils the workings of power and its material effects" (342). One finds here, then, something closer to Valentine's version of optimistic modernism, celebrated by Sanchez-Pardo as a "superb disruptive potential" (342).

The power of literature to disrupt, intervene, undermine, etc. is a topic raised by both studies because both have been written in the context of another institutional question: in the era of cultural studies, should departments of cultural studies replace departments of literature? Or should literature maintain a separate place, and for what purpose? Valentine's book, for all its claims for the oppositional stances taken by Woolf, Coleman, and White, brings up this topic with great ambivalence. On the one hand, Valentine rejects the notion that "the sensitivity of modernist practitioners was so advanced that they were hyperaware of the rhetoric of politics and science going on around them" (129). Yet this "hyper-awareness" is very close to the qualities Valentine discerns in the texts of Woolf, Coleman, and White, allowing her to make a claim for the value of these women's writing *qua* women's writing that is ultimately a political, not a literary one. On the other hand, Valentine's book ends with: "Literature, especially literature written by women, or people called mad, or both, should be treated as literature, not as case notes or therapeutic practice. To do otherwise misrecognises the ambitions and achievements of those writing, and the field to which that literature contributes" (202). Sanchez-Pardo's view of literature is, ultimately, redemptive. In her conclusion, she writes "What does a writer do when the world collapses but write? In writing and reading, we search for meaning and perspective and lessons to be shared. Even in its most extreme cases the discourses of melancholia and trauma offer a kind of survivor's guide, not just for those who suffer from some traumatic loss but for anyone who is, after all, only human" (393). One might build on Valentine's concluding statement a case for maintaining the study of literature as a field separate from that of cultural studies, and from Sanchez-Pardo's a post-post-structuralist appeal for an appreciation of literature's ability to supply meaning and construct the world anew, rather than toss readers into a terrifying delirium of infinite play. "Let us then leave it to the poets to tell us what the dream is," Woolf wrote in *Three Guineas*.

Madness and melancholia are marketable. One can promote literature as an elite enterprise, accessible only to those with the right educational or emotional background, and create around it an aura of extraordinary passion—in the sense of both enthusiasm and suffering. The studies under review, by exploring Woolf's mental distress and her literary work in connection with that of other modernist writers and in the context of institutional histories and the post-World War I culture of loss, resist singling Woolf out for special fear or adoration as a mad genius. "Genius," indeed, is explicitly analyzed and properly problematized by Valentine. In a culture that often weds the cult of the suffering artist to commercial gain in the non-academic marketplace, and to pedagogical seduction in the classroom, there is still something to be said for that.

—Rishona Zimring, *Lewis and Clark College*

Hearts of Darkness: White Women Write Race. Jane Marcus (New Brunswick: Rutgers UP, 2004). xiv + 219 pp. 18 b&w illus.

In the vast field of contemporary feminist thought, the singularity of Jane Marcus's contribution is characterized by the decided advantage of her huge intellect and an unhesitating commitment to difference as an analytical tool in the feminist investigation of a recalcitrant social order. Cast in manifesto form in *The Future of Difference*, an early volume of feminist critical theory first published in 1980 and reprinted a third time in 1988, the idea of difference was said to carry, in the words of Alice Jardine, one of the book's editors, "high epistemological and political stakes" (Eisenstein and Jardine xxvi) for the future of feminism. Jardine underscored the concept's timely intervention in the transition in feminist discourse "from an original emphasis on the commonality of the female experience to a recognition that, if we are to give form to a new vision, we must constantly examine *every* cultural presupposition as we explore the possibilities of comprehending, communicating, and ultimately changing our experiences" (xxv; emphasis in the original). Marcus captured the sentiment's revolutionary character in an essay provocatively titled "Storming the Toolshed" (1982), at once expressing solidarity with her peers and warning against the threat of appropriation if "the practitioners became absorbed into the academy and stopped combining political activism and the position of 'outsidership' with their scholarly work" (138).

The activist consciousness brought to bear on Anglo-American feminist criticism a quarter century ago enunciated a clear strategy for investigating the nexus between gender ideology and the founding texts of Western literary culture. In particular, the emphasis placed on the renderings of women's experiences in these texts raised enough questions about the established literary tradition and female talent to demand the reconfiguration of an alternative trajectory of women's artistic development. Virginia Woolf held a towering presence in this reconstructive project largely due to Marcus's pioneering scholarly work. Invoking the courage of Woolf's own position as "outsider," Marcus fashioned a brand of Woolf criticism that has served for over two decades as a significant locus of gender differences in modernist literature and spawned in the process a new generation of fervent Woolf critics seeking to tend a similar relationship with the writer. Marcus's determined urgency to place Woolf on the threshold of a differentiated female aesthetic can be explained by what Marianne DeKoven refers to as modernism's "unprecedented preoccupation with gender," expressed variously as "a male modernist fear of women's new power ... misogyny and triumphal masculinism" (DeKoven 174). Thinking through Woolf, Marcus produced a formidable critique of modernism's displacement of masculine anxiety into a discourse of sexual excess marked by the gendered idioms of male power and privilege. Her rehabilitation of Woolf from the ineluctably bourgeois aesthete of patriarchal myth to a resolute socialist-minded feminist and, ultimately, to superordinate status in Women's Studies, is an enduring tour de force in the history of contemporary literary criticism.

In her latest book, *Hearts of Darkness: White Women Write Race*, Marcus makes a pivotal turn on a familiar terrain to provoke debate and inquiry on racial difference. Race, about which Benjamin Disraeli said "there is no other truth" (qtd. Firchow 1) is, according to Marcus, not only modernism's darkest secret, ensnaring male and female writers alike, but also a susceptible element of Anglo-American feminism given its reluctance to seriously engage the subject. For Marcus, the decoupling of race and gender is at the heart of the conflicts in feminism. Indeed, *The Future of Difference* may have anticipated the current problem when it undercut its own revolutionary ethic with the admission that "[t]he issue of differences of class among women is not addressed here, and although the issue of race and ethnicity in relation to feminism is broached, it is by no means fully explored" (Eisenstein and Jardine xxiii). In the intervening years, race and ethnicity became spheres of influence in feminist and gender critiques but the burden fell disproportionately on African American, Third World, and postcolonial critics to provide the scope and quality of the interrelationships and the dynamics of power at play. In the difference-prone discourses of Anglo-American cultural feminism, the profile of race has not been raised to the level of gender differences.

The editors of the recent book of previously published essays *Female Subjects in Black and White: Race, Psychoanalysis, Feminism* (1997), for example, described their collaboration as emblematic of the theoretical anxiety of racial difference within feminism: "This anthology has been a site of challenge, frustration, and revelation. Soliciting, editing, and organizing these essays has made us painfully aware that the encounter between a predominantly white psychoanalytic feminism and African American cultural formations reveals as many stubborn incompatibilities as it does transformative possibilities. . . . What has made this endeavor difficult is also what gives it value—for it is the first of its kind" (Abel 1). The epilogue, a personal perspective on the reading and teaching of Toni Morrison's *Beloved* aptly titled "Fixing Methodologies," points the way to a new direction in feminist criticism, where race, gender, and culture interact unabashedly within the conventions of an "othered" space. "By exploring the novel from the point of view of African cosmology," the author writes, "one sees it for what it could be in the world: a prayer, a ritual grounded in active remembering . . . why it is that so many of us are wounded, fragmented, and in a state of longing. Then, perhaps, we might move beyond that fracturing to those actions that might result in communal healing . . . " (in Abel et al. 370). As one of the book's editors, Barbara Christian imprints her legacy and the promise of feminist difference in these words. She died three years after its publication.

In its quest for a change of white women's hearts in writing and reading black female subjects, *Hearts of Darkness* could actually be renamed *Female Subjects in Black and White* as proof of the way "books continue each other, in spite of our habit of judging them separately"(Woolf 84). But the primary intertext of Marcus's book is Joseph Conrad's *Heart of Darkness* (1899), an important touchstone for probing the ideologies of Empire. Conrad's novel is perhaps the most popular of modernism's shadowy myths of African otherness behind which writers of the age tried to peer into their own hearts to deflect the unseemly. It is invoked and then decentered to allow for a re-visioning of the mutually constitutive process between colonialism and the producer of colonial culture. In *Hearts of Darkness* the dynamics of racial gender are expressed in the interplay between difference and complementarity, authority and subjugation.

The book brings together in six chapters new and previously published essays featuring three familiar subjects of Marcus's research—Woolf, Djuna Barnes, and Nancy Cunard. A number of the chapters were originally presented as lectures before academic audiences in the United States and abroad. In addition to serving the greater community, the essays are debated in the classroom, which has become a site of knowledge production for Marcus and new generations of students. The essays' antiphonal chords derive from their origin as evocative argument. The prefatory chapter, "The Empire is Written," provides an overview of the book's political context and content and the justification for the deployment of a postcolonial reading strategy. Here Marcus captures her own psychic, intellectual, and political shifts and those of her subjects:

> *Hearts of Darkness* is an attempt to trace those fictions of racial fantasy that formed my own imagination and that, I believe, of many people of my own generation. In this book the reader will find the author constantly at odds with herself. . . . In a new century the questions still before me concern the responsibility for writing those once vilified texts into classic status in a new social imaginary. If it was once the critic's role to argue the case for canonizing such works, perhaps it is now her role to question their status and explore their limits. (22-23)

The statement's pensive and tentative tone marks *Hearts of Darkness* as a transitional book, one that charts the memory of a movement and simultaneously maps its future. As the prelude to the fighting words contained in Marcus's book, however, the statement is conspicuously chastening. If I were asked to speculate, I would first look for a cause in the disappointing reaction to Marcus's rereading of *A Room of One's Own* in "A Very Fine Negress." Could that have shaken her confidence in the hard-fought ideological struggles of the later decades of the last century? To compound the problem, her book makes clear that for every gifted woman recovered, there are scores still unknown. There is the example of Nancy Cunard in chapters five and six, who, Marcus argues, must be restored in African American and Pan-African cultural histories. Finally, she makes the powerful argument throughout the book for the reemergence of African women and the African continent from a plethora of Western myths. We can begin to weave these threads together as we usefully ask how we reengage the pressing need for rebuilding coalitions across racial, cultural, gender, sexual, and class divides.

— Tuzyline Jita Allan, *Baruch College, CUNY*

Works Cited

Abel, Elizabeth, et al. *Female Subjects in Black and White: Race, Psychoanalysis, Feminism*. Berkeley: U of California P, 1997.

DeKoven, Marianne. "Modernism and Gender." In Michael Levenson, ed. *Modernism*. Cambridge: Cambridge UP, 1999.

Eisenstein, Hester and Alice Jardine. *The Future of Difference*. New Brunswick, NJ: Rutgers UP, 1985.

Firchow, Peter Edgerly. *Envisioning Africa: Racism and Imperialism in Conrad's* Heart Of Darkness. Lexington, Kentucky: U of Kentucky P, 2000.

Landau, Paul S. and Deborah D. Kaspin. *Images & Empires: Visuality in Colonial and Postcolonial Africa*. Berkeley: CA: U of California P, 2002.

Marcus, Jane. "Storming the Toolshed." In Robyn R. Warhol and Diane Price Herndl, eds. *Feminisms: An Anthology of Literary Theory and Criticism*. New Brunswick, NJ: Rutgers UP, 1991: 138-53.

Woolf, Virginia. *A Room of One's Own*. NY: Harcourt, Brace, Jovanovich, 1929.

Virginia Woolf, the Intellectual and the Public Sphere. Melba Cuddy-Keane (Cambridge: Cambridge UP, 2003) x + 237 pp.

Melba Cuddy-Keane's outstanding *Virginia Woolf, the Intellectual and the Public Sphere* puts to rest any lingering doubts about the significance of Woolf's criticism by delineating a new context in which to read it—as an intervention in a truly open public sphere, re-imagined to include women and workers. In this elegantly argued monograph, Cuddy-Keane shows how Woolf shifted the conversation of literary value to include both "bad books" and readers from beyond the Oxbridge elite, especially women and working-class readers. In so doing, she shows, Woolf used criticism to extend the reaches of the public sphere.

Woolf's nonfiction has always held an uneasy place in her oeuvre. In the century since Woolf published her first piece (December 1904), readers have expressed ambivalence towards her extraordinary success as an essayist and reviewer; praise for her essays has often gone hand in hand with labels of femininity or, more recently, complicity with aesthetic capitalism (which may be much the same thing). Cuddy-Keane dismisses this, building instead upon the work of those critics who made Woolf's nonfiction texts and sources readily accessible and placed that work in context. Perhaps the most important contribution of this book is that it takes Woolf's status as a major intellectual as its starting point and spends its energy assessing her considerable contribution.

In contrast to more critical assessments of Woolf's contributions to *Vogue* by Jane Garrity and Lois Cucullu, Cuddy-Keane argues that Woolf's involvement in the Worker's Educational Association (WEA) taught her to navigate issues of class and cultural hierarchy that typically made social action difficult for other liberal elites. Thus, in writing for *Vogue*, "Woolf ... comes closer to the aims of workers' education than does the supposed leader in the development of English studies" (95), the prominent Victorian professor Walter Raleigh. But having better class politics than Raleigh, a real old lad, is no achievement. Well-taken as her point is, I wished for more.

This is an important book, a smart book, and a well-written book. It will be easily accessible to Woolf scholars. Even so, and although it is a book that is much about the common reader, that lauds the common reader, and celebrates Woolf's respect for the common reader, it is not a book for common readers. In itself, that seems a fine and reasonable choice: it is hard to imagine a different one. Nonetheless, the irony that academic books seem to equate difficulty with legitimacy is not lost on Cuddy-Keane or this reviewer. We, as a profession, seem to have trapped ourselves in a bind, a bind that, this book suggests, Woolf's nonfiction may help us think our way through.

Cuddy-Keane's aim is to locate Woolf "in a different context—one that involves public debates about books, reading, and education and, by extension, the changing construction of audiences and reading practices during her time" (8). To do this, her most influential precursors are Raymond Williams and Jonathan Rose. Williams' *Keywords* is a model here and this book puts the words *democratic* and *highbrow* in their full Woolfian cultural context. Cuddy-Keane writes, too, of what she calls Woolf's "modernist historicism," noting that as early as 1906, "Woolf was ... thinking of history as a dialogic interaction between the historical text and the historian's understanding" (149). At the same time, she elegantly resists classifying Woolf as postmodernist *avant la lettre*: "Woolf's foregrounding of the constructed nature of history does not, however, erase the historical object" (151).

Less well known than *Keywords* but just as central is Jonathan Rose's monumental *The Intellectual Life of the British Working Classes*, in spite of that book's "increasingly angry ... accusation that modernists not only disdained the lower classes but deliberately cultivated difficulty as a way of maintaining ascendancy" (4). Given her engagement with Rose, I would like to have heard Cuddy-Keane say more about her understanding of the sociology of reading in relation to Woolf as a teacher of reading, perhaps by contrasting her assessment of Woolf's intervention in the public sphere with Lawrence Rainey's cranky, antifeminist analysis of modernist audiences or with Janice Radway's much more congenial celebration of the American middlebrow. In spite of this quibble, overall, the arguments of others assist but do not dominate. Occasionally, however, Cuddy-Keane introduces a major theorist only to leave the ideas behind a few pages later. It feels a little unfair to lurch one's brain into thinking about Woolf in connection to Foucault or Kant only to find the allusion to be minor. Ultimately, however, I am gladder of the mention of fresh ideas from critics such as Isobel Armstrong and still resonant ones from Roman Jakobson than I am for a book that dutifully cites all the members of an easily identifiable theoretical constellation.

The book opens with a brisk and helpful overview of Woolf's experiences with education: her lack of higher education, her work as a teacher at Morley College, and her observation of Roger Fry's success as a lecturer. This combination of experiences, Cuddy-Keane argues, led to the emergence of a pedagogical Woolf, one who was radically committed to education for readers of all classes, one whose "endorsement of the 'common reader' was a significant intervention in public debate" (2). Recounting Woolf's reflections on these experiences, Cuddy-Keane speculates that Woolf turned her pedagogical impulse to her writing, where she could command the kind of attention that, lacking Fry's charismatic gift of performance, she could not in person, This is not, Cuddy-

Keane convincingly demonstrates, a failing, but a different—and more lasting—kind of success.

Her section on reading is one of her strongest. She discusses at some length Woolf's contribution to a symposium in a WEA journal on the question "What is a Good Novel?" The only woman among eleven, Woolf's contribution, according to Cuddy-Keane, differs significantly in content from the others: rather than define "good novels," Woolf tells "her readers how to go about forming their own" opinions: she "emerges as a teacher whose concern is to teach the students how to think" (171). Here, she conveys the significance—aesthetic and political—of Woolf's insistence that evaluation occur after both pleasure and historical contextualization. This is Woolf at her best as a teacher and Cuddy-Keane's reading of this neglected prose fragment represents the book at its best. Here and on many occasions throughout, her thorough research has uncovered forgotten gems, polished them, and set them in a rich context. Similarly fascinating and valuable are her readings of Leonard and Virginia's joint 1927 BBC broadcast, "Are Too Many Books Written and Published?" "The Plumage Bill," and the unpublished sketch, "The Fascination of the Pool."

From the vantage point of the essays, it is impossible to doubt Woolf's deep connection with ordinary readers—for all her snobbishness elsewhere, she could always connect herself to other readers and writers, whatever their class. That is why the otherwise strangely remote and class-bound essay "Memories of a Working Women's Guild" remains so interesting. For when Woolf considers working women not as workers or activists but as writers, she is immensely sympathetic to them and, by consequence, to us.

As important to this book as the emphasis on pedagogy is the effort to recuperate the term *highbrow*, to offer the highbrow as a possibly welcome and active figure in the public sphere. The book asks a hopeful question: "Can highbrow culture be a border-crossing zone where 'common' and 'professional' intellectuals meet?" (15). Cuddy-Keane challenges what she sees as an assumption that, because Woolf was a highbrow, she was not a full participant in the public sphere. Here is an instance where the lack of explicit engagement with feminist criticism creates a blind spot. For the widespread critical reluctance to recognize Woolf as a participant in the public sphere is twofold: some feminists find her *TLS* contributions complicit in the mainstream while male participants in the public sphere have labeled her "highbrow" as part of a thinly veiled anti-feminist attack. A closer reading of the conflicts would have led to a sharper point. In either case, Cuddy-Keane is undoubtedly right to find that Woolf's "true antagonist" is "a whole discursive system"; the alternative Woolf proposes is focused on "a respect for the reader's intelligence and the reader's intellectual needs" (31).

The novels are a deep background for this book; her nonfiction is its focus. The book is divided into two parts: cultural context and critical practice. The first section has two long chapters, "Democratic highbrow: Woolf and the classless intellectual" and "Woolf, English Studies, and the making of the (new) common reader"; the second half explores "the theory and pedagogy of reading." As these categories might indicate, there is considerable overlap between the sections. This is both an advantage and a disadvantage: the book is coherent, clear, and smoothly written, but the lack of emphasis on the trajectory of Woolf's career in this otherwise strongly historicist book is sometimes puzzling. Although it is difficult to count precisely, it is safe to say that Woolf wrote over four hundred substantial nonfiction pieces in her career. About half of these were written in the twenties. Of the 21 essays Cuddy-Keane discusses in detail, half are also from the twenties. The thirties essays are heavily weighted to 1930-34 with discussion of only one essay after 1934 ("The Leaning Tower"[1940]). This is an implied argument in itself, as much recent work on Woolf's political writing has argued for an increase in activism, and a turn more firmly to the left, in the thirties. Though she never says so, Cuddy-Keane's argument can be seen as the pedagogical and literary prelude to the more explicitly political and feminist work of Christine Froula, Brenda Silver, and others; it may perhaps also be a declaration of preference. It would have been helpful to know.

Cuddy-Keane makes brilliant use of her own term, "the trope of the twist" to discuss Woolf's refusal to reduce complex issues to banalities, her ability to engage with current polemic and, by altering the terms of the debate, to add to that debate. The article in which "the trope of the twist" appears is not reprinted here, nor is Cuddy-Keane's influential work on *Between the Acts* or her work on modernist historicism. This is one of the pleasantest and most impressive surprises about the book: there is nothing recycled about it. It draws on and benefits from her expertise, but it is its own project, full of new material.

While researching this book, Cuddy-Keane grew curious about Woolf's note that the library copy of *The Common Reader* was "spotted with readers" (113), so she went to find that same book, hoping for some illuminating marginalia: "Opening the book, I found, to my surprise, *literal* spots splattered over a great many pages: smudges that appeared to be thumb marks but also orange spots, brown spots, pink spots—looking like tea, marmalade, jam, and lipstick" (113). "I was delighted," Cuddy-Keane continues, "that Woolf—who so frequently used the metaphor of eating to describe her own reading—should have herself been delighted by the literal tokens of eating on her page. Perhaps, I thought, there is no better sign for her work as a democratic highbrow, working for the integration of literature into our daily lives" (114). This is Cuddy-Keane at her best: serious and diligent, sincerely committed to accessible reading and education, but with a lovely, welcoming light touch. Elsewhere, she writes that Priestley's style "can be described as informal, matey, and pugilistic" (24) and we need read no more to imagine how oppressive such a style would have been to Woolf. For her part, Cuddy-Keane has an impressive way of ending sections with a fillip and does so in her best, most optimistic and inviting way at the end of the final chapter: "The next words must be written by you" (193). With the thoughtful intervention of *Virginia Woolf, the Intellectual and the Public Sphere*, read we must and write we will.

—Anne Fernald, *Fordham University*

Bloomsbury Rooms: Modernism, Subculture, and Domesticity. Christopher Reed (New Haven: Yale University Press, 2004). viii+315 pp.

On the front cover, I see a detail of Duncan Grant's *The Kitchen* of 1914, with a dreamy woman's face at bottom left, cuddling a blue-eyed baby, a standing caryatid figure just above her, and behind her, a woman preparing something or other, her hands—putty-colored—in circular form above her head, while various goblets, bowls, and bottles sit upon a shelf. The scene is at once calm and active, the colors—yellowish, green, pink, light blue, black, ochre—at once cheerful and melding together in a peaceful and productive place.

Sounds like the domesticity part of the subtitle, doesn't it? Between the starkly differing terms of Heroism and Housework, such as Reed compares and contrasts them in his introduction to the "competing ideas of the modern," the case is clear, as are his predilections. The case makes sense, the venue is just what we would expect, and given the path opened by Woolf's *A Room of One's Own*, these rooms and environments—46 Gordon Square for "the company of the young" as Vanessa Bell describes the inhabitants, Roger Fry's Durbins, and the rooms of John Maynard Keynes and Dadie Rylands at King's College—fit precisely and in fact brilliantly (given Reed's flowing prose) along that path. It eventually leads to Byzantium, with Post-Impressionist Primitivism and "Greek Loves," and then on to Omega, to the wartime situation and places, and finally to a very convincing effort to "re-imagine" modernism through its private and gay culture, the subculture of the title.

A word about seriousness: seriousness in the boring sense is just that, boring. This book is anything but boring. When Reed arrives at the last chapter, about "The End of Amusing," you see just what he means. Ornament goes. Triviality is nowhere here. This is in fact a book I wish I could have had the knowledge and, well, the zip, to write (and I am sure that many others wish they could have written.) Reed has done his homework, and I'd be just delighted if he would do mine. His history of architecture and decoration, of the Bloomsbury group in all its comings, goings, shiftings, and loyalties, and of pre, post, and middle modernism is impeccable. And let me state what seems to me his central idea right now: About 1930, Bloomsbury was excluded from the modernist mainstream, because its path (see above) did not lead to an International Style. Period.

Straight off, one of the most gripping analyses for me was the way in which the Abstract Expressionists were into the heroic: Barnett Newman with his very, very virile-wishing *Vir Heroicus Sublimus* (!!!), Robert Motherwell's love of the large format (he used to say to me: "Oh, how I wish I had a wall to paint on," he longed for a housepainter's brush, actually painted on the floor with a six-foot handle, and his *Reconciliation Elegy* in the East Wing of the National Gallery in Washington speaks LOUDLY).

No, the Bloomsbury group was into domestic, small, calmer space. That their designs and passion for designing may have seemed "decorative" (dreaded word) is the issue here. Wyndham (the AntiBloomsbury) Lewis longed for energetic goings on and loathed the Bloomsbury group, whom he attacked hysterically (in both senses) in his over, overlong *Apes of God.*

What has always fascinated me is the collective spirit of the Bloomsberries and the individual strength of its central characters: Keynes the economist, Woolf the writer, Carrington the journal-keeper, Duncan Grant and Vanessa Bell the painters, Clive Bell the critic, and the amazing Roger Fry, the Renaissance man, going in every direction: writing, painting, developing the Omega workshop, and on and on. They were deeply given to "anti=authoritarian individualism," to adopt Lewis's eccentric punctuation, and just as deeply group-oriented: bravi, say I.

Hooray for contradictions. For unforgettably elegant design and radical dissent, for high culture and deep primitivism.

Lytton Strachey (now who could write better than Lytton?) meditated on the group sensitivity: "We find satisfaction in curves and colours, and windows fascinate us, we are agitated by staircases, inspired by doors, disgusted by cornices, depressed by chairs, made wanton by ceilings, entranced by passages, and exacerbated by a rug." And that is precisely the kind of writing that goes—as does our Virginia's—with these rooms, houses, temperaments, art works.

What especially fascinated me as a reader, along with much, much else, was the description of the persons dwelling in the rooms and their ancestors and acquaintances: from Julia Margaret Cameron's "exaggerated self-regard" to Augustus John's bohemianism and would-be "gypsy persona" to the Stephen sisters' "self-conscious bid to reconfigure their lives—socially and

REVIEWS

aesthetically—on terms that seemed to them modern." My hero in the group has always been Roger Fry. As Frances Partridge, beloved above all by so many of us, used to say, he was of all of them the one she found most invigorating. He had only to come to lunch, and everything picked up. Indeed, we can imagine it, as Vanessa mentions his "quite peculiar charm and rightness."

France, France. It was easier to be homosexual there, deeply part of the anti-bourgeois Mediterranean culture. They were there, yes, and they were in Italy and loved its "passionate primitivism," they traveled in Turkey and all over, and, bringing back ideas and reinforcement of their libertarian natures, they thought, and fought against convention in Britain. Feminism and Byzantine aesthetics went sublimely together.

They loved the Ballets Russes and the legs of Nijinsky, they loved their friend Picasso's cubist paintings and purchased his *Pots et citron* of 1907 (and Duncan Grant actually supplied the paper for one of his collages from a wallpaper roll found in his hotel closet). They went in for abstraction in 1913-14, and went in and out of much else.

Still lifes, still rooms, like moments of being: they remained, even after the postwar shift away from abstraction to a certain representational mode. Accusations of their "slouching toward fashionable" simmered to the surface, their drag parties were a howling success (Woolf as Sappho, Grant as a wolfhound surrounded by kennel maids in evening gowns, played by Dadie Rylands, Douglas and Angus Davidson, and the like), and they became, in the eyes of the world, linked with the younger Sitwells, and (here it comes) "amusing."

And now I see the whole painting of which the cover was a detailed part. To the left of the madonna scene is a maid at the teatable, and to the right of the housekeeper is the filled-out form of an unidentifiable shape on the cover: a naked boy. As Reed says of the complete picture, it seems "to express a tentative delight in its unexpected integration of themes: unveiled masculine eroticism and familial domesticity associated with the feminine." In short, the author sums up, a kind of haven, a kind of Eden during wartime.

As I write this now, at the beginning of October 2004, I could wish—we might many of us wish—that we might find any sort of Eden. That it is so very unlikely only enhances the gorgeousness of presentation and the ultimate conviction of this book's defining motif: that an unconventional subculture, highly creative and motivated, is the best possible defense against authoritarianism.

— Mary Ann Caws, *Graduate School, City University of New York*

Virginia Woolf As Feminist.
Naomi Black. (Ithaca: Cornell UP, 2004) xiv + 247pp.

Woolf studies has seen a shift from the 1920s to the 1930s over the last decade, but recently something of a *Three Guineas* renaissance has emerged. At the 2004 Modernist Studies Association Conference in Vancouver there were five papers on Woolf's 1938 text. It is no surprise that in a time of increased military involvement on the part of the West, critics turn to Woolf's pacifist essay. *Virginia Woolf as Feminist*, the first book to focus solely on *Three Guineas*, is part of this trend; Naomi Black addresses contemporary militarism and terrorism —Kosovo, 9/11, Chechnya—in order to emphasize the continuing relevance of Woolf's ideas about women and pacifism.

Black's project is one of recuperation. Woolf's feminism and her clearest explication of that feminism, *Three Guineas*, have been misunderstood. It is not only the style, format, publishing history and response to *Three Guineas* which has eluded explication, according to Black, but Woolf's central argument itself: that the roots of domination and power hierarchies generally (not just militarism) lie in sexism and that women's agency can bring about social transformation.

My problems with this book lie not in its focus on *Three Guineas* or its insistence on the radicalism of Woolf's feminism, but in its assumptions about the articulation of that feminism, an assumption belied in the title. The title *Virginia Woolf as Feminist* is initially perplexing; in 2004 do we see Woolf as anything *but* a feminist and if we don't then doesn't the title serve to dismiss its contents. It quickly becomes clear that the title originates in and relies upon a separation of Woolf's fiction and non-fiction. *Three Guineas* represents Woolf's fullest articulation of her belief system, an explicit argument that is consistently expressed here and in a cluster of related essays. Again, attention to Woolf's non-fiction is certainly overdue, but such a separation along feminist lines seems unsustainable. For Black, the innovation of Woolf's fiction is "unrelated to politics or to feminism in the normal senses of the word" (13) and overturning the literary canon is not "feminism as such" (13). This seems an entirely retrograde step, a sidestepping of recent criticism which has elucidated the politics of Woolf's use of color, for example, or her narratology; studies which fuse the aesthetic and the political. Black in fact undermines her own argument about the "raw form" of Woolf's feminism, when she emphasizes the fictionality of *Three Guineas*, and the impossibility of identifying "real life" referents for the societies named in the text. I find too that Black's welcome drive to contextualize the creation, revision and publication of the text jars with her insistence that this is the "best, clearest presentation of Woolf's feminism" (1), a feminism which is "recognizably the same over time" (2). This kind of argument is reminiscent of early criticism that saw *Between the Acts* as the culmination of Woolf's imaginative vision. For Black, *Three Guineas* is the "central piece of dry land" in a collection of "shallow reefs and islets of feminist writing" (17). What is submerged becomes explicit in her 1938 "much maligned" masterpiece (1). Again, this seems to ignore and evade recent Woolf scholarship, which explores Woolf's antipathy to totalizing belief systems, her subversion of the monologic or didactic.

Having moved beyond this troubling positioning of *Three Guineas*, I was ready to welcome illuminating accounts of the text's various contexts. Unfortunately, many of the chapters failed to deliver here either. Black places Woolf's argument in the context of the various individuals and women's organizations which constituted interwar, British feminism: the Stracheys, Margaret Llewelyn Davies, the People's Suffrage Federation, the Women's Co-operative Guild, the National Union of Women's Suffrage Societies, and the Women's Freedom League. While such contexts are not new (indeed Black herself has published on this topic), it is a useful reminder of the feminist networks within which Woolf moved. However, in the third chapter when Black traces the evolution of the text from a lecture delivered to the Junior Council of the London and National Society for Women's Service to its publication in 1938, one feels that this is a much too familiar narrative to warrant its own chapter.

From here Black moves into a reading of the text itself, based around a reframing of conventional descriptors of the text: *Three Guineas* is *not* a polemic or pamphlet, it is based around twelve rather than three letters, its narrator is not Woolf and its societies are not based on real ones (For International Liberty, Newnham Fund, and LNSWS). Black then traces Woolf's arguments through letters in the text, culminating in her key refutation: that this is not a text about war, but about "the hierarchy, the domination that distorts all social relationships" (98).

Black then discusses a selection of Woolf's letters and essays which represent the "emerging contours" of her feminism (99), the "outlines of a position that can be seen fully developed in *Three Guineas"* (101). She treats epistolary exchanges with Desmond MacCarthy in the *New Statesman*, and essays such as "A Society," "Women and Fiction," "Memories of a Working Women's Guild," and "Thoughts on Peace in an Air Raid." While hampered by the bizarre claim that she does "not want to exaggerate how much identifiably feminist material Woolf wrote" (99), Black's readings do illuminate the pieces themselves, particularly her discussion of the "Introductory Letter" to *Life As We Have Known It* and exchanges between Woolf and members of the Women's Co-operative Guild.

One of the most original chapters is an analysis of the different versions of *Three Guineas*. This is where the book really comes into its own, providing genuinely new contexts. Black compares the British and American editions, as well as the version serialized as "Women Must Weep" in the *Atlantic Monthly*. She discusses the title's allusion to Charles Kingsley's poem "The Three Fishers" (134), the absence of endnotes, as well as various textual omissions and additions.

The final chapter, "Feminism in the Third Millennium," deals with contemporary responses and applications and it is here again that the project falters. While Black outlines some of the text's blind spots for a 21st century audience (divorce, sexuality, abortion, class) and forays into the question of racial difference with an interesting section on the imperial contexts of the word "guinea," she argues that neither Virginia Woolf, nor her feminism are outdated. The cursory references to Afghan women's organizations or Chechen feminism seem tokenistic and out of place. Surely the strength of Woolf's argument is its specificity, the careful contextualization of her arguments and embedding of the abstract in the particular. Women's potential for an alternative vision is the result of particular social circumstances, therefore the specificity of her argument and examples underlie the feminism of the text. To relate *Three Guineas* to the position of women in contemporary sites of military conflict would be a valuable project, but would require detailed discussion of the differences as well as the links between the Britain pre-WW2 and the current situation in the ex-Soviet Union or the Middle East. Given contemporary debates about the neo-imperialism of Western feminism (and of course Woolf's famous phrase "as a woman my country is the whole world" can be read in this light), the brevity of Black's treatment of these links seems misjudged. The tension within post-1980s feminism between political collectivity and identity politics (a tension which Black acknowledges [10]), is one which Woolf addressed in the 30s in the class specificity of *Three Guineas*. Ironically then, Black's erasure of the specific histories of Chechen nationalism or Islamic fundamentalism in Afghanistan in her gestures of solidarity is to ignore one of the key features of Woolf's feminism in *Three Guineas*, which of course the book sets out to elucidate. Also Black's careful attention to the feminist contexts in which the book was produced is undermined by her treatment of the present day situations to which *Three Guineas* is to be applied.

This book seems full of missed opportunities. It doesn't engage with archival material relating to *Three Guineas* (now available on-line) and only makes passing reference to the, now published, eighty-odd letters from common readers (remarkable given the chapter dedicated to reactions to *Three Guineas*). Recent scholarship relating to the photographs, or to the Fawcett Library goes unacknowledged. Black does not hide the genesis of this book: "I began this process in my edition of *Three Guineas*...here I present a discussion that is less closely tied to the requirements of a scholarly edition and more directed toward understanding Virginia Woolf's feminism" (11). The combination of largely expository material and a problematic framework suggest that the transition from Shakespeare Head edition to research monograph has not been entirely successful.

— Anna Snaith, *King's College London*

Lily Briscoe's Chinese Eyes: Bloomsbury, Modernism, and China. Patricia Laurence. (Columbia, SC: University of South Carolina Press, 2003) xxvi + 488 pp.

In *Lily Briscoe's Chinese Eyes: Bloomsbury, Modernism, and China*, Patricia Laurence makes a convincing—and provocative—case for a truly global understanding of modernism. While Laurence is not the first critic to recognize the need for a less Eurocentric focus on the part of modernist scholars, she here provides a clear example of what this change in approach would look like in practical terms. Her study of the Bloomsbury group in England and the corresponding Crescent Moon group in China (sometimes referred to as "the Chinese Bloomsbury"), details the individual cultural exchanges that took place as artists and writers from both communities traveled, literally and intellectually, into one another's territory. The sheer scope of Laurence's research is impressive. A Woolf scholar by training, Laurence ventures bravely into the world of Chinese literature, art, and politics—and emerges with a fascinating, if necessarily abridged, cultural history of important early twentieth-century Chinese writers, artists, and intellectuals. Many Woolf scholars will be unaware of the Chinese figures discussed by Laurence, or of their connections to the Bloomsbury group, and will be grateful for the new information this book offers.

Laurence maintains that the personal and working relationships that formed between members of the Bloomsbury group and members of the Crescent Moon group operated outside the imperialist model in which much postcolonial and postmodern criticism would situate them. Instead, Laurence contends, such relationships were mutually beneficial and produced overwhelmingly positive results for the work and lives of those involved, in ways that have not previously been recognized by scholars. The book's immediate objective is to reveal the various forms and discourses of modernism that existed in China during the early twentieth century, and, in so doing, to "reconfigure international modernism." However, the author's personal travels in China form the backdrop to her narrative, and signal her larger goal—the reinsertion of place, and of individual works and figures, into literary studies.

Laurence constructs her detailed study around the love affair of Virginia Woolf's nephew Julian Bell and the Chinese artist Ling Shuhua, the wife of the dean at Wuhan University, where Julian taught English literature for seventeen months after graduating from Cambridge University. It was the discovery of a packet of letters between Bell and Ling Shuhua, included in a group of Bloomsbury papers being sold at a Sotheby's auction in 1991, which first sparked Laurence's interest in the people and places that would lead her to write this book. The study radiates outward from these two figures to a web of individuals who meet and come together in an often dizzying fashion over the course of Laurence's study. Previously unpublished writings, and rarely seen photographs of Julian Bell, Ling Shuhua, and their associates, along with artwork from both communities (most notably a beautiful reproduction of Ling's "friendship scroll"—a handscroll that contains artwork and writing from members of both the Bloomsbury and the Crescent Moon groups), aid Laurence in challenging East-West polarities, as she makes her case for the importance and the reciprocity of the relationships she delineates.

In addition to Julian Bell and Ling Shuhua, the central figures of the book include Virginia Woolf, Vanessa Bell, G. L. Dickinson, Xu Zhimo, E. M. Forster, and Xiao Qian. Laurence divides her work into five chapters, each of which allows her to approach her topic from a different angle. Still, the book is less a progressive argument than an enthralling and wide-ranging exploration of individual writers and artists and their experiences with cross-cultural exchanges.

The vast quantities of material with which Laurence deals can be overwhelming at times, as the reader is asked to keep straight any number of unfamiliar names and events (unfamiliar, at least, to the reader who is not well-versed in Chinese literary, political, and cultural history), yet in a sense this underscores Laurence's main point. That is, it is the intricate and complicated relationships between individuals that must be accounted for and examined before conclusions are drawn about a given community's work or its effects or influences—and this is always a massive operation, which cannot be simplified or abstracted for purposes of convenience. In her introduction to the book, Laurence declares that her project "was begun in the belief that present literary theory in America and China is quicksand unless grounded in specific lives, and historical and literary conversations and communities" (22), and it is plain that she intends this quite literally. An appendix to the work offers a helpful index of Chinese and British figures, which allows the reader to navigate more easily through the sometimes labyrinthian pathways of the book.

The first chapter, "Julian Bell, 'Performing Englishness'" focuses on the life of Woolf's nephew Julian Bell, and particularly upon the year and a half that he spent teaching English literature in China and establishing personal and intellectual connections with the scholars and artists to whom he served as a conduit for many of his British relatives and companions. Margery Fry, the sister of Roger Fry, was the first of the Bloomsbury group to meet Ling Shuhua and her husband Chen Yuan, encountering the couple during a 1933 visit to China sponsored by Boxer Indemnity Funds. She connected Julian with the society of artists and intellectuals with whom he would spend his time abroad. After Julian's death in the Spanish Civil War in 1937, Ling Shuhua would sustain a long-term correspondence with both Julian's aunt, Virginia Woolf (who provided necessary encouragement and practical advice to Ling Shuhua as she completed her autobiography), and his mother, Vanessa Bell, who would bond with Shuhua as a fellow painter.

The second chapter, "Literary Communities in England and China: Politics and Art" focuses upon the backgrounds and the aesthetic programs of the Bloomsbury group in England and the Crescent Moon group in China, both of which thrived in the 1920s and early 1930s. By far the shortest of the five chapters, this chapter argues that both communities took up a deliberately apolitical approach to their art, as they felt the pressure of the turbulent political conditions that surrounded them—the Sino-Japanese war in China and the onset of World War II in England. Laurence maintains that this situational coincidence prepared the ground for the literal exchanges that would take shape among members of the two groups, as it rendered their interests and concerns naturally compatible.

Chapter Three, "East-West Literary Conversations" moves into more direct comparisons of the thematic and perspectival approaches of the two groups. The first half of the chapter focuses upon G.L. Dickinson, a Cambridge don and historian, and Xu Zhimo, the founder of the Crescent Moon group. The British concern with "civilization" is contrasted with the idea of "subjectivity" toward which Laurence argues that some Chinese writers were moving at the end of the Republican period. The second half of the chapter explores the longtime friendship between E.M. Forster and Xiao Qian, a Chinese journalist and writer. An examination of the correspondence between the two men leads to a discussion of the problems faced by writers like Forster in incorporating "unacceptable" themes such as homosexuality into the British novel, and concludes that connections with China nonetheless enabled modern British authors to incorporate ideas and perspectives into their work that would have proved untenable otherwise.

Chapter Four, "Chinese Landscapes Through British Eyes" turns to "Chinese landscape through the eyes of painters and writers who are removed from mainstream British discourse about China" (223). It provides detailed accounts of the correspondence that formed between Ling Shuhua and Virginia Woolf and Vanessa Bell. Generous excerpts from these letters, written over the course of decades, make for informative reading. Excerpts from Ling Shuhua's autobiography and from the short stories she produced with the assistance of Julian Bell are included here as well. Some pages from one of these stories, "Writing a Letter," are reproduced, with Julian's corrections and marginalia, in the work's appendices.

Chapter Five, "Developing Modernisms" argues that the literary and aesthetic exchanges described over the course of the book contributed to an "international modernism," which took shape in the years 1900-1949, and was reflected in any number of forms and locations, many of which are here treated in detail by Laurence.

The title of the book comes, of course, from Virginia Woolf's *To the Lighthouse*, where it is Lily Briscoe, the female artist who will not conform to societal conventions, but insists instead upon her art and personal integrity, who is described by Woolf as viewing the world through "Chinese eyes." In Laurence's words: "Lily's 'Chinese eyes' suggest not the Empire's foraging glance toward the distant lands of China and India for trade and gain, but the new aesthetic voyaging in the East during the modernist period" (10). In Laurence's interpretation, China functions for British modernists not as a subjugated or colonized place, but as a location in which freedoms and possibilities that are unimaginable elsewhere begin to open up: "As the modernists in England looked to the East, a vast mass of new cultural, philosophical, aesthetic experiences and perceptions emerged at the beginning of the twentieth century and would challenge British perceptions. Lily's embodiment of 'Chinese Eyes'—Woolf's brilliant cultural, political, and aesthetic stroke—suggests then not only the incorporation of the Chinese aesthetic into the 'English' artist, but also European modernism's and, now, our own questioning of our cultural and aesthetic place or 'universality'" (10).

Overall, Laurence's work is engaging, original, and thoughtful in both its approach and analyses. One might wonder whether Laurence's enthusiasm for her subject matter leads her to idealize, to a certain extent, the relationships between the Bloomsbury group and the Crescent Moon group. Surely the exchanges between members of the two groups were not wholly exempt from the imperialism that governed political and economic relations between England and China. Laurence's own evidence suggests as much, and she seems to acknowledge at points that it is the *extent* to which these artists and writers adopted what Edward Said calls "contrapuntal perspectives" outside the imperialist attitudes that governed larger relations between their two countries that is ultimately of interest. Irrespective of one's feelings about Laurence's larger claims, however, the material she presents is an exciting contribution to Woolf studies, and to literary scholarship more generally. *Lily Briscoe's Chinese Eyes: Bloomsbury, Modernism, and China* is delightfully and eminently readable, and should be of interest not only to those who study Woolf and British modernism, but to anyone interested in thinking seriously about the directions in which a more inclusive literary scholarship might, or should, be moving.

—Randi Saloman, *Yale University*

Violence and Modernism: Ibsen, Joyce, and Woolf.
William A. Johnsen (Gainesville: UP of Florida, 2003) xv + 168.

William A. Johnsen's *Violence and Modernism* addresses a question that concerns many modernist scholars in an age of terrorist threats and the "war on terror": what can modernism teach us and our students about the experience of, and appropriate reaction to, acts of violence? Johnsen's response, delivered through readings of the works of Ibsen, Joyce, and Woolf, is that modernism analyzes the violence of nations, parties, and cultures to posit a "postsacrificial" response to violence and oppression. These writers, Johnsen argues, reject self-sacrifice as well as the demand that those who commit violence be forced to taste it themselves. They thus suggest, in the words of René Girard, "the time has come for us to forgive one another. If we wait any longer there will not be time enough" (qtd. on 141). The timeliness of Johnsen's argument, and his often insightful readings, will make readers wish that the book were less antagonistic in tone and better researched, particularly when Johnsen turns to Woolf.

Girard provides the theoretical underpinning of the book, particularly his mimetic hypothesis and theory of the scapegoat. Although Johnsen also draws on Northrop Frye's "conception of *literature as a whole*" (vii), it is Girard that Johnsen most turns to in order to show how modernist writers themselves theorize collective acts of violence. The first chapter of *Violence and Modernism* thus summarizes "Girard's hypothesis for cultural mimesis" (5) and then turns to discussions of *King Lear*, a play that focuses on the violence of characters who "cannot know what they do" (18), and *Nineteen Eighty-Four,* which "imagines the end of the modern in the ruthless hijacking of the comprehension of scapegoat practices in order to perfect them in perfect violence" (33). This first chapter suffers from an unnecessarily defensive posture, which leads Johnsen to make statements such as "anyone certain that they have disproved the mimetic hypothesis by conjuring up an example of pure desire should be sent to their room" (3). This attempt at humor turns academic dialogue into a parent-child affair that seems disrespectful of Johnsen's readers. When Johnsen sticks to analysis of literary texts, which show that "modern literature finalizes Western literature's progressive *thematization* of the scapegoat mechanism" (18), he is on surer ground.

Johnsen's analysis of Ibsen focuses on *Pillars of Society* and *An Enemy of the People.* Together, these plays "theorize different aspects of the hypocrisy of modern sacrificial solidarity" (53) and specifically demonstrate "the way that public leaders qualify themselves for public concern and approval through apparent and staged acts of self-sacrifice" (140). This persuasive reading is one of the timeliest aspects of Johnsen's book, encouraging readers to examine contemporary claims of self-sacrifice with skepticism, but the argument becomes troubling when Johnsen encourages readers to reexamine Tomas Stockmann, the scapegoat who unites the crowd in *An Enemy*. According to Johnsen, this play reveals "the error symmetrical to Peter's [the town mayor's] excessive sense of virtue: Tomas's excessive sense of persecution, the one whose sacrifice and persecution proves his innocence and virtue. Tomas Stockmann is the forerunner of the great subaltern texts of this century, which maintain their virtue by the measure of their (unjust) persecution" (64-5). Leaving aside the snide—and unsubstantiated—dig at an entire category of world literature, Johnsen's argument raises troubling questions about whether a "postsacrificial" orientation toward collective violence necessitates a relativism that would see those who oppress as no more culpable than their victims. Johnsen seems to assume that many in the academy view oppression as a badge of moral superiority, and while his reading of Woolf later suggests a universal sympathy for scapegoat and oppressor alike, his argument veers toward a dismissal of the victim that will trouble some readers.

Two subsequent chapters treat Joyce's early work, touching on "The Sisters," "The Dead," and *A Portrait of the Artist as a Young Man*. Johnsen is particularly interested in the evolution of Joyce's use of irony, which he identifies as "the technique of modern rivalry, artistic as well as sexual," because "a defeated rival is necessary to the ironist's sense of superior being" (77). In view of this necessity, "it takes a revolutionary change of heart to renounce resentment and rivalry [and with these, irony] *unilaterally*" (78). One revolutionary turns out to be Gretta Conroy. Contrasting Gabriel's reaction to the history of Michael Furey's self-sacrifice with that of Gretta, who views her first lover's self-induced death as an unnecessary mistake, Johnsen argues that readers of modernism need to learn to read as Gretta reads: to reject irony and emulation of self-sacrifice. As Joyce's career progressed after *Dubliners,* he developed an even more radical critique of self-sacrifice that saw victims as complicit with their betrayers (86). Johnsen contends that Joyce then moved to complicate irony, which makes the modernist artist the "enemy of the people" (93). Stephen refuses to sacrifice himself—to participate in collective violence—and readers should also refuse to sacrifice him through an ironic interpretation that only incriminates the self. Instead, if we read Stephen as Gretta might read him, as a father might read him, we discover a "potential zone of resistance in a characteristically ironic situation" and "resist the dominant mode of modernism-as-ironic modernization" (106).

Johnsen's final chapter, "Finding the Father: Virginia Woolf, Feminism, and Modernism," ranges across *A Room of One's Own, Mrs. Dalloway,* and *To the Lighthouse* to position Woolf as moving the farthest beyond "futile competitive and vengeful modernizations" (112). Woolf does this, Johnsen argues, by researching the operations of patriarchy to explain the history of oppression to women but also, and more important, to consider how she herself—and the women who inspired her—could have come into being under patriarchy. According to Johnsen, Woolf uncovers the "hidden historical and structural origins" of modern feminism "within the patriarchy" (120), a strategy that helps Woolf analyze and come to terms with her own anger.

Johnsen's analysis of Woolf's novels thus aims to show that she gradually moves from anger and rivalry toward a radical forgiveness of oppressor as well as oppressed. He characterizes the narrator of *The Voyage Out* as a "modernist snob" who is ironic "towards characters and the narrative conventions" alike (120) but sees *Mrs. Dalloway* as turning from irony to admiration and understanding. In this novel and *To the Lighthouse*, Johnsen perceives a sympathy for characters who "are the anonymous but necessary antecedents of [Woolf's] own thinking" (121), a sympathy that encompasses Richard and Mr. Ramsay as well as their female counterparts. It is Woolf's treatment of Mr. Ramsay that Johnsen sees as most significant, arguing that the trip to the lighthouse allows James, Cam, Lily and the novel's readers to "see what Woolf saw that enabled her to write this book, what contemporary criticism would dare not let us see, a patriarch mysteriously reconfigured to bless [. . .], not tyrannize" (134). This reading is central to Johnsen's larger claim that Woolf let herself admire—as well as castigate—the patriarchs who "sponsored" women even as they oppressed them, a dual orientation that helps to explain why *Three Guineas* advocates a society of outsiders "who refuse to participate in the mirror mechanisms of the patriarchy" (135). It seems significant that Johnsen only briefly touches on *Three Guineas*—three references that largely function as comparisons to *Room*—a text that would have complicated his focus on the "positive reciprocity" between Woolf and her father(s) (138). As Brenda Silver notes in her 1991 "The Authority of Anger: *Three Guineas* as Case Study," the range of responses to Woolf's polemic suggests that sexual politics plays a role "in the perception and construction of tones of voice" (346). It is unclear how Johnsen perceives Woolf's tone in *Three Guineas*, but his relative silence on a text that many readers hear as distinctly angry enables him to posit a kind, gentle Woolf rather than an impassioned cultural critic.

Although Johnsen's readings of individual texts are often insightful, they are accompanied by curmudgeonly swipes at various features of contemporary literary criticism. Instead of simply making an argument about how one might theorize "the historical preference [. . .] for the tradition of Judeo-Christian writing," for example, Johnsen must slip in a sarcastic comment in the place of my ellipses: "or 'privileging,' to use the critical term of late-modern pseudoscientific skepticism" (17). These types of observations pepper the book and make it seem that Johnsen expects a hostile reading; because they are often unnecessary, one wishes that an editor or reader had counseled their removal.

Johnsen's discussion of Woolf demonstrates other ways in which his impatience with, and indeed ignorance of, the direction of recent criticism limits the potential of his argument. His comments on feminist criticism suggest that Johnsen works with an outdated caricature of a large and diverse body of inquiry: "the great deconstructive move of feminism is to ferret out complicity with the patriarchy, to expose the bad faith of the fathers everywhere" (138). The lone feminist Johnsen seems to have consulted as he worked on Woolf is Jane Marcus, whose *Virginia Woolf and the Languages of Patriarchy* (1987) comes in for particular criticism. Leaving aside Johnsen's reductive representation of Marcus's argument ("Jane Marcus has argued for Woolf as a socialist writer bent on dissolving the patriarchal family, but Woolf did not mean children to do without fathers and mothers" [134]), it is clearly impossible for him to argue that feminists have misrepresented Woolf's "new feminism" and "new modernism" based on the works of one critic, however influential. Had Johnsen consulted additional feminist work on Woolf, such as Christine Froula's 1994 "St. Virginia's Epistle to an English Gentleman; or, Sex, Violence, and the Public Sphere in Woolf's *Three Guineas*," he would have been forced to develop a more nuanced argument about Woolf's feminist response to violence. The omission of Froula's work from Johnsen's bibliography is particularly glaring as it, like his study, puts Woof into dialogue with René Girard to make a similar argument: "*Three Guineas*'s thematic treatment of the scapegoat mechanism and its explicit refusal to substitute new scapegoats for old make it a prophetic text" (Froula 38). While the sheer volume of criticism on Woolf daunts many who want to participate in the ongoing conversation, Johnsen has simply ignored pertinent work and engages a straw-woman instead.

To the question of what modernism can teach about the appropriate response to violence, Johnsen's study replies that texts by Ibsen, Joyce, and Woolf in particular follow a tradition properly called "Abrahamic, another term that has been hijacked away from its originary sense of ending human sacrifice" (141). To work in this tradition ourselves, Johnsen suggests, we need to end our purported preoccupation with victims, which results in new cycles of scapegoating, to extend a universal forgiveness to persecutor and persecuted alike. While readers will find Johnsen's readings of texts such as Joyce's "The Dead" original and insightful, his characterization of current literary criticism and theory—and of feminist criticism in particular—will strike many as off the mark. If Johnsen counsels a universal forgiveness, the work of feminists and others seems to have been excluded from that offer, leaving us still to wonder if we have time enough to understand and pardon one another.

—Celia Marshik, *SUNY Stony Brook*

Works Cited

Froula, Christine. "St. Virginia's Epistle to an English Gentleman; or, Sex, Violence, and the Public Sphere in Woolf's *Three Guineas*." *Tulsa Studies in Women's Literature* 13 (1994): 27-56.

Silver, Brenda R. "The Authority of Anger: *Three Guineas* as Case Study." *Signs: Journal of Women in Culture and Society* 16 (1991): 340-70.

The Library of Leonard and Virginia Woolf: A Short-title Catalog
Compilers and eds. Julia King and Laila Miletic-Vejzovic (Pullman, Washington: Washington State UP, 2003) xx + 251 pp.

The title of this catalog is misleading, for it is not a catalog of the Library of Leonard and Virginia Woolf but of that part—admittedly the bulk—of their Library that is held by Washington State University. There are a number of books, such as Clive Bell's copy of *Lady Chatterley's Lover*, that are included in the *Catalog* but were never owned by the Woolfs. Similarly, most of the books written by Leonard and Virginia were acquired by WSU Libraries from elsewhere (iii-iv). Even to talk of the Woolfs' Library sounds pretentious, for, however much they cared for books, they appreciated them for their contents and were never book collectors as such. Many books passed through their hands in the course of their lives: many were sold, many were given away. We might as well accept the simple definition of their "Library" as being that collection of books and printed matter that Leonard Woolf owned when he died on 14 August 1969: there were "probably about 9000 volumes" (Holleyman 1) split between Monks House and his Victoria Square house in London. It is difficult to be precise about the total number of books, because there are a number of multi-volume sets (or "items"), such as Sir James Stephen's *Essays in Ecclesiastical Biography* (2 vols., 1849), *Œuvres complètes de Voltaire* (70 vols., 1784-9) that Leonard took to Ceylon in 1904, and Sir Leslie Stephen's own copy of the *Dictionary of National Biography* (63 vols., 1875-1901). The arbitrariness of that definition of the Woolfs' Library is thrown into relief when one remembers that Virginia died over twenty-eight years earlier and when one also realizes that in the WSU collection are "some 400 books from Cecil Woolf, which Leonard had sold to him over the years" (iv)—or had Leonard only "loaned [them] to his nephew" (Luedeking)? It may not even be possible now to list those 9000 volumes with total accuracy. While the majority were sold to Washington State University, some were bought by the University of Texas and many books written by Leonard and Virginia were donated to the University of Sussex by Trekkie Parsons. Sussex also received translations of Virginia's works published in foreign languages (some of the duplicates are in Virginia's bedroom in Monks House), and it is debatable whether these can be exactly identified. And what, for example, happened to Leonard's "nearly complete file of the daily issue of *The Times* covering many years" (Spater 61)?

A few years ago, Washington State University libraries added to its on-line catalog individual bibliographical details for each title in the collection. The on-line catalog of the collection may be accessed via: click on "Author"; enter: "Library of Leonard and Virginia Woolf" in the box provided, and click on "Search." The first page appears, showing twelve books in alphabetical order by title; currently, there are in all 246 pages with a total of 2950 entries. There are, however, a number of mysteries that cause unease. Why is Augustine Birrell's *The Collected Essays* (3 vols., 1922) indexed as *Selections* in the on-line catalog? Why are James Thompson's *Biographical and Critical Studies* (1896) and Sir James Stephen's *Essays in Ecclesiastical Biography* (three editions: 1849, 1860 & 1867) in the *Short-title Catalog* but not in the on-line catalog? Holleyman also lists all three titles (V/s.I, 47, 49 & 40) and is much more informative than the *Short-title Catalog* regarding the annotations and inscriptions.

Until the collection appeared in the on-line catalog, researchers were restricted to using the late George Holleyman's *Catalogue of Books from the Library of Leonard and Virginia Woolf* (1975). Later, Elizabeth Steele made a couple of valiant efforts to help researchers by publishing two addenda (1983, 1987) to Holleyman. The main problem with Holleyman is that it only lists "2,617 items comprising 3,740 volumes" (Holleyman 9). In practice, what gave rise to Holleyman's infamous reputation was its pagination, although it also contains errors and omissions. Holleyman consists of fifteen sections each separately numbered without running heads. Having consulted the index, anyone who then attempts to track down the entry for a book will know how Zuleika Dobson felt when she tried to use *Bradshaw* to find out how to travel by train from Oxford to Cambridge. Personally, I have solved the problem by writing the section codes at the top of each of the 274 pages.

Researchers wish to see Holleyman totally superseded and would like to welcome the *Short-title Catalog*. Unfortunately, they will not be able be able to do either. The *Catalog* has no index. One is therefore only on safe ground if one wishes to know whether a particular author is represented in the collection. Where a book has no obvious author, it could be almost anywhere in the *Catalog*, even though Laila Miletic-Vejzovic states that the "entries are arranged in alphabetical order by author or title" (v). When Margaret Llewelyn Davies sent Virginia Woolf the manuscript of what became the famous *Maternity: Letters from Working Women* (1915), Woolf wrote to her: "Do publish those letters.... They are so amazing." (*L2*, nos. 712, 721). Davies did publish them, of course, and introduced the collection, although her name did not appear on the title-page. The book is listed in the *Catalog* under "Women's Co-operative Guild."

A researcher might wish to know which books about Ceylon are in the collection. The *Catalog* is of course of no real use, although quite a few items are listed under "Ceylon" because they have no obvious author. It is perhaps unfair to demand this amount of assistance from a book. Instead, we can turn to the on-line catalog and, having reached the first page of 12 titles (as explained above), we can click on "Limit/Sort" at the bottom of the page, then choose "Words in the TITLE" from the dropdown list and type "Ceylon" in the adjacent box. A satisfactory 41 items will appear: from *Art and Architecture of Ceylon, Polonnaruva Period* to Bella Woolf's *The Twins in Ceylon* and Dorothy Fernando's *Wild Flowers of Ceylon*.

Thus it is clear that the on-line catalog is more helpful and flexible than the *Short-title Catalog*, although as indicated above the on-line catalog seems to have its drawbacks too. Returning to the example of *Maternity*, we find that the *Short-title Catalog* gives fewer details than the on-line. Only the latter tells us that "WSU Archives copy came with a letter from Margaret Llewelyn Davies [editor], to Virginia and Leonard Woolf thanking them for help and encouragement with this book." (Even so, one cannot find the book by searching on "Words in the AUTHOR" = Davies.) *Maternity* is not in Holleyman (it is in Steele [1983], p. 311), but Maurice Baring's *Translations, Ancient & Modern* (1925) is. A short letter from the author to Virginia Woolf is pasted inside the front cover. This is confirmed by both the *Short-title Catalog* and the on-line catalog, but only Holleyman quotes the letter in full. There are many examples of this sort, and so Holleyman and Elizabeth Steele's addenda remain indispensable.

While it is difficult to get an overview from a computer catalog, it is difficult to index all "fields" in a book. The report of the death of the book was an exaggeration, but here we are between the devil and the deep sea. It is hard not to flounder. Diane F. Gillespie's informative and interesting introduction to the *Short-title Catalog* ends with a word of caution about the Woolfs' Library which, perhaps unkindly, I would apply to the *Catalog* itself: "Drawing conclusions from a list of books . . . requires caution and often a look at the book itself" (xviii-xix).

—Stuart N. Clarke, *Independent Scholar*

Works Cited

[Holleyman, G. A.] *Catalogue of Books from the Library of Leonard and Virginia Woolf . . . now in the possession of Washington State University. . .* Brighton: Holleyman & Treacher, 1975 (limited edition of 250 copies).

Luedeking, Leila. "Contents of the Woolf Library." *Virginia Woolf Miscellany* 22 (Spring 1984): 2.

Spater, George A. "The Monk's House Library." *Virginia Woolf Quarterly* 1.3 (Spring 1973): 60-5.

Steele, Elizabeth. Appendix B: "An Addendum to Holleyman: Books on Literature in the Woolf Library Owned by Washington State University and the University of Texas." *Virginia Woolf's Literary Sources and Allusions: A Guide to the Essays*. New York: Garland Publishing, 1983.

——. Appendix B: "Second Addendum . . ." *Virginia Woolf's Rediscovered Essays: Sources and Allusions*. New York: Garland Publishing, 1987.

Notes on Contributors

Melba Cuddy-Keane is Professor of English and a Northrop Frye Scholar at the University of Toronto, and a former President of the International Virginia Woolf Society. She is the author of *Virginia Woolf, the Intellectual, & the Public Sphere* (Cambridge UP, 2003) and numerous essays and chapters on Woolf, narrative theory, and cultural history. Her edition of the previously unpublished BBC broadcast by Leonard and Virginia Woolf, entitled "Are Too Many Books Written and Published?" will appear in the *PMLA* special issue devoted to the History of the Book (January 2006).

Angela Frattarola is a lecturer in the Expository Writing Program at New York University, where she recently finished her PhD in Literature. Her dissertation, "The Rhetoric of Sampling: A Study of Narrative Technique in the Twentieth-Century Novel," theorizes and appropriates the music term sampling into literary studies in order to discuss aurality and resonance in the twentieth-century novel. Through close readings of the novels of Woolf, James Joyce, and Samuel Beckett she demonstrates a typology of sampling, which includes sampling historical styles, "found sounds," and intra/inter-textual material. This dissertation also probes the relationship between technological innovations, particularly those related to sound and music, and modernist literature.

Ruth Hoberman is Professor of English Literature at Eastern Illinois University. She is the author of *Modernizing Lives: Experiments in English Biography 1918-1939* and *Gendering Classicism: The Ancient World in Women's Historical Fiction,* and co-editor, with Kathryn N. Benzel, of *Trespassing Boundaries* (Palgrave/Macmillan 2004), a collection of essays on Woolf's short fiction. Her current research focuses on the literary depiction of museums, objects, and aesthetic taste in early twentieth century British literature.

Ann Martin is an Assistant Professor of English at Dalhousie University. She has published articles on Djuna Barnes and on urban Canadian Modernism, and has recently completed a study of the role of fairy tales in Anglo-American Modernist works. Her current research addresses the significance of the automobile in the prose fiction of Dorothy L. Sayers.

NOTES ON CONTRIBUTORS

Kathryn Simpson is Lecturer in English at The University of Birmingham, England, where she teaches courses on nineteenth and twentieth century fiction and film. Her research interests focus on the interrelationships of sexuality and creativity in the work of Virginia Woolf, H.D., and Gertrude Stein. Her current research is concerned with exploring the operation of the gift economy as it works in conjunction with market and libidinal economies.

Helen Southworth is Visiting Assistant Professor of Literature at the Robert D. Clark Honors College at the University of Oregon. Her work has appeared in *Tulsa Studies in Women's Literature* and the *Journal of Modern Literature*. Her book, *The Intersecting Realities and Fictions of Virginia Woolf and Colette*, was published by Ohio State University Press (November 2004).

Policy

Woolf Studies Annual invites articles on the work and life of Virginia Woolf and her milieu. The Annual intends to represent the breadth and eclecticism of critical approaches to Woolf, and particularly welcomes new perspectives and contexts of inquiry. Articles discussing relations between Woolf and other writers and artists are also welcome.

Articles are sent for review anonymously to a member of the Editorial Board and at least one other reader. Manuscripts should not be under consideration elsewhere or have been previously published. Final decisions are made by the Editorial Board.

Preparation of Copy

1. Articles are typically between 25 and 30 pages, and do not exceed 8000 words.

2. A separate page should include the article's title, author's name, address, telephone & fax numbers, and e-mail address. The author's name and identifying references should not appear on the manuscript.

3. A photocopy of any illustrations should accompany the manuscript. (Black-and-white photographs will be required for accepted work.)

4. Manuscripts should be prepared according to most recent MLA style.

5. Three copies of the manuscript and an abstract of up to 150 words should be sent to: Mark Hussey, English Dept., Pace University, One Pace Plaza, New York NY 10038-1598. Only materials accompanied by a self-addressed, stamped envelope (or international reply coupon) will be returned.

6. Authors of accepted manuscripts will be asked to submit two hard copies and an electronic version. Authors are responsible for all necessary permissions fees.

Please address inquiries to: Mark Hussey, English Department, 41 Park Row Rm. 1510, New York, NY 10038. Email: mhussey@pace.edu
Fax: (212) 346-1754.

www.ingramcontent.com/pod-product-compliance
Lightning Source LLC
Chambersburg PA
CBHW021825300426
44114CB00009BA/322